Cultural Studies Goes to School

Cultural Studies Goes to School

Reading and Teaching Popular Media

David Buckingham and
Julian Sefton-Green

UK Taylor & Francis Ltd, 4 John St., London WC1N 2ET
USA Taylor & Francis Inc., 1900 Frost Road, Suite 101, Bristol, PA 19007

First published 1994

A Catalogue Record for this book is available from the British Library

ISBN 0 7484 0199 7
ISBN 0 7484 0200 4 (pbk)

Library of Congress Cataloging-in-Publication Data are available on request

Typeset in 10/12pt Baskerville
Typeset by Franklin Graphics, Southport

Printed in Great Britain by Burgess Science Press, Basingstoke on paper which has a specified pH value on final paper manufacture of not less than 7.5 and is therefore 'acid free'.

Contents

List of Figures

Acknowledgments

The research underpinning this book started in 1989 and lasted for four years. Over that period of time, a large number of people contributed to its progress. First and foremost, we would like to thank the students and staff at Northumberland Park Community School, Tottenham, London for their enthusiasm and support. Alan Cotterell and John Watson encouraged the growth of Media Studies at the school, and most of the staff at one time or another were probably inconvenienced by us as the students took the subject into their own hands. Special thanks to John Bradshaw, Joan Deslandes and the English department for allowing us to colonise their offices to tape small groups of students. Dave Carrington and Terry Genin also helped us use a range of practical media-production equipment to the full. Pete Fraser of Latymer School worked with us developing some of the A-level work.

Our thanks also to Jenny Grahame, Ken Jones, David Lusted and Lyn Thomas for their insightful comments on the manuscript, and to several PGCE, MA and INSET groups who suffered our excitement with apparent interest. The Central School of Speech and Drama was generous in its support, and the Institute of Education financed a year of 'recent and relevant experience'. Our respective families put up with endless phone calls and excuses.

Above all, we want to thank the students whose work we have discussed. They were keen that we use their real names. It is to them that we would like to dedicate the book, in the hope that maybe they might enjoy and see some point to our angst-ridden deliberations on their learning.

Some of the book has already been published. An earlier version of Chapter 2 appeared in the NATE journal *English in Education* (Vol. 27, No. 2, Summer 1993) and was reprinted in *Teaching English*, edited by Susan Brindley (Routledge, 1993). Chapter 3 appeared in another guise as Untidy, depressing and violent; a boy's own story, by Julian Sefton-Green in *Reading Audiences*, edited by David Buckingham (Manchester University Press, 1993).

Part of Chapter 8 was published in *The English and Media Magazine* (No. 26, Spring 1992).

> But the schools (and society, and not only the young) must learn new instructions on how to react to the mass media. Everything that was said in the 60s and 70s must be re-examined. Then we were all (perhaps rightly) victims of a model of the mass media based on that of the relationship with authority: a centralised transmitter, with precise political and pedagogical plans, controlled by Authority (economic or political), the messages sent through recognisable technological channels . . . to addressees, victims of ideological indoctrination. We would only have to teach the addressees to 'read' the messages, to criticise them, and perhaps we would attain the age of intellectual freedom, of critical awareness . . . This was another dream of '68.
>
> What radio and televsion are today, we know — incontrollable plurality of messages that each individual uses to make up his own composition with the remote-control switch. The consumer's freedom may not have increased, but surely the way to teach him to be free and controlled has changed.
>
> (Umberto Eco, 'Reports from the Global Village', 1983)

Series Editor's Introduction

At a recent seminar, leading Slovenian educator Eva Bahovec raised what has been the key issue facing literacy educators for the past two decades: the extent to which literacy teaching should focus on the reproduction of dominant cultural texts and knowledges, and the extent to which it should aim towards critical analysis and contestation. In the opening quote to *Cultural Studies Goes to School,* Umberto Eco calls for the latter: 'the age of intellectual freedom' where we teach 'victims of ideological indoctrination' to read and write with 'critical awareness'.

The issues raised by Eco as 'another dream of '68' are still relevant. Bahovec's immediate concern was the task of building educational policy and curriculum in Slovenia. There, critical media studies and literacy have taken on some urgency in the context of the predatory expansion of multinational capitalism and global corporate culture into a previously insulated economy. Many Slovenians are contending with MTV and Disney, Benetton and Hyundai for the first time. In the face of new forms of capital and consumerism, childhood and youth culture are being reconstructed in relation to new and hybrid images, texts, identities, and indeed, forms of 'ideologidal indoctrination'.

The work of Bahovec's fellow teachers, and the work of intellectuals, academics and writers in the 1980s is testimony to the futility of top-down ideological imposition in education. Working within a directive, lock-step Yugoslav educational system, many Slovenian teachers and writers found ways to produce alternative knowledge, to generate and publish polysemous texts, counter-theories and counter-constructions. In many Eastern European and postcolonial education systems, cultural critique, production and transformation was sustained in overt and covert forms against significant odds. A similar case could be found in the Australian state of Queensland in the 1980s. There, under the watchful eye of one of the most reactionary state governments in English-speaking countries, teachers and students developed consistently innovative approaches to media studies, counter-racist and counter-sexist curriculum.

These are examples of how teachers, students and communities can reshape the practices and consequences of literacy in local contexts, often in classrooms where centralised, conservative edicts and policies work against their interests. In the British context where David Buckingham and Julian Sefton-Green work, many teachers report that the National Curriculum is closing down curriculum options, pushing them towards narrow examination-driven teaching. In these situations, whether and how literacy education can be used for reproduction and critique is as much an empirical question as a theoretical one. It depends greatly on the politics of schooling, and on the kinds of cultural strategies, tools and artefacts available to teachers and students. In this way, how literacy is shaped depends on local struggles over 'official knowledge' (Apple, 1993), local struggles like those that occur everyday as Buckingham and Sefton-Green's students critique and analyse, build and reconstruct media texts.

In this light, we can revisit Eco's 'dream of '68'. In the early 1970s, there was widespread optimism that innovative pedagogies could 'emancipate' students. These ranged from the radically apolitical to the explicitly political, from 'child-centred' progressivism to 'free school' models, from cultural nationalism to liberationist theology, from the 'negotiated curriculum' to 'deschooling'. As Buckinghamm and Sefton-Green note, assumptions about the capacity of critical pedagogies to promote social agency and change remain central to many media literacy projects. Yet the continuing debate over whether literacy can be 'empowering' or 'disempowering', 'liberatory' or 'domesticating', 'reproductive' or 'critical' may be fundamentally misleading. It is driven in part by the product guarantees of particular approaches and in part by attempts to identify universal practices and properties of literacy.

It is naïve to assume that any approach to literacy has definitively positive or negative political effects. If we put aside claims about universal cognitive and social effects, we are in a much better position to describe the local complexity and possibilities of literacy education. Part of this description can focus on how literacy education constructs differing kinds of cultural knowledge and social competence — identities and ideologies that are linked to students' access to the material and symbolic resources of communities and economies.

Cultural Studies Goes to School provides us with valuable arguments for moving beyond simple axioms about the power of literacy.

Drawing from Buckingham's influential work on media education, it begins with a re-analysis and re-grounding of classroom practice in contemporary debates, issues and theories of critical literacy and cultural studies. Focussing on Sefton-Green's London urban classroom, it provides a chronicle of teachers' and students' everyday work in classrooms and communities. What emerges is a documentary record of the possibilities of using literacy education for the construction of knowledge, texts and identities.

Many previous attempts to develop cultural studies curriculum have taken their lead from literary theory, cinema and film studies. In some schools, unwieldy alliances between media and literature study have shaped how 'cultural studies' and 'media studies' are done. As a result, what could have been an innovative field of study has, in many cases, been co-opted into a new space for the literary.

What Buckingham and Sefton-Green here document is a fuller range of productive work in the classroom, including work in music, photography, dance and rap. These intertextual and multimodal analyses and performances become sites where students research and document, map and explore the politics of identity: converging and contradictory representations of gender and colour and class. As Buckingham and Sefton-Green show, the students' texts are rich, polyvocal and, at times, profoundly ambiguous.

Secondary student 'Pony', for instance, constructs narratives that are pastiches and transformations of various cultural texts: *Batman, Escape from New York*, etc. His characterisation of Plaz as hero, stitched together from a range of other TV and cinematic texts, cannot be taken as a simple positive or negative image of reconstructed masculinity in urban culture. Plaz is hardly the hero as moral examplar typical in traditional literature study. Nor is he the romanticised 'voice' of the 'oppressed' sought by critical pedagogy. As Buckingham and Sefton-Green point out, 'Pony's' text is an expression of the moral and political ambiguity of 1990s masculintiy. His narrative frames up the tensions of the relationship between authority and marginality, 'pro-social behaviour' and 'anti-social activity', violence and justice in patriarchal society.

Other students develop powerful affirmative statements of gendered identity and women's power, complex analyses of Asian identity and class exclusion. Taken together, the students' texts are powerful representations of postmodern identity — representations that raise as many questions as they are likely to resolve. These questions have educational ramifications that just cannot be avoided any longer: what are the new cultural forms that people must deal with? How can schools, teachers and classrooms deal with the hybrid cultural and gender identities produced by and experienced in postmodern conditions?

Cultural Studies Goes to School is a vanguard book, because of its refusal of formulaic approaches to critical literacy, because of its rich documentation of students' complex 'readings' and 'writings' of the cultures and worlds they live in, and, most of all, because of its teachers' and students' commitment and persistence. As Nicky's rap, *The Female Force*, says:

This is Rheality
Local versatility
This is Rheality
Go! Go! Go!

Allan Luke
San Diego, California
September, 1994

References

Apple, M.W. (1993) *Official Knowledge: Democratic Education in a Conservative Age*, London: Routledge.

Chapter 1

Introduction: Reading and Teaching Popular Media

I am afraid that the interests of our children are not served either by some of the examination boards. One recently defended the use of a hamburger advertisement in a public exam by claiming that it provided just as important food for thought for children as our great literary heritage.

They'd give us Chaucer with chips, Milton with mayonnaise. Mr Chairman, I want William Shakespeare in our classrooms, not Ronald McDonald.

(Education Secretary John Patten,
speaking at the Conservative Party Conference, 1992)

In recent years, the place of popular culture within the school curriculum has become an increasingly controversial political issue. The growing interest in media education at all levels of the education system has re-awakened traditional anxieties about 'cultural value' in their most absolutist form. We are regularly asked to express our outrage at teachers who have abandoned *Pride and Prejudice* in favour of *'Allo 'Allo,* or who dare to replace comprehension tests with the analysis of soap operas. Such things, it is argued, amount to a conspiracy to subvert Civilised Values. We are urged to choose between Bob Dylan and Keats, Madonna and Mozart, *Neighbours* and *Middlemarch,* as though the same set of critical standards could be brought to bear and definitive judgments agreed upon. To enjoy and to study the one, it would seem, is automatically to exclude the other.

As we write, late in 1993, the Conservative Government's revised proposals for the English curriculum have been temporarily stalled, largely as a result of the concerted opposition of teachers — although it seems unlikely that they have been permanently defeated. Among other things, these proposals would effectively remove any requirement for English teachers to teach about the contemporary media. In their place is a renewed emphasis on 'our great literary heritage', a heritage defined in increasingly narrow and prescriptive terms.

On one level, it is not hard to see why the Conservatives might want to prevent children from developing a critical perspective on advertising, as John Patten does here. Yet, his speech was merely one of a series of high-profile statements by education policy-makers which have condemned the negative influence of television and other media, and roundly mocked the idea that anybody might do anything as foolish as teach about them. Thus, Michael Fallon, former schools minister, condemned television for turning children into 'passive, unimaginative voyeurs', and called for the popular Australian soap opera *Neighbours* to be banned. Meanwhile, the National Curriculum Council chairman David Pascall expressed concern about the 'pervasive diet of cartoons, sloppy speech and soap operas' that he saw as undermining the 'cultural development' of young people. And John Major himself ridiculed the notion of studying soap opera, assuring the Conservative faithful that 'there'll be no GCSE in *Eldorado*'.[1]

From this point of view, the role of English teaching is clear: it is to maintain and police necessary distinctions between the timeless values of 'art' and 'literature' on the one hand, and the disposable trivia of popular culture on the other. In these debates, Shakespeare has become the symbolic talisman of cultural value: 'having read Shakespeare', being able to talk about Shakespeare, seems to serve as an indispensable component of what it means to be a civilised British citizen. In this struggle for the souls of our nation's children, *Neighbours* seems to have been cast as the unlikely villain. The purpose of reading Shakespeare, according to this perspective, is not just a matter of learning to 'appreciate' what is self-evidently good: it is also about learning to see through what is self-evidently *bad*. By contrast, watching *Neighbours* is condemned as a passive, mindless pursuit, which is at best a waste of time, and at worst a dangerous form of voyeurism. Consuming popular media is seen to require no intellectual or cultural competencies, and thus to develop none.

Yet this debate about education and cultural value, such as it is, needs to be seen as part of a much more long-term historical process. It is perhaps inevitable that the English curriculum should be a focus for much deeper concerns about changes both in the social order and in the national culture — although, to its enormous cost, those concerns have been increasingly defined by the political Right. In order to explain how this has occurred, we need to give a brief sketch of the broader context.[2]

To some extent, the history of education in Britain in the post-war period could be seen as one of growing teacher autonomy. Although in practice there has been a considerable degree of consensus about what is to be taught, curriculum development and assessment in the 1970s and 1980s were increasingly entrusted to the teachers themselves — an approach which is very different from the centralised, state-controlled systems of many other European countries, for example. However, the late 1970s began to see the emergence of arguments for a core curriculum, and this eventually led to the emergence of a National Curriculum in the late 1980s. It is worth remembering, however, that those arguments did not just arise from the political Right. The liberal Left has also often argued for a core curriculum — albeit more in terms of equality of access and opportunity than in terms of 'standards' or the need to preserve the 'national culture'.[3] And yet, while there remain fundamental tensions and contradictions in Conservative policy on education, the National Curriculum — and in particular the apparatus of standardised assessment that has accompanied it — undoubtedly represents a powerful assertion of centralised state control.

In terms of the *content* of the curriculum, however, its implications have been somewhat more ambiguous. Certainly, the definition of some subjects reflects a highly traditional right-wing perspective. History, for example, appears to stop at around 1968(!), and to place its major emphasis on *British* history, if not quite on a celebration of the glories of empire. Other, more dangerous areas of the curriculum have effectively been excluded altogether: if, as Margaret Thatcher once argued, there is no such thing as society, there is clearly no need for such things as Social Studies.

In the case of English, most teachers had similar fears. The committee that produced the report that established the framework for the English National Curriculum was chaired by Brian Cox, an academic who had been one of the key figures in the right-wing group that produced the Black Papers in the early 1970s.[4] However, the curriculum that emerged was very much in the middle ground. What it offered was a notion of English as a kind of 'broad church', which in many ways acknowledged a good deal of the best current practice in English teaching. At least it did not do what many teachers had feared, which was to return to a narrow canon of literary texts, to prescribe a single method of teaching reading or to insist on a very mechanistic notion of literacy skills.

Most significantly from our point of view, the Cox Curriculum also allotted a role for media education, alongside aspects such as drama and information technology. While the compulsory elements of media education were in fact comparatively marginal, and were largely confined to *non-fictional* media, the Curriculum documents did contain plentiful references to media work, as well as some detailed examples of classroom activities.[5] For those of us involved in media education, this represented a major opportunity. Although 'progressive' English teachers had been teaching about the media for many years, the Cox Curriculum finally made this a statutory entitlement for all children aged 5-16 years old. In the few years that followed, there were significant increases both in the provision of training and in the publication of books and teaching materials for media education.

In general, most English teachers were justifiably relieved about the Cox Curriculum, although perhaps to the extent that they were rather reluctant to acknowledge its limitations and contradictions — which we would argue were fairly fundamental. Despite the token references to multicultural literature, and to the importance of students' home cultures, the Cox Curriculum maintains what Ken Jones has termed 'a resolute blankness towards the cultures of school students and of the communities in which they live'.[6] As Jones argues, Cox effectively reduces relationships of power and inequality to mere cultural 'difference' (although this is a criticism that we believe also applies to many more 'progressive' approaches to English teaching). In this context, it is perhaps not surprising that the broader challenge to English teaching which is posed by media education should have been diluted or ignored.[7]

More recently, however, the whole terrain on which this debate is being conducted has shifted alarmingly to the Right, to the extent that we have all been forced into a defence of the Cox Curriculum. Far-reaching proposals to revise the English curriculum, largely instigated by a right-wing pressure group, the Centre for Policy Studies, have currently been 'postponed' in the light of a more extensive review instigated by the Dearing Report. Nevertheless, the proposals remain representative of current Conservative thinking on education. Essentially, they represent an attempt to return English teaching to a much earlier era. For example, they seek to replace the very subtle and interesting work that was developed, in the wake of the Kingman Report, around the notion of 'Knowledge about Language' — and which was eventually refused publication by the Government — with the teaching of 'correct', formal grammar.[8] There is now a much greater emphasis on standard English, to the point where teachers would be required to correct the spoken English of very young children, even when they hear them splitting infinitives out in the playground. There is a prescribed list of recommended texts, weighted much more heavily in favour of pre-twentieth-century authors. And the required approach to the teaching of reading flies in the face of at least 20 years of research about how children learn to read.

Predictably, in the light of statements like those quoted at the start of this chapter, the proposed revisions almost entirely exclude media education, aside from the odd token references — and even these references fail to distinguish between teaching *through* media and teaching *about* media. It might still be possible, for example, for students to make a radio programme as part of their work in speaking and listening, but any idea that they might *study* radio programmes, or consider the conventions of radio presentation, is out of the question. Meanwhile, film, television, popular music, video games — all the media that form the major leisure-time activities of the vast majority of young people — are simply not mentioned.

These developments are obviously part of a much more broad-ranging project of social change which Conservative governments have been engaged in for the past 15 years. They represent an attempt to return to a vision of an earlier society, a vision of unity and stability that is embodied in 'our great literary heritage'. They reassert a notion of Englishness, of national identity, that ignores the changing, multicultural nature of contemporary British society, not to mention our continuing economic decline. Ultimately, perhaps, they are seeking not to conserve aspects of what currently exists, but to return to a mythical golden age that may never have existed at all.

Clearly, these are tendencies that we wish to oppose. The vast majority of English teachers have always argued for a notion of literacy that is not merely confined to functional skills. They have emphasised that children's competencies in using language cannot be abstracted from the social contexts and relationships in which they are acquired and used. The development of literacy, in this sense, is an inherently social and cultural process; and as historical and cross-cultural studies have shown, forms of literacy are inevitably plural and diverse.[9] Our aim here is to argue that this 'cultural literacy' now needs to be even more broadly defined. Contemporary culture is, by and large, *electronically mediated* culture: the book is no longer the single privileged means of representation that it may have been in earlier times. Literacy in the late 20th century therefore cannot be seen as something that is confined to one particular medium or form of expression.[10] It is not simply a matter of learning to read and write print texts, but rather something that applies across a range of media. The competencies and understandings that children are developing in their encounters with media texts, largely *outside* school, are both valid and important in themselves, and also form part of a continuum that includes, and may be transferred across to, their encounters with books and with print.

For this reason, we would argue that teachers — and particularly English teachers — should be centrally concerned with popular culture, and with the media that children actually read and watch and enjoy. We do not believe (as the Conservatives seem to do) that this is incompatible with looking at 'literature', although we would have a rather different view of what literature teaching might be about. We would argue that English teachers should be concerned with the whole range of cultural products, from Shakespeare plays to hamburger advertisements. Any text that we might choose to use in our classrooms will come already surrounded by assumptions and judgments about its cultural value, which students themselves will inevitably articulate and wish to debate. The crux is surely that they should be able to *question* the processes by which such judgments are made, as well as their social origins and functions, as part of their study of the text. And while we cannot avoid acknowledging the many differences between such cultural products, we do not believe that our primary concern should be to police the distinctions between them in the name of some arbitrary and unquestioned notion of cultural value.

On one level, then, our argument for teaching about popular culture is an argument for a wider notion of English, for something that we might want to call 'Cultural Studies', although in the end the term itself is neither here nor there. However, as we shall indicate, this critique of English is not merely about extending the range of objects of study. We ourselves both studied English at élite Universities, and then trained to become English teachers; and we have both taught in departments that include Media Studies alongside English and Drama. Yet in becoming media teachers, and in seeking to make the case for media education in the various institutions in which we have worked, we have inevitably been led to challenge English — not merely on the grounds of its narrow preoccupation with 'literature', but also on the grounds of the basic theoretical assumptions that it makes about language, subjectivity and culture.

The work that we describe in this book took place almost exclusively in specialist Media Studies classes at GCSE and A level (school years 10–13). While separate examined Media Studies courses have already existed for more than 20 years in Britain (albeit under a range of different titles), these have recently undergone a considerable expansion. Since the introduction of the GCSE in the mid-1980s, the number of candidates in Media Studies has steadily increased; numbers at A level (which commenced in 1989) are growing by 50 per cent each year. While Media Studies remains an optional subject, it has rapidly moved in from the margins. For example, most of the students whose work is considered here were among the first Media Studies cohort in the school; although by the time they had left, Media Studies had become one of the largest options at GCSE level and the most popular subject at A level.

For the reasons we have indicated, this work proceeds from very different premises than those of mainstream English teaching. In many ways, our approach remains strongly indebted to 'progressive' English, particularly in its emphasis on the richness and validity of students' out-of-school cultures. Yet ultimately, we do not believe that media education is something that English teachers can simply take on board as an additional element that will fit easily alongside poetry or drama. While Media Studies has developed rapidly as a separate subject in its own right, we believe that it represents a challenging, contemporary version of English teaching, that should be at the heart of the subject rather than a mere bolt-on extra. It is in this encounter between English and media education that we hope to offer a much more fundamental reconsideration of the aims and purposes of teaching about culture.

We should emphasise, however, that we are not seeking merely to vindicate media education, or to offer a glowing account of 'best practice'. Throughout its history, media education has been characterised by some extremely grand assertions about its ability to empower and liberate students, and to revolutionise the curriculum. While these inflated claims may prove inspiring in the short term, we believe that they are ultimately debilitating, not least because they set expectations that can rarely be achieved. Like a good deal of so-called 'critical pedagogy', media education often employs a form of utopian rhetoric that can only be sustained by those who remain at a distance from the messy realities of schools and classrooms.

Ultimately, while we would share the notion of media education as a *political* practice, we also want to raise some difficult questions about its underlying assumptions and motivations. In particular, we want to move beyond the notion of media education as a means of 'demystifying' students, or dispelling their 'false consciousness', and thereby ensuring their consent to positions that we would define as 'politically correct'.[11] This approach is often based on a view of ideology as a form of 'misrepresentation',[12] and of young people as merely passive dupes of media ideologies. It sets up the teacher as the bearer of 'hidden realities' and of truly 'objective' methods of analysis, and assumes that students will merely accept these once they are revealed to them. In many ways, as we shall argue, this approach to texts embodies a pedagogy which has much in common with traditional forms of literary criticism. In our view, it is an approach that largely fails to recognise the nature and extent of students' existing knowledge of the media, as well as the difficulty and complexity of classroom practice.

In this respect, the origins of this work lie in the book *Watching Media Learning: Making Sense of Media Education,* published in 1990, to which we both contributed.[13] *Watching Media Learning* arose from the work of a teachers' research group, which met over a three-year period to share and discuss evidence from classroom practice in a manner which had not previously been attempted. At least in some quarters, it has been seen as a 'second generation' book in media education, one which moves beyond the political certainties of the early pioneers to consider the complexities of what actually takes place in classrooms. In the process, it begins to sketch out a new theory of 'media learning' which we hope to take further in this book.

Two major issues which were considered in some detail in *Watching Media Learning* are revisited and developed here. The first concerns the relationship between students' existing knowledge of the media and the 'academic' knowledge that we make available in schools. The structure of this book reflects these two kinds of knowledge. The first part is concerned with the students' *existing* knowledge of the media, both as 'readers' and as 'writers'. Here, we look at evidence from surveys and interviews with students about their media preferences; and at examples of their own productions in a range of media. The second part of the book is concerned with the ways in which that knowledge is mobilised and transformed in teaching and learning. Here, we look at the students' written and practical work with a view to identifying what and how they have learnt about the media. As we shall indicate, this relationship between the everyday competencies students bring to the media classroom and the critical, theoretical discourses that they subsequently encounter there is far from easy or straightforward.

The second (and related) issue that we have taken up from *Watching Media Learning* is that of the relationship between 'theory' and 'practice' in media education — in other words, between students' critical analysis of the media and their involvement in practical production, for example of photographs or video tapes. Over the past decade, practical work has come to be recognised as a central aspect of media teaching, partly as a result of the growing accessibility of the technology involved, but also because teachers have increasingly abandoned their fear that students will merely 'imitate' dominant media. Yet the question of *what* students learn from practical work and *how* it is to be evaluated remains a central problem, which we are still pursuing.[14]

Perhaps the major difference, however, between this book and *Watching Media Learning* is that we are much more centrally concerned here with students' own perspectives, and with what they might be learning. In this respect, and to some extent in the range of pedagogies that we describe, we come much closer to the concerns of 'progressive' English teaching than to the traditional critical/analytical approach of Media Studies. Yet in a sense, we also want to hold progressive English teaching to its word. We want to begin by acknowledging our students' existing cultural practices and identifications, which must necessarily include the diverse ways in which they use and interpret commercial media. However, we do not want merely to romanticise or reclaim them in the interests of some illusory form of 'authenticity'. On the contrary, we want to point to ways in which media education can enable students to reflect upon their existing understandings and practices, make them systematic and thereby challenge and move beyond them. Media education, as we see it, is far from being the soft option envisaged by Conservative critics: far from simply celebrating what students already know, it offers a challenging, rigorous basis for learning about contemporary culture.

The research described in this book emerges from a collaboration which has lasted for four years. During this period, Julian was a teacher in a comprehensive secondary school in North London, while David taught (and still teaches) in initial and in-service teacher education at the Institute of Education, London University. Such collaborations are not always easy to achieve: there is a sorry history of academics exploiting teachers and claiming the credit for their work. At least to begin with, David's role in the classroom situation was not always consistent, to the extent that some students were intrigued about his work, while others expressed a justified scepticism about whether he actually had a job at all. In certain cases here, he was simply an observer in lessons, 'hanging around'; in others, he took groups or individual students off to interview them about some aspect of their work. In most cases, he was involved in jointly planning the lessons, in many instances, in teaching. While different parts of the book were initially drafted by each of us separately, much of the writing has been genuinely collaborative.

The school in which we worked is situated in Tottenham, North London. Tottenham is probably best known for its football team — whose ground overshadows the school — and, more significantly, for the 'riots' that took place there in the early and mid-1980s, largely in response to heavy-handed racist policing. In 1985, following the murder of a policeman in one of these disturbances at the Broadwater Farm estate, three black men were convicted after police had forced 'confessions' from them, in one of the most notorious miscarriages of justice in recent years.[15]

The school draws its pupils from an almost exclusively working-class neighbourhood, which includes Broadwater Farm and other large council estates. The students are very ethnically mixed, although the largest groups are black Afro-Caribbeans, Greek and Turkish Cypriots and white British. There are also smaller groups of Asian and Chinese students. The level of material deprivation in these students' lives, and of the other problems (such as crime and illness) that often accompany it, is high by any standards.

The London Borough of Haringey, in which the school is situated, has suffered for many years from its 'loony left' image, and has been systematically starved of financial support by successive Conservative governments. As a result, the Haringey education service is significantly underfunded compared with those in more middle-class areas: special-needs provisions and the youth service have both been progressively run down, while mainstream schooling is increasingly being deprived of basic resources.

To state the obvious, this is a very particular situation. Our whole experience as teachers (and subsequently in teacher education) has been exclusively confined to inner-city London secondary schools, which are ethnically diverse and predominantly working-class. In this respect, our 'biases' reflect those of the broader Cultural Studies tradition on which we have drawn. We cannot generalise from our work to the very different problems involved in teaching middle-class students, younger children or in predominantly white schools. Nevertheless, we hope that the account that we offer is sufficiently detailed to be recognisable, if not familiar, to other teachers.

In some ways, the research we have undertaken is very much in the tradition of classroom-based 'action research' — and here again, we have learnt a great deal from the example of English teachers in this field.[16] We would share the broad political and epistemological standpoints adopted in much of this work — for example, the notion that educational research should be responsive to teachers' own perceptions of their needs and problems, and the rejection of empiricist and instrumentalist approaches.[17] Particularly in the context of growing centralised control of education (for example, through assessment and teacher-appraisal), we would see this kind of self-reflexive research as an essential way of sustaining the notion of teaching as a *profession* rather than merely a system of 'delivery'.

Our approach is also, however, informed by academic work carried out in the field of Cultural Studies, and particularly by the tradition of empirical research both on media audiences and on youth culture.[18] Over the past two decades, this research has moved well beyond traditional views of young people as passive victims of the media, and the behaviourist assumptions on which these views are based. Audience research has increasingly emphasised the diverse ways in which media texts are read and used by different audiences in different social contexts. Likewise, research on youth culture has focused on the ways in which young people appropriate popular forms of cultural expression, as well as the activities that surround them, in order to construct their own social identities. From this perspective, the media are seen not as all-powerful forces of socialisation but as symbolic resources which young people use in making sense of their experiences, in relating to others and in organising their daily lives. They offer opportunities for experimentation with alternative social identities, if only at the level of fantasy or aspiration — although of course the identities and perspectives that they make available are far from neutral. In applying this approach, therefore, we are looking at how young people actively establish and articulate their own tastes and preferences, the different ways in which they interpret what they read and watch and listen to. Yet in locating this work on media within the wider context of Cultural Studies, we are also seeking to emphasise the various social processes and relationships of which readings of texts form only a part.

We will have much more to say about this approach in due course, although it is worth noting here some important differences between our own work and previous research in this field. First, the work described in this book uses a broader range of methods than most research in Cultural Studies. In gathering the data, we have used both observation and individual and small-group interviews and surveys; and most significantly, we have considered students' own productions in a range of media, including their written reflections on their work. In effect, we are looking at students not merely as consumers, but also as *producers* of popular culture, and we want to pay attention to the differences between these two roles, rather than simply collapsing them together. Inevitably, it has only been possible for us to reproduce here a small amount of the work carried out. Nonetheless, we hope that our analysis begins to suggest some of the interest and complexity, as well as the potential value, of this approach for future research in this field.

Secondly, in analysing the data, we have sought to develop a more sceptical and self-reflexive approach than is usually adopted in Cultural Studies research. We have tried to 'read' the data, not as transparent evidence of what students really think or feel but as a form of *social action* that needs to be related to the social contexts in which it is produced. From this perspective, what students say about popular culture, and the texts they produce, are part of the process by which they construct their own social identities. Although this process, inevitably, is defined in terms of social power — for example, of social class, gender, ethnicity and age — we would see the meanings of these categories not as pre-determined but as actively constructed in social relationships themselves.[19]

Lastly, and most significantly, this research has a rather different purpose from strictly academic work in Cultural Studies. In recent years,

Cultural Studies researchers appear to have been undergoing a painful process of soul-searching. Some very fundamental questions have been asked both about the power-relationships between researchers and their 'subjects', and about the political purposes of empirical research.[20] Recent debates around the work of writers like John Fiske and Paul Willis[21] have pointed to the dangers of a vicarious, even narcissistic, identification with 'the people', and of the superficial populism that is seen to accompany it. Yet in some cases, researchers have attempted to resolve these problems by recourse to ever more grandiose political rhetoric about 'empowerment' and 'cultural struggle'. In this context, there is a significant danger that the detailed empirical study of cultural processes that is fundamental to the Cultural Studies tradition will come to be replaced by a kind of postmodernist navel-gazing that we would regard as little more than an academic luxury.

Our approach here is different in a number of ways. Firstly, we want our arguments to remain grounded in the empirical data. This does not mean that we reject 'theory', nor does it make us vulgar empiricists. However, it does mean that we want to question the social functions of 'theory', and to consider the relationships between theories and lived experiences. As will become apparent in the second half of the book, this is a central aspect of our argument about pedagogy. Our dispute, in this context, is not with theory but with 'theoreticism' — with the privileging of theory that seems to have become an essential element in the institutionalisation of academic Cultural Studies courses.

Secondly, we want to consider our *own* role in the work that we describe, rather than seeking simply to efface it. We want to reflect upon our own position as researchers and as teachers, and to encourage the reader to question our own readings of the material. In particular, we seek to draw attention to the power relationships between ourselves (both as adults and as teachers) and our 'subjects' (both as young people and as students), recognising that these fundamentally determine what we can know and how we can know it. In this instance, however, we are very much *participant* observers. We are not simply explicating what young people are doing, or seeking either to defend them or to enable them to speak on their own behalf (even assuming that this were possible). As teachers, we are not under any illusion that we can simply abolish these differences of power or knowledge. On the contrary, as we shall argue, they seem to us to be an indispensable aspect of the pedagogic process.

Ultimately, however, we are not interested in the production of academic knowledge for its own sake. We are researching our own practice in order to encourage others to reflect on theirs, and thereby improve what we all do. For all their political rhetoric, academics in Cultural Studies rarely seem to reflect on their own pedagogic practices — whether this means the pedagogy of academic writing, or of the teaching that they presumably do to earn a living.[22] We feel that there are some hard questions to be asked here about the social functions of academic discourse, and about the social investments of middle-class academics who are so interested in studying working-class popular culture. On the one hand, there is the danger that such a study will serve merely as a new form of cultural capital, and thus implicitly reinforce academic cultural superiority. On the other hand, there is the danger of an illusory identification with the subjects of our research — a kind of nostalgia, perhaps, for a youth that was not quite as misspent as we might have liked. Neither of these, we would argue, are tenable positions for teachers, who spend their working lives in the company of 'the Other' rather than simply theorising about them.

Our title, *Cultural Studies Goes To School*, thus brings several of these emphases together. On the one hand, we are arguing for a fundamental reconsideration of what it means to study culture, and particularly popular culture, in schools — albeit in extremely hard times. And while we are mainly focusing on media education, and indeed on specialist Media Studies classes, we are also arguing for a rethinking of the central discipline of English, and pointing to the need for a more inclusive approach. On the other hand, we are also 'importing' Cultural Studies methods and perspectives into the study of school classrooms, and particularly of students' work. Again, while our central focus is on students' reading and writing of media texts, we also want to move beyond this emphasis on texts, and to situate these activities within their broader social and cultural contexts. In the process, however, we are also implying that academic Cultural Studies might have something to learn from 'going to school', and from reflecting upon its own pedagogic practices, as we shall be doing in this book.

Notes

1. Michael Fallon, quoted in *The Sun* 14 May 1991; David Pascall, in a speech entitled 'The Cultural Dimension in Education', delivered to the National Foundation of Arts Education, London, 20 November 1992; John Major, speaking at the Tory Party Conference, 7 October 1992. For a dissection of these and other recent arguments, see Pete Fraser (1993).
2. See Ken Jones (1990) and (Ed.) (1992).
3. See, for example, Raymond Williams (1961) and David Hargreaves (1982).
4. See Jones (1992), introduction.
5. Especially in 'Non Statutory Guidance'; see Bowker (1990) for detailed indications of how media education relates to the Cox Curriculum.
6. Jones (1992).
7. For a discussion, see Buckingham (1990a).
8. Carter (1990) and Alistair West (1992). This work will be considered in more detail in Chapter 8.
9. See, for example, Graff (1979), Heath (1983) and Street (1984).
10. For problems with literacy metaphor, as with reading, see Buckingham (1989). For an extension of this argument, see Buckingham (1993a).
11. See Buckingham (1986).

12. For a critique of this notion, see Thompson (1990).
13. Buckingham (1990b).
14. Currently being investigated in the research project *Making Media,* directed by Buckingham, Grahame and Sefton-Green, due to be published in 1995.
15. See Rose (1992).
16. For example, Talk Workshop Group (1982).
17. See Carr and Kemmis (1990) for a thorough philosophical rationale for teacher research.
18. For brief critical reviews of these traditions, see the introductory and concluding chapters of Buckingham (1993b). More extensive surveys are contained in Turner (1990) and Harris (1992). Important recent examples of this work would include: on audience research, Hodge and Tripp (1986) and Seiter *et al* (1989); and on youth culture, Willis (1990), McRobbie (1991), Morley (1992) and Nava (1992).
19. This approach is developed in more detail in Buckingham (1993b) and Buckingham (1993c).
20. Walkerdine (1986) and Ang (1989).
21. Notably around Fiske (1987), Willis (1990); see Buckingham (1993b, Chapter 10) and Buckingham (1993c Chapter 11) respectively.
22. Harris (1992) makes some interesting observations on this issue.

Part One

Reading and Writing

Chapter 2

Making Sense of the Media: From Reading to Culture

Public debates about education and culture often invoke deep-seated anxieties about the influence of the media on young people. The concerns about 'sloppy speech' and 'voyeurism' noted in our introduction are merely one aspect of a much wider phenomenon. Ultimately, the threat which seems to be posed by studying popular culture in schools derives not simply from the need to preserve particular 'standards' of cultural value but from much more fundamental concerns about the negative moral, intellectual and political effects of the media.

The view of young people as the 'dupes' of popular media has a long history, and is regularly espoused by critics of all political persuasions. For many on the Right, the media are often seen as a major cause of moral depravity and violence; while they are routinely condemned by many on the Left for their reinforcement of racism, sexism, consumerism and many other objectionable ideologies. What unites these otherwise very different views is a notion of young people as helpless victims of manipulation, and as extremely vulnerable and impressionable. In this account, the text is seen to be all-powerful, while the reader is powerless to step back or resist: 'reading' or making sense of media texts is regarded as an automatic process, in which meanings are simply imprinted on passive minds.[1]

As we shall indicate in more detail in Chapter 7, these views have implicitly informed the dominant rationales for teaching about popular culture. The notion of education as a means of defending or 'inoculating' young people against the influence of the media is one which unites apparently 'conservative' and 'radical' approaches. It assumes that young people are subject to a process over which they have no control: they need to be trained to make choices and judgments because they are seen to be incapable of doing this for themselves. This is a view we wish to contest, not only because it is ineffective, but also because we believe it seriously mistakes the nature of young people's relationship with the media.

Our aim here, however, is not simply to demonstrate that young people are, on the contrary, extremely active, critical and sophisticated 'readers' of popular media. At one level, this is something we take for granted; and it is certainly a view which would be supported by a growing body of research.[2] Yet in a sense, this argument remains within the terms of the debate we have outlined. To claim that young people are active and sophisticated readers is only relevant if the opposite argument is assumed to have any purchase.

Our intention in this chapter is to move on from this debate, and to offer the beginnings of an alternative approach. We will be considering our students' uses of a wide range of media, including television, films on video, popular fiction, newspapers, magazines, popular music and computer games. There are obviously important differences between these media, and all are worthy of more sustained attention than they typically receive, or than we will be able to give them here. The case studies included in later chapters will explore particular media in greater depth. Our aim here is rather more general: we want to raise some broad questions about how young people read and use popular cultural texts, about how we might gain access to these processes, and how we might conceptualise them.

In the process, we want to move beyond the familiar notion of reading as an isolated encounter between reader and text. We want to look not so much at the relation between the reader and the text as at the ways in which meanings and tastes are socially established and circulated. Rather than merely concentrating on how young people read particular texts, we also want to consider the *social functions* that their readings perform. Broadly speaking, we want to move away from a notion of reading as merely a matter of individual 'response', and to redefine it as part of a broader process of social circulation and use, which we might term 'culture'.[3] Such an approach takes us beyond limited anxieties about 'effects' — of the kind that seem to be informing current educational policy — and beyond the assumptions about readers that appear to underlie them.

Maps of Culture

One common characteristic of these debates is the assumption that the media, and young people's use of them, are somehow homogeneous. In order to obtain a more detailed picture, we conducted an extensive survey of students' media use at the beginning of year 10 (age 14). This included a series of questions about their access to media technology, and about their use of television, videos, radio, popular music, computer games, newspapers, magazines and books. Despite the occasional objection to our 'nosy' questions, 112 students completed the questionnaires satisfactorily. Space precludes a detailed presentation of the data, but the following summary indicates some key tendencies.

Considering the economic deprivation of the majority of these students' families, they appeared to be relatively 'rich' in terms of their access to media technology in the home, both for consumption and production. Almost two-thirds claimed to have access to more than three television sets. Almost all (96 per cent) had access to a video recorder, while 44 per cent had more than one. Almost all had access to a radio, cassette player and walkman, while 60 per cent had more than three cassette players and 43 per cent had compact disk (CD) players at home. Almost all (94 per cent) had access to still cameras, and half to three or more, while one-fifth had a video camcorder. Three-quarters had a musical instrument and a home computer in the family. While the figures for television and audio ownership are roughly in line with national figures,[4] those for the ownership of VCRs, camcorders, CD players and home computers are significantly higher than average. At the same time, almost half (43 per cent) had fewer than 100 books in the house, while only 15 per cent claimed to have more than 300.

The survey also revealed an interesting relationship between shared tastes and those which were confined to particular groups. Unsurprisingly, more popular media were more likely to provide the grounds for shared tastes. On average, television appeared to be the most popular medium: 90 per cent claimed to watch 7 of the 10 popular programmes that we named either 'sometimes' or 'always', while 32 per cent claimed that they always watched five or more. When the students were asked to list up to three other programmes that they watched, 195 titles were named, although there were only 69 different titles. Similarly, 87 per cent had seen seven or more of the popular video titles that we named; while among the 174 additional titles, there were 91 different ones. In these instances, then, while there was undoubtedly considerable diversity in students' viewing, there was a high degree of commonality around popular texts.

This was less the case with other media. In the case of radio stations, for example, 34 per cent said they listened to Capital Radio ('mainstream' pop music), 30 per cent to Kiss FM (dance music) and 23 per cent to WNK (a local station specialising in black music); yet 19 additional stations were mentioned, with a significant group of black pirate stations being named, mainly by black students. Similarly, in the case of books, 60 per cent said that they had read two or less from our list of popular authors and genres; while 64 per cent were unable to name any single book that they had read. Of the 75 additional titles mentioned here, only five were named more than once. Books — even popular books of the kind we suggested and the students themselves mentioned — would seem, at least on the basis of this survey, to be very much 'uncommon culture'.

Tastes also varied systematically in terms of social factors such as gender and ethnicity. Thus, some media appeared to be more 'gendered' than others. While books were the least popular medium in the survey, girls were significantly more interested in them than boys. Of the 36 per cent who named any book, only one-quarter (or 9 per cent of the total sample) were boys, and only three of these named more than one title. On the other hand, playing computer games appeared to be less gendered (at least among this group) than some critics have argued. While all but one (98 per cent) of the boys claimed to play computer games, 78 per cent of the girls also did so; of these, the vast majority owned their own system.

Gendered tastes were also evident in relation to specific titles, particularly in the case of books and magazines. Predictably, only a couple of boys ticked *Just Seventeen, Sweet Dreams* or Mills and Boon books, although a slightly higher proportion of girls (albeit still very few) ticked James Bond books and WWF wrestling magazines. Such divergencies also occurred in the case of some television and video titles, although they were less marked. For example, while 75 per cent of girls claimed that they always watched *Neighbours*, only 44 per cent of boys did the same; the figures for *EastEnders* were 45 per cent and 27 per cent respectively. On the other hand, while 23 per cent of boys claimed they always watched *Sportsnight*, only 5 per cent of girls did, and a high proportion ticked 'never'. Video viewing among boys was slightly higher overall, but there were only minor divergencies, for example with *Lethal Weapon* and *Nightmare on Elm Street* (in both cases seen by 13 per cent more boys than girls). While few professed any interest in television news (10 per cent of boys ticked 'always' as against 6 per cent of girls), many more claimed to read either of the two main tabloids at least sometimes (boys 84 per cent, girls 78 per cent).

In the case of ethnicity, similar patterns emerged. Among the 49 responses from black students (44 per cent of the total), there was clear evidence of 'black' tastes and preferences. While many of the texts named by black students were also named by whites, this was predictably much more the case with mainstream 'black' television than with more specialist music or magazines. Even in the case of programmes like *The Cosby Show*, however, black students tended to express stronger preferences, for example by ticking 'always' rather than 'sometimes'; and they were much more likely to watch the slightly more 'specialist' *Fresh Prince of Bel Air* (90 per cent black, 52 per cent white). In the case of music, the mainstream pop of Capital Radio was much more popular with white students (47 per cent white, 22 per cent black), while the reverse was true with the local black music station WNK; and nearly all the pirate stations were named by black students.

At the same time, this identification of specifically 'black' tastes was significantly inflected by gender. Among the boys, 80 per cent said that they watched *The Fresh Prince of Bel Air* and 98 per cent *The Cosby Show*, although this was split evenly between 'always' and 'sometimes'. By contrast, 98 per cent of the black girls watched these programmes, all claiming to do so 'always'. The boys named only one 'black' film (*Juice*), and no 'black' magazines or books were added; only one claimed to have read a Maya Angelou book, and while 37 per cent read *The Voice* (the black British newspaper), 25 per cent said that they never did so. By contrast, the girls added *Desmonds* (the black British sitcom) and also supplied three additional titles for 'black' films, which were all named more than once. Only one girl said she never read *The Voice*, while 84 per cent said that they did, and 16 per cent claimed to have read a Maya Angelou book. Black girls were also more likely to name books by black writers and 'black' magazines, particularly *Black Beat*, which was named by 28 per cent. Responses to the questions about radio and music also indicated the girls' clearer identification with specifically 'black' tastes.

Of course, the reliability of this information is questionable. Our sample is small, and we would not claim that these students are necessarily representative of broader demographic categories. In this sense, the results merely serve to set the scene for the slightly more detailed observations that follow, and for the more extensive qualitative studies contained in later chapters. Questionnaires obviously do not provide a completely accurate measure of students' media uses and preferences, let alone their *meanings* for the students themselves. Nevertheless, the fact that people *claim* to watch or read or listen to particular texts is itself significant. As we shall argue, defining one's tastes — even in the apparently 'neutral' context of a questionnaire — is in itself a social act: it is part of the broader process whereby young people construct and define their social identities.

The key issue here, which the results do at least begin to indicate, is that of social diversity. As we have noted, debates about young people and the media often assume that both are homogeneous. 'Young people' are treated as a single social group, defined primarily in terms of their difference from adults.[5] Likewise, the differences between media and between texts are often elided; 'the media' or 'popular culture' are seen as unitary and undifferentiated. Even researchers and teachers broadly sympathetic to young people's use of the media tend to resort to notions of 'common culture' or assertions to the effect that 'this is "their" culture'.[6] Yet, as our summary begins to indicate, the picture is one of commonality *and* diversity: and while this varies systematically between media and between texts (television is more of a shared medium than books, for example, and *Neighbours* is more shared than *News at 6*), it also varies between different social groups. Furthermore, the differences even between such apparently similar programmes as (for example) *The Cosby Show* and *The Fresh Prince of Bel Air*, or *Neighbours* and *EastEnders*, are clearly significant for their readers. And while the reasons for these differences may partly be found in the texts themselves, they may emerge much more clearly in their social use and circulation.

Ultimately, however, the key question is how we understand these differences. Perhaps inevitably, a survey of this kind tends to construct social differences in merely demographic, distributional terms, by lumping individuals together to stand for broader social categories. At this level, it tends to confirm some of our informal 'intuitions' — for example, about boys' and girls' reading — while upsetting others, thus suggesting hypotheses for further investigation — for example, about girls' use of computer games, or about the differences between girls' and boys' definitions of 'black' culture.

Yet at the same time, we want to move beyond such a view of difference, which sees it primarily in terms of distribution. This is because the differences that we are concerned with are essentially to do with power relationships. Claiming specifically 'black' tastes, for example, is not merely a neutral act, a statement of what you individually happen to like. On the contrary, claiming particular tastes and preferences and discussing readings of specific texts are part of the process by which individuals come to define their identity and social position in relation to others, and thereby to situate themselves in broader relationships of social power.

Social Readings

These processes of social use may be identified, at the most obvious level, in the ways in which texts themselves are physically circulated. In Tottenham, as in many other inner-city communities, the piracy of videos and computer games and the home taping of favourite music tracks are widespread — and of course the reasons for this are partly economic. The large majority of students' video viewing appeared to be of pirate tapes, often obtained through well-organised networks in the local area. Students regularly spoke of having seen films that were not yet officially available on video, and had only recently been released in the cinema — and indeed often volunteered to obtain them for us. Similarly, the high cost of computer games made outright purchase comparatively rare: even among the devotees, the majority of the games that they possessed were illegal copies. Swapping and borrowing texts was thus a means whereby tastes and relationships were formed, and where evaluations and judgments were established and debated.

In the case of some other media, however, this was much less the case. As we have noted, there was very little evidence of books having been exchanged by students, and also a general sense in which reading books appeared to be a much more private activity. Against our expectations, this also seemed to be the case with comics. Here, the economic value of old or special editions of comics tended to prevent them from being shared, for fear that they would be damaged. Darren, a comics enthusiast, spoke of how he kept his comics in special envelopes, only taking them out to read 'for reference' — although this sense of the essentially private nature of comic reading was tempered by his experience of specialist shops and comic marts, and the knowledge that his interests were much more widely shared (see below).

Yet there were many instances in which the act of reading or viewing was described as an essentially collective activity. Recent studies of television viewing, for example, have focused on the ways in which it is located in the broader context of family interaction and the routines of domestic life.[7] The meanings of television viewing as an activity, and of specific programmes, are themselves partly mediated by the social relationships that surround them, and gender and age are unavoidably significant here. The definition of what constitutes 'appropriate viewing' for young people, for example, is subject to a constant process of negotiation — and in many cases, a war of attrition — that takes place around the family television set. As we shall indicate in Chapter 6, many students demonstrated a clear and often ironical understanding of these processes; while most had access to additional sets, and thus the opportunity for private viewing, there was a sense in which, for better or worse, television was seen to be a 'family' activity. On the other hand, collective video viewing — for example, the enthusiasm for horror among some teenage boys — might be seen as a 'youth culture' phenomenon, whose significance derives partly from its function as a form of competitive male bonding and partly from the evasion of parental regulation that it often entails.[8]

Our research did not take us beyond the boundaries of the school, yet similar processes were undoubtedly at work here. The collective reading of girls' magazines or the informal discussion of computer games that take place outside lessons, in the playground or during registration at the beginning of the day are familiar aspects of school life. Indeed, such activities might partly be seen as a form of resistance to the institutional constraints of the school: having a quick blast on your Walkman between classes, or surreptitiously reading *Just Seventeen* in the middle of a boring lesson, may serve as a kind of 'escape attempt', albeit one which runs the risk of official censure and temporary confiscation.

Some of the interviews we recorded with students in this age group provided further opportunities to observe these processes at first hand. Of course, removing groups of students from lessons, taking them to a room elsewhere in the school and asking them a series of questions about their preferences is bound to set up an 'artificial' situation, however informal we might attempt to make it. Such interviews may be likely to cue a 'critical' discourse about the media — or alternatively to encourage apparently 'subversive' responses — and we would be unwise to take what is said at face value.[9] Nevertheless, at least part of what took place here *did* seem to replicate what occurred on other occasions, particularly when we stopped asking questions and just let the students talk amongst themselves.

This was certainly the case, for example, in an interview with a group of 14-year-old girls which focused on teenage magazines such as *Just Seventeen* and *Big*. Their reading was very much a collective activity: they described how they would 'flick through' the magazines at break or lunch times (and occasionally during lessons), reading out each other's horoscopes, 'gossiping about this page and that page' and admiring the pin-ups (a style of reading that is of course encouraged by the design of the magazines themselves). Once the 'interview' had finished, they continued to read the magazines we had provided, commenting on Michael Jackson's plastic surgery, ogling Tom

Cruise, discussing how male strippers had appeared on *EastEnders*, admiring the computer graphics and sharing the free perfume sample.

In discussion, the girls were very definite in identifying the magazines as 'theirs': they described them as 'for kids' like themselves, and as 'realistic', 'up to date' and 'telling you about life'. While they acknowledged that boys might secretly read these magazines, they agreed that, as Suna put it, 'they would feel funny going round with *Just Seventeen* in their pocket, thinking they're hard'. To this extent, the magazines appeared to speak to their own sense of positive female values: unlike boys, they argued, girls were 'more understanding' and 'caring', they showed their feelings and were more interested in 'long relationships . . . making it last'. By contrast, boys were defined as 'immature': 'they just act like they're still in junior school . . . getting their magazines out and reading computers "yeah, I've got that computer, you haven't"'. Yet at the same time, there was a sense in which the girls' reading was selective. While they enjoyed the 'gossip' and the horoscopes, they admitted that, in Suna's words, 'you believe the bits you want to believe'. Similarly, while they acknowledged that the problem pages did reflect some of the realities of 'teenage life', and might be valuable if they weren't able to talk to their parents, they also agreed that 'you have to go your own way'.

As this example suggests, the collective reading of texts can be part of a broader process of constructing social relationships and thereby defining individual and group identities. In this case, the discussion of the magazines is part of the way in which the girls actively and positively define themselves, both in terms of age and gender, as teenage girls with teenage girls' interests and concerns that are distinct from those of adult women or boys.

A more extended example of the gendered aspects of this process emerged from a series of interviews about computer games.[10] Despite the fact that many girls played computer games and possessed their own systems (as our survey indicated), there was little doubt that this was perceived as a primarily male domain. Rather like adult men talking about their cars, the boys' main preoccupation was with comparing the capabilities and prices of different systems. A clear hierarchy of systems emerged here — portables, super systems, mega systems, master systems, wonder mega systems — which was established partly in terms of the capacity of the disks ('meg' or 'half meg'), and partly in terms of the potential attachments (whether you can have more than one joystick, or whether you can connect it to a CD player, or even a karaoke!). The primary criteria for judging the quality of games were those of realism — for example, in terms of the detail of the graphics, the inclusion of realistic sound effects and the smoothness of the movement — and complexity — for example, the number of levels or options, the complexity of the rules and the inclusion of 'secret codes'. Both criteria are clearly dependent on the memory capacity of the computer.

Computer magazines had an important role to play here. They helped to establish a specialist terminology — for example for the generic classification of games (shoot-em-ups, beat-em-ups, platform games, and so on) — and provided a basis for informed consumer choices (for example, about the quality of graphics, or about 'presentation' and 'playability'). Much of the discussion took the form of a projection: looking forward to games and systems that the boys would be buying in the future, and awaiting the UK release of games that were currently available only as Japanese imports. The boys preferred the 'unofficial' computer magazines, largely on the grounds that they seemed to promote a kind of 'critical consumerism', for example by warning readers about 'bodge jobs' that had been badly translated from one system to another. The boys were very aware of the high profit margins on games; and, as we have noted, most of the games in their own collections were in fact pirate copies.

Although the playing of computer games is usually an individual activity, there was also a sense of a collective process here. The detailed comparisons of systems, and the sharing of information about new products, which took place in our interviews were similar to those processes which took place daily during class registration, as groups of boys huddled round copies of the new magazines. Learning to play new games (particularly pirate copies, which came without an instruction book) was itself a partly social process, in which players would swap hints, additional codes and 'cheats' which had either been discovered accidentally or gleaned from magazines. From the boys' point of view, this was a medium that was distinctively 'theirs'. While they acknowledged that girls might play, it was argued that they would probably use their brothers' machines; and if they did own their own system, it was unlikely to be a high-status one. Yet significantly, the 'gendering' of computer games was seen to be at least partly a function of peer-group talk: as Dean said, 'if [girls'] friends don't talk about it, they don't talk about it'.

Predictably, the girls were much less committed and enthusiastic, although they were also more reflective, about computer games. Their accounts of the games that they had played emphasised their predictability, but they were also keen to distinguish between the games that they themselves preferred — 'fantasy ones . . . where you have to make decisions about what to do' — and those which boys were seen to enjoy. According to Kerry, 'the boys like all the fast games, 'cause they don't have to use their brains . . . it's something they can do without thinking about it.' They also argued that the 'publicity' for computer games was 'geared for boys' and that the games were largely 'designed for them'. Although Kerry was more enthusiastic about 'violent' games than the other girls (and this was a preference which extended to a taste in 'gory' books), she was also explicitly critical of the sexism of the games: 'You never see a woman on *Streetfighter* . . . the woman is never the heroine, she just sits there going "help me! help me!", and he has to save her, but you never see the man in trouble and the woman saving.'

As in the girls' discussion of teenage magazines described above, the girls' comments on the games fed into broader criticisms of boys. These were partly on the grounds of intelligence: boys, it was argued, couldn't read, and even when they did appear to be reading — for example, computer magazines and pornography — they were only 'going for the pictures'. Interestingly, boys' lives were described as much more limited than their own. Like the magazine readers, they argued that girls tended to go out more, and had a wider range of interests. While boys were 'hooked' on computer games, girls had 'better things to do with their time'.

In both cases, therefore, talk about popular texts served as a means of establishing group identity and group membership, defined primarily here in terms of gender. Yet largely because they did not perceive themselves to be the 'primary' or at least the intended audience, the girls were much more explicit about this, and more reflective, than the boys. In attempting to explain the reasons for their sense of exclusion, the girls were thus inevitably more critical both of the games themselves (for example, on the grounds of their 'sexist' and violent content) and of the boys who play them. Like many adult critics, they effectively pathologised the 'fans' as mindless addicts — although it is notable that the boys themselves also attempted to displace the potentially negative effects of game playing onto other people, in this case 'little kids' who would fail to perceive the unrealistic nature of the material, and thus be encouraged to imitate it.[11] By contrast, the boys were almost too close to the experience, and for this reason could only define it in insiders' terms — for example, by using the specialist terminology derived from the magazines. Yet in a sense, it was not really in their interests to be reflective, at least in this context: talk about the games was primarily a means of asserting group membership through the sharing of specialist expertise, and any questioning of the pleasures of the games was only likely to disrupt this.

Many of these arguments can also be applied to 'race' and ethnicity, although in a rather different way. As our survey results imply, black Afro-Caribbean students (and particularly black girls) appeared to have a much more explicit, 'conscious' cultural identity than other ethnic groups. While this may to some extent be a local phenomenon, the reasons for it are of course related to much broader historical and political movements.[12] Certainly, in the school, and in the local area, the assertion of a positive black cultural identity has a very wide cultural purchase. For a minority of black students, this was a matter of articulating a specifically 'black' political perspective, and of informing themselves about black history: hence, for example, the significance of *The Voice* newspaper, and of the work of certain black American and Caribbean writers.

Yet for the majority of both black and white students, it was in the area of popular music and fashion that this issue held a particular significance. Black musical genres such as hip-hop, rap and ragga were perceived by most students to carry high status: they were seen to embody a kind of 'hardness' and 'realism' which were regarded as essential for survival in the inner city. As we shall indicate in more detail in Chapter 4, there were a number of white students whose preference for these styles was clearly related to their broader attempts to redefine their own cultural identity. Yet for some black students, this in turn created a problem.

In one of our interviews, two black students, Leon and Damien, engaged in an extensive debate about this relationship between taste and the peer group. They had conducted a survey of musical preferences as part of their Media Studies coursework (to be described in more detail in Chapter 6) and had been surprised to discover that their own taste for ragga music was shared equally between black and white students. From their point of view, ragga (a kind of combination of rap and reggae) was the most distinctively 'black' of all popular music genres, although the reasons for this were hard to define: it was partly a matter of the use of Caribbean dialect, although it was also to do with the 'different beats' and the music's perceived lack of commercial appeal. Damien argued that white people who claimed to listen to ragga were 'lying' (or at least exaggerating), primarily in order to fit in with their peers: '[If] they listen to ragga, they're in with the in crowd . . . if they listen to something else, they might not be with the in crowd'. While this may partly be true, it nevertheless comes close to a 'commonsense' adult dismissal of young people's preferences — which implies that they merely 'follow the crowd', whereas adults themselves are implicitly seen to be much more discerning (the strangely 1960s phrase 'the in crowd' is perhaps revealing in this respect).

When it came to considering their own tastes, however, there was a good deal more ambivalence about the role of the peer group. At different points in the discussion, each boy accused the other of merely following the crowd, and yet also admitted doing so himself — although such admissions were subsequently retracted. The relationship between music and associated styles of dress proved to be particularly problematic here. For example, Damien accused Leon of wearing 'ragga clothes' — 'suits and stuff' — although Leon retorted that this was 'just clothes . . . just what I like'. This led on to some speculation about the origins of ragga style — 'someone has to buy it first before it's in' — although the processes by which styles were disseminated remained a mystery: was it simply that 'everyone buys it because it looks good', or was it that baggy clothes made it easier to dance to the music? Damien went on to challenge Leon, asking him if he would wear country and western clothes ('big hats') if everybody else did: Leon's admission that he would, while perhaps ironic, appeared to confirm Damien's argument that he merely 'followed the fashion'.

Nevertheless, when it came to their white peers, the boys maintained that their professed interest in black music might simply be a form of hypocrisy — or at least that their behaviour at home might be different from that at school:

Damien: I didn't expect as much white people to listen to ragga as black people. That's why I think people was a bit lying, 'cause they're with their friends in school and their friends listen to it, they just write it down as well, but when they're actually in their home, the black people would play like ragga music loud in their house and dance to it, whereas I don't think the white people would do that. They might say they do, but . . .

Leon: They just play it and just do something else.

Damien: They wouldn't be listening to it.

The boys are attempting to deal with a difficult contradiction here. They know — or at least seem to have discovered — that black music carries high status for many of their white peers. Yet they also want to hold on to the notion that there is something distinctively 'black' about the music they enjoy, or at least about the way they use it. When pressed, they found this hard to define, although there was definitely a sense in which black artists who had 'gone commercial' were seen to have abandoned their specific appeal to a black audience. This was most transparently the case with Michael Jackson, who was condemned for being 'ashamed of what he is'. Similarly, they rejected white appropriations of black styles, for example in the case of the white rapper Vanilla Ice, who was fiercely dismissed as a 'copy' and a 'fake'. Yet underlying this debate is a more fundamental tension, between their apparent discovery that race 'makes no difference' and their knowledge that it *does*. Commonsense theories of fashion, which reduce taste to a matter of individual whim, or alternatively to a slavish following of the crowd, or which provide merely functional explanations ('baggy clothes make it easier to dance'), did not ultimately seem to offer a satisfactory explanation of the complexity of the process. While the establishment of taste is clearly seen here as a social, interpersonal process, it is not, however, something that can merely be dismissed (as it often is) by resorting to simplistic notions of 'peer pressure'.

However, it is important to avoid a determinist approach to these issues. In particular, we should beware of assuming that black Afro-Caribbean culture can be made to 'stand in' for all kinds of ethnic culture, or that it is itself simply homogeneous. The explicit or 'conscious' relationship to cultural products that we have noted here seemed to be rather different from the more ambivalent, at times even ironic, approach of some of the Greek or Turkish Cypriot students, for example. In one particularly hilarious interview, two Greek Cypriot girls engaged in extended, but highly affectionate, parodies of their parents' cultures and accents, and of the advertisements featured on local Greek radio. They seemed to be particularly inspired by the British-Greek Cypriot comedy duo 'Donna and Kebab' — although they also strongly rejected the character of the kebab-shop owner 'Stavros', played by the white British comedian Harry Enfield. At the same time, they were keen to assert 'we're proud to be Greek!' and spoke with great enthusiasm about Greek food and Greek festivals — although in fact both girls were born in the UK, and neither had ever visited Cyprus. Justifiably, however, they seemed to be claiming the right to satirize their 'own' culture, and *denying* that right to outsiders. As we shall indicate in later chapters, there was a sense in which these 'minority' cultures, such as Greek and Turkish Cypriot or Hong Kong Chinese — or at least the cultural *differences* between them and the dominant white British culture — were regarded as less 'visible' than Afro-Caribbean culture; and there was a feeling among some students that they would like to keep them that way, for fear that a greater degree of visibility would leave them vulnerable to racism. Again, the reasons for these differences relate to broader political and historical factors.

A second issue here concerns the interpenetration of different ethnic cultures — a phenomenon which has been seen as part of the cultural 'syncretism' of contemporary inner-city life.[13] In particular, as Leon and Damien's observations suggest, black Afro-Caribbean and Afro-American culture has a considerable degree of salience for many white working-class young people. Yet the fact that particular texts are popular does not necessarily mean that they are read in the same way — indeed, one might well argue that their ability to permit a wide range of readings is one of the major reasons for their popularity in the first place. To choose an extreme case, *The Cosby Show* is clearly popular among white South Africans and among black Britons for very different reasons. Leon and Damien, for example, acknowledged the way in which the show made reference to black history and to aspects of black culture (such as food) which might be less apparent or significant to white viewers. Likewise, they argued that, despite his attempts to appeal to a white audience, (MC) Hammer had retained specifically 'black' elements both in his music (for example, his references to gospel) and in his style of dance. On the other hand, different texts obviously possess a different potential for appropriation: it is unlikely that the group Public Enemy will ever gain a large following among white South Africans; and it is perhaps because of their resistance to this kind of appropriation by white audiences that Leon and Damien valued them so highly.

In our account thus far, we have attempted to define reading as an inherently *social* process. This has two main dimensions. Firstly, it involves a recognition that the 'meaning' of a text is not established by the reader in isolation. On the contrary, meanings are defined in and through social interaction, and particularly through talk. As John Fiske has argued, talk about popular media can be seen as part of a broader 'oral culture'.[14] The meanings which circulate within everyday discussions of texts are 'read back' into individual responses, thereby generating a dynamic interplay between 'social' and 'individual' readings — and perhaps ultimately rendering the distinction itself irrelevant. What we 'think' about texts and how we use them in our daily lives depend to a great extent on how we talk about them with others, and on the contexts in which we do so. Reading is thus inevitably a process of *dialogue*.[15]

Secondly, looking as it were in the opposite direction, talk about popular media also serves functions involved in constructing and negotiating social relationships. In considering how individuals use and talk about what they read, therefore, we are effectively examining the ways in which they socialise themselves into group membership, and thereby construct their own cultural identities. In defining their own tastes, individual readers also develop hypotheses about how *other* people read. For example by distinguishing between 'fans' and less committed readers, or in terms of gender or ethnicity, they define themselves as readers in terms of what they are not as well as in terms of what they are — and indeed, in the case of popular music, this may be particularly significant. As we have indicated, this process is likely to be complex and tentative, particularly when it comes to 'buying into' membership of other social groups. Yet it is also, crucially, an active process. As we have shown, tastes and preferences are socially distributed, and they serve as markers of social distinctions and positions — and thus of power relationships; yet the *meanings* of those distinctions and positions — what it means to be black or white, male or female — are not simply given but are actively reconstructed and renegotiated through social interaction.[16] It is through such processes that 'readings' become 'culture'.

What underlies this approach is a broadly post-structuralist notion of subjectivity, not as singular and fixed, but rather as multiple and constantly changing.[17] From this perspective, identity is seen to be constructed at least partly through and in relation to the 'subject positions' that are embodied in discourse; yet those subject positions themselves are seen as diverse and potentially contradictory. The media are regarded here not as powerful forces, inexorably conditioning young people into predetermined social roles; on the contrary, they provide heterogeneous 'symbolic resources' which young people may actively use in seeking to define and to resist the various social identities that are available to them. Of course, the meanings and pleasures that can be constructed from texts, and the subject positions that are available to their readers, are not infinite. The 'activity' and autonomy of readers is clearly circumscribed, although in ways that will vary for different readers in different contexts, and for different texts. Ultimately, however, this relationship between the 'power' of the reader and the 'power' of the text is one that cannot be defined in the abstract, or determined in advance. Yet the crux of our argument is that both *are* defined *in relation to each other*: in accepting that the text is somehow 'readable' in the first place, we also inevitably agree to become its reader, and we do so at least partly in the terms that the text permits. In reading, and in talking about what we read, we are thus simultaneously defining our identities as readers.

Rethinking Reading: Profiles, Histories and Positions

One of the difficulties of this emphasis on the social process of reading is that it can easily lead to the assumption that social groups are much more homogeneous, and the boundaries between them much more rigid, than they actually are. Such an approach leads to a determinist account of reading, in which readers are seen to read in a particular way *because* of their gender or ethnic background, or because of some other given 'fact' about their social position.[18] Such an account inevitably tends to ignore the diversity and complexity of individual readings and tastes.

As we have suggested, different readers may make sense of one and the same text in quite different ways — and to a greater or lesser extent, this diversity of readings is something that texts may well invite, or at least allow. Furthermore, individual readers will inevitably read a range of different texts, and any given text that they read will be perceived in this broader context. Perhaps particularly for young people, the kinds of texts that they read and prefer will change quite dramatically as they mature. By comparing what they are reading with their other experiences of reading, both contemporaneously and historically, readers will come to recognise what *kind* of thing it is that they are reading, and what it can and cannot do for them.

These points may all appear quite obvious, but they do begin to identify some of the parameters of what we have termed the *social process* of reading. There appear to be three distinct but related aspects here, which we will term reading *positions*, reading *profiles* and reading *histories*. To restate: each text (for example, by virtue of its specific textual properties, its address to its readers and its intertextual relationships with other texts) makes available a broader or narrower range of *reading positions*, and also closes off others; that is, it invites the reader to read it in some ways but not others, and demands, and thereby develops, particular kinds of competencies. In reading, and in sharing what they read, readers also define themselves. In semiotic terms, this is a process that has both a synchronic and a diachronic dimension. Thus, readers can be said to have *reading profiles* — that is, as they read a range of texts at any given time, and they situate a particular text by comparison with other texts, defining it in terms of what it is and is not. This process also changes over time: readers have *reading histories*, and as their experience of texts widens, so the way that they situate the text also changes. It is through these processes that young people develop their cultural competencies as readers, while simultaneously constructing identities for themselves as particular *kinds* of readers. We would like to illustrate these points by considering four brief examples.

The first is drawn from a series of interviews relating to Britain's most popular — and indeed most notorious — daily newspaper, *The Sun*.[19] What was particularly striking about these interviews was the remarkable degree of ambivalence that students expressed. On the one hand, they were all regular readers of *The Sun*, and actively chose it in preference to other newspapers. While there were clear gender differences here — with the boys reading it primarily for the sports coverage, and the girls preferring the 'gossip' about stars and royalty — there was also a way in which the paper seemed to speak to their shared sense of class and generational membership. Unlike the so-called 'quality' newspapers, which were seen to be directed at middle-class readers, *The Sun* was defined as being for 'working people' like their parents — and by extension themselves; and it was also described as 'easy to read' and therefore more appropriate for young people. The political news featured so heavily in other newspapers it was often condemned as 'boring', and as the domain of adults. For the few students who expressed any interest in politics, this seemed to be catered for by their other reading: Anthony, for example, also read black newspapers such as *The Voice* and *The Gleaner*, which he described as 'more realistic, more true'.

On the other hand, though, *The Sun* was also condemned by many students for its hypocrisy and dishonesty — for its tendency to 'lie', to 'exaggerate' and to 'bullshit'. While these complaints related primarily to false predictions about the soap operas and scurrilous gossip about the stars' private lives, they occasionally extended to 'straight' new stories. Gemma and Lyndsey, for example, complained about the paper's biased coverage of the Gulf War, arguing that 'they told lies' about Saddam Hussein and that 'they didn't show the bad things what other people had done'. Eda (who is not black herself) also criticised the 'racist' way in which the paper referred to black people, and offered a comment which seemed to sum up much of this ambivalence: '*The Sun*'s a hypocrite, it's a liar and it's sometimes racist. I don't know why I read it.'

What emerged very clearly from these interviews, however, was the students' sense of the *place* of *The Sun* in relation to other types of reading. By comparison with the genteel restraint of *The Independent*, for example, the paper appeared to be valued for its vulgarity, its plain speaking and its crude rejection of pomposity and pretension. While it was certainly distrusted in comparison with television news, it was also distinguished in this respect from the *Daily Sport*, whose stories about eight-stone babies and children born with beaks were described with great hilarity. *The Sun* was defined by most students as a 'rubbish paper', but one they enjoyed nevertheless, because it served particular functions very well: 'reading *The Sun*' was not seen as an exercise in responsible citizenship but simply as a means of relaxation, and as something it would be wrong to take too seriously. To imply that the paper is a kind of biblical text which is studied and obeyed, or that it is responsible for merely imposing reactionary views on its passive readers — as many critics appear to suppose[20] — may well be to miss the point.

These students' reading of *The Sun* was thus part of a broader *reading profile*. Their sense of its limitations and of its positive functions for them derived partly from a comparison with other texts. Yet, as we have noted, this process may also have a historical (or diachronic) dimension. The next two case studies, which relate to girls' and boys' reading, illustrate this sense of *reading histories*.

As we have noted, the girls in the age group studied in this book were generally much more enthusiastic readers of books than were the boys — a fact which will come as little surprise to most English teachers. Furthermore, there were clear distinctions between the kinds of books that they read out of school and those that they read *in* school. In fact, their leisure reading was fairly diverse, covering a range of genres including crime fiction, humour, adventure stories and horror; and some black students also stated a preference for black writers such as Maya Angelou and Alice Walker. It was romances and sexy bestsellers, however, that formed the staple of most girls' reading diets.

Interestingly, many of the girls appeared to be at a point of transition in their reading careers: many were leaving behind teenage romances such as the *Sweet Valley High* and *Sweet Dreams* series, and moving on to more 'adult' fiction by the likes of Jackie Collins. Their discussions of the romance were often quite ambivalent as a result, as the following extract shows:

Sophie: [I read] Mills and Boons books, that's just when I haven't got a book. But some of the stories in them are really boring, because they're really soppy, one of them stupid love stories.
Natasha: Yeah, sex and violence.
Carol: So predictable.
Sophie: There was one of them I read —
DB: Sex and violence, what in Mills and Boon?
Natasha: Yeah, it seems like that to me.
Carol: Not really.
Sophie: They're a bit soppy for me. But there was one that I read, 'cause I got a whole load, 'cause I don't normally read at home, and I got a whole load, and I don't even look at them, but I did look at one of them, I can't remember what it was called, but it was quite good, it ended up, it wasn't as predictable as all the rest, because like all the rest you could say 'Oh, he's gonna jump off the cliff and commit suicide'. You knew what was gonna happen on the next page.
DB: But they're not all like that, you're saying?
Girls: No.
Carol: The writers. It varies, with the writers.

The hesitations and backtracking in Sophie's contributions here suggest a strong desire to disclaim her earlier preferences. On the one hand, she seems to be able to make generalisations about the genre, and to suggest possible distinctions within it; while on the other hand, she says that she only 'looked at' one of the books. While their criticisms are partly to do with artistic quality — the complaint about the stories being 'predictable' — Natasha also introduces a discourse of moral judgment, albeit one which the others recognise is less appropriate here. While Sophie and Carol acknowledge the familiar criticisms of romances, and thus implicitly distance themselves from the 'typical' unenlightened reader, they are also concerned to make distinctions here. Although she doesn't go into detail, Carol's last comment would imply that she is actually a rather experienced and discriminating Mills and Boon reader.

The hesitations here might partly derive from an implicit acknowledgment that Mills and Boon is culturally low-status stuff, although it may also reflect the fact that it is not seen as 'adult' enough. In this group, for example, the critical discourse did not seem to extend to Jackie Collins, who was praised without reserve. Indeed, following a subsequent class in which we examined definitions of 'literature', it was Sophie who 'borrowed' David's copies of Jackie Collins's *Rock Star* and Joan Collins's *Prime Time,* and subsequently failed to return them! Here, and in other groups, it was generally agreed that Jackie Collins's novels would not be seen as appropriate reading for school, although this was primarily on the grounds that they were 'adult' in a way that most class readers were not, rather than for reasons of literary value (see Chapter 7).

In this instance, then, there is a sense in which the girls' historical transition from one type of reading to another leads them to revise or at least recontextualise their earlier preferences.[21] Questions both about modality — about how 'realistic' the stories are perceived to be — and, implicitly, about ideology — for example, about the ways in which they reinforce misleading 'soppy' notions of romantic love — come into play at this stage as a result of their wider experience both of reading and, of course, of life in general.

A different, and somewhat more explicit, instance of this notion of 'reading history' comes from an interview with two comic readers, Darren and Mark. Darren, whom we have mentioned briefly above, was increasingly becoming involved in the specialist networks of comic readers, going to comics shops and marts, trading back issues and buying a readers' newsletter.[22] In the process, he had developed clear preferences for particular writers and artists. Both boys had been comics fans for many years, having begun by collecting *Dandy* and *Beano* and then moving on to DC and Marvel. Within this transition, Darren also saw himself as having made the move from simpler comics, such as *Punisher,* aimed at children and which he described as being simply concerned with 'action and fighting' — to more complex 'Mutant comics' aimed at older teenagers and adults.

The long history of some comic heroes was also significant here: having a collection of comics, which one could 'flick through for reference', ıade it possible to recall characters' past lives, and thereby to fill out the background to current story lines. Much of the appeal of Marvel comics in particular would appear to derive both from their wealth of intertextual references and from their self-reflexivity — characteristics which clearly serve to construct a reading position based on notions of expertise and 'insider knowledge',[23] It was almost as though Darren had 'grown up' with characters such as Batman, Spiderman and the Incredible Hulk, as they themselves had become more complex and mature, and had developed what he called 'realistic' and 'normal' private lives in addition to their less realistic public personae. For example, he noted the changes that had occurred in the character of Batman: 'He's changed, 'cause he never used to come out at night and be a dark man, like a vigilante; he's bad as well as good . . . I think it's a bit more for adult readers now.' In the case of the Batman films, he argued that a *different* kind of reading was available to a specialist reader such as himself as compared with the general audience:

> Darren: I think it helps if you read the comic, if you read a few Batman comics, before you see the new film, so you get an understanding of the character, what he's really like. 'Cause some people thought it was rubbish, but they didn't really know what he's really like, didn't understand it . . . They didn't understand the way he acts; they didn't really understand that much about his background.

What Darren defined as more 'adult' comics were also distinguished by their engagement with 'realistic' social issues:

> Darren: *X-Man* — that's a good comic. It may talk about racism or something like that, and things like that . . . It slips into the plot as well. And it changes with the times. Like before they may talk about, 'cause it's an American comic, like the Cold War and stuff like that, to do with Russian spies and stuff like that . . . [They tell you about] like people on the streets, like poverty and stuff like that.

Darren thus had a clear sense of his own history as a comic reader, with a past and a potential future. His knowledge of the wider comics culture enabled him to recognise that this was not simply a 'childish' preoccupation. While he had not attended comics conventions himself, largely because this was beyond his means, he knew that there were adults who did so; and while he felt he had now 'moved on' from his earlier preferences, he acknowledged that there were other comics and graphic novels, aimed at what he called 'mature readers', that he might come to enjoy in the future. Typically, however, both Darren and Mark claimed that they did *not* read books outside school — although the emphasis both on a long-term engagement with more 'realistic' characters and on the seriousness and complexity of the themes, might suggest that in many ways reading comics served similar functions to those which reading books might serve for some adult readers.

Finally, the *social character* of reading can also be traced more closely, in the ways in which individuals interpret specific texts or genres. Studies of television soap operas, for example, have provided very clear illustrations of the ways in which this particular genre enables readers to move between different 'reading positions'.[24] Talk about TV soaps often fluctuates between a position of close engagement with the text — in which it is described as, to all intents and purposes, 'real' — to one of considerable distance, in which the artificiality and implausibility of the characters and storylines are criticised and mocked. What Christine Geraghty has called 'the oscillation between involvement and distance'.[25] is one of the characteristic pleasures of the genre.

This was certainly the case with the students we interviewed here. Elizabeth and Manivone, for example, were both regular viewers of at least four soap operas. Both in our interview and, in some cases, in lessons, they would engage in extended debates about the moral rights and wrongs of the characters' behaviour — for example, condemning Michelle in *EastEnders* for acting like a 'slag', or speculating about whether Sophie in *Home and Away* was pregnant with David's baby. Yet their discussion of the programmes was also characterised by a constant barrage of satire and condemnation. They complained about implausible and predictable story lines, poor acting and wobbly sets, and professed great amusement at the prospect of characters being 'killed off'. Elizabeth argued that *Eldorado* was so 'predictable' that 'you don't really have to watch it': she claimed to watch the programme with the sound turned down because 'you know what they're saying'. This distanced perspective also appeared to derive from the 'secondary texts' that surround the programmes — for example, the plot predictions, and the information about the actors' private lives that regularly appears in the popular press.

Here, too, there was a sense of the girls' having a reading history — although — as in the case of the romance readers, their move towards more 'adult' viewing led them to be more critical both of the realism of the programmes and of their ideology. Thus, for example, the girls discussed the marriage of Scott and Charlene in *Neighbours* (which had taken place roughly four years previously) as follows:

Elizabeth: Because I was younger, I thought that was really good . . .
Manivone: Yeah, but you know, they give people what they wanna see, isn't it? They think it's 'Aaahh', it's sweet. That's what people wanna see.
Elizabeth: When I think back to it, I think, like little girls, they're sort of expected to get married at, how old was she? She was really young. Get married and start going all lovey-dovey, and get a family and go and move to Brisbane . . . Is that what they expect us to do? Like when I was younger —
Manivone: — that was just to write them out.
Elizabeth: But you don't do things like that.
DB: So you don't think the programme gives you kind of, like, sort of advice about life?
Manivone: No!
Elizabeth: But it sort of, 'cause it gets us talking about it, that's the thing. 'Cause when we start talking about *Home and Away*, like whether or not we would let Meg, if she was older, if we would let her go with Blake and everything. That's the one good thing about it.

Manivone: They do the obvious thing, though, don't they?
Elizabeth: Yeah, they do, it's really obvious . . .

Of course, it is possible that this 'critical' discourse was prompted by the interview situation, although it seemed to emerge spontaneously at the very start. Clearly, this discourse is a powerful one, in the sense that it might enable one to present oneself as superior to the 'ordinary viewer', who is somehow taken in by the programme and believes it to be real. In this extract, for example, Manivone suggests that the programme might be giving 'people' what they want to see — although she clearly does not include herself in this group of people. Yet in fact, the girls subsequently denied that anybody of their own age would be likely to 'take the programmes seriously' in this way — although they were prepared to entertain the possibility that 'little kids', and perhaps the occasional 'psycho', might do so. Both girls described how they would laugh at the programmes while they were on — even at moments of high drama — suggesting that this was not a position adopted simply as a form of impression management. However, as Elizabeth's penultimate comment here suggests, the programmes also seem to construct an arena in which they can discuss their own more 'personal' concerns — although, as she implies, this kind of discussion does not necessarily have to rely either on the terms provided by the programmes themselves or on the belief that they are realistic.

The fact remains, however, that both girls were regular viewers of these programmes — as indeed were most of their peers (as our survey indicated). So why did they watch them? Elizabeth sought to explain this simply in terms of 'boredom', while Manivone argued that there was 'nothing else to watch'. They seemed to agree that viewing was a habit they had picked up in junior school and had merely carried on. Nevertheless, their discussion indirectly reveals some more complex reasons. As we have noted, there is a sense in which the critical distance that these programmes permit (if not encourage) enables the reader to experience a kind of personal 'empowerment', a sense of superiority both to the text and to the characters. Indeed, in Elizabeth's case, this sense seemed to extend to the programme's producers:

Elizabeth: I just think, this is what they, these people with all this money, this is all they can come up with. Like, I thought they had brains. If they had gone to universities and everything, to become film directors, is this all they can come up with? 'Cause it's so rubbish. I was thinking, like, I could do better than that, and I'm 14, and how old are they?

At the same time, the enduring popularity of soaps might also be seen to derive from the diversity of 'reading positions' that they make available — not merely in terms of distance and engagement but also in terms of the range of characters (and thus possibilities for 'identification') that they seem to provide. In effect, they offer diversity within commonality:[26] they represent a form of 'common culture' that permits difference, even if it does not directly encourage it, and that enables viewers to exert a degree of deliberate control over the reading process that may be less possible with other genres.

While it would be tempting to see this degree of control as broadly positive — and even as 'educational'[27] — we need to be wary of reaching easy conclusions about its political consequences. The fact that young people are able to be 'critical' of the media — on both aesthetic and ideological grounds — does not necessarily mean that they can create their own meanings, irrespective of the constraints exerted by the text. Their critical 'resistance' to a given text should not be generalised into broader assertions about their resistance to all texts, or indeed to broader ideological or political resistance. The diversity and ambiguity of some aspects of popular culture and of the ways in which they are read by audiences, are very far from infinite.

Conclusion

Our aim in this chapter has been to offer an account of the reading process which moves beyond individualistic notions of 'response'. Rather than regarding meaning as something which is produced in the isolated encounter between the reader and the text, we have focused on the *social* production and circulation of meaning. This approach is an inevitable consequence of the broader social theory of literacy that we are adopting in this book.

As we have argued, making sense of the media is a process in which individual and collective identities are defined and negotiated. In making meaning, and in establishing our own tastes and preferences, we are simultaneously defining the meanings of our own social lives and positions. While there are undeniable constraints on this process — constraints which are variously material, historical and discursive — it is also one which is characterised by a considerable degree of diversity and complexity. Our illustrations of this complexity in this chapter have necessarily been brief, and have largely been subordinated to our more general argument. In the three case studies that follow, we offer more detailed examples, ones which will enable us to explore these issues in greater depth; while in the final chapter of this part of the book, we will examine how our students themselves understand and reflect on the processes that we have described.

Notes

1. See Buckingham (1993b), introduction.
2. For example (among others) Hodge and Tripp (1986), Palmer (1986), Buckingham (1987a, 1993b and 1993c), Moss (1989), Sarland (1991).

3. See Sarland (1991, Ch. 9), and his critique of 'Englishy' notions of reader response. Sarland's 'revised model' of response is somewhat contradictory in places, but it does offer fruitful points of connection with recent research on media audiences, such as the work referred to in Note 2 above.
4. See, for example, Wober and Fazal (1986).
5. See the introduction and conclusion to Buckingham (1993b).
6. Notably Willis (1990). Our emphasis on the heterogeneity of contemporary popular culture is echoed in some recent work on 'postmodernism', such as Collins (1989).
7. Morley (1986), Palmer (1986), Lull (1990) and Buckingham (1993c, Ch. 5).
8. Wood (1993).
9. See Buckingham (1993c, Ch. 3).
10. See Buckingham (1993d).
11. This kind of displacement is characteristic of talk about television: see Buckingham (1993c), Cullingford (1984).
12. See Fryer (1984); but also the discussion of the local context of the 1980s riots in Rose (1992).
13. Gilroy (1987); see also Hewitt (1986) and Jones (1988).
14. See Fiske (1987a).
15. See Bakhtin (1981).
16. It is here that we would distinguish *our* notion of 'taste' from that of Bourdieu (1984), whose approach is ultimately determinist: see Mander (1987).
17. For empirical instances of this approach, see Henriques *et al* (1984) and Davies (1989).
18. See Jordin and Brunt (1988), Buckingham (1993c, Ch. 3).
19. For a fuller account, see Buckingham (1992).
20. For example, Searle (1989).
21. See Moss (1993).
22. See Barker (1993).
23. See Collins (1989).
24. See Ang (1985) and Buckingham (1987a; and 1993c, Ch. 4).
25. Geraghty (1991).
26. See Buckingham (1987a).
27. Hodge and Tripp (1986), Liebes and Katz (1990).

Chapter 3

A Boy's Own Story: Writing Masculine Genres

In the last chapter, we examined some of the readings our students made of the popular texts that they consumed in the contexts of home and leisure time. This chapter offers a more extended case study, based not on reading but on writing. We want to focus on one long story written by a year-10 student called 'Ponyboy'. 'Pony' is in fact a working-class Greek Cypriot boy whose real name is Michael — or rather Michaelis. Michael had assumed the name of Ponyboy Curtis, the hero of S. E. Hinton's novel *The Outsiders,* at the age of 12, and had obstinately refused to be addressed otherwise ever since. As we shall go on to argue, this question of fantasy identities was also central to his writing, and in particular to the story that we shall be considering.

The focus of our account is the way in which 'Pony's' writing *re-works* the masculine pleasures that he derived from popular texts such as Marvel comics and action-adventure films within the more formal demands of the 'school story'. The following extract from one of his earlier stories, written in year-8, and the teacher's comments that accompanied it, exemplify some of the tensions that exist between 'popular' and 'educational' definitions of culture and literacy:

> he shot but Zartan bloked it with the sword. Zartan gave him a double kick, he went down zartan picked up the swore and droke it through Dark storms head Dark storm try to get up but he fell he was dead zartan was relifed but frostbite got up and shot a freeze at Zartan.

At the end of 14 pages, the teacher (Julian) wrote: 'Action packed although I find all the battles a little difficult to follow — spelling and punctuation — we must have a talk. I prefer knowing more about character and scene than just the action, it adds to the overall effect.'

As most English teachers would confirm, boys are often highly committed to these action-packed sagas, to the extent that they will frequently share them as group readings amongst themselves in much the same way that they gather around computer magazines, or swap videos. Yet there is a clear sense here of the teacher reading the story for a very different purpose from the one which motivated the writer. In fact, the teacher's comments offer a revealing insight into some of the hidden values of English. Although he doesn't explicitly condemn the emphasis on violence and action, he does try to recuperate the story by claiming that 'the battles are a little difficult to follow'. The emphasis on the mechanical details of the transcription — 'spelling and punctuation' — bring the violence back to the teacher's territory; and the comments about 'character and scene' stem from a critical repertoire that seems implicitly Leavisite in origin. Indeed, the implied model of good writing behind these mild criticisms might be that of the 'classic realist' novel, with its emphasis on 'rounded' characters and good, solid descriptions.

This is not to say that the teacher's criticisms are not a valid way of developing the writer's skills. Rather it is to suggest that evaluation of this kind often ignores the positive skills that are exemplified in boys' writing such as this. Indeed, stories of this kind reveal a literary competency that is culturally, generationally and ethically at odds with the dominant values encoded in the teacher's remarks.

This kind of response to boys' writing is far from unique. Indeed, we would argue that the vast majority of English teachers perceive such writing as a weakness and a problem. As Charles Sarland has suggested, this is encouraged by the way in which English teachers are often socialised in the dominant practices of their profession, without considering the wider implications of literacy.[1] Furthermore, a great deal of research on the education of boys has tended to represent them as a problem — for example, in terms of their attention-seeking and disruptive behaviour or their control of a scientific and work-oriented curriculum. English is often perceived as a feminine subject; and it is certainly one in which boys' level of achievement is significantly lower than that of girls'.[2] It is common currency amongst English teachers that boys read less than girls, a finding confirmed by our survey reported in Chapter 2. And if they do read, it is unlikely to be anything that would be perceived as worthwhile: scientific manuals, pornography, violent science fiction action stories or comics.

In this chapter, we want to analyse a 6000-word story called *Plaz Investigations* that 'Pony' produced in the summer of 1990. Like most first novels, *Plaz* is unfinished. It is in three sections and is a third-person narrative, although at times the narrator explicitly ascribes authorial insight to the protagonist. The first chapter is entitled 'The choice' (crossed out), and describes how the Tottenham schoolboy Plaz ends up protecting an 'attractive brewnet' Sam from kidnapping thugs who turn out to be the FBI. Reluctantly, Plaz rescues Sam and her friend Danual and escapes with them back to the future (8963 AD, to be precise) where he becomes 'a freelance peace keeping agent' or 'bounty hunter'. The second and third parts, entitled

'The wrong case', deal with an adventure where Plaz is hired by an image-conscious and impotent police force to kill various gang leaders. His adventures take him through time and space, including a visit to 'his ex-home town Tottenham' and he gains a mechanical or robotic arm in the process. A couple of pages before the manuscript breaks off, he is employed on a third adventure to capture a gang who have escaped from a high-security prison. Needless to say, he is successful in this mission, and has many battles along the way, in which he kills the major evil characters of that time, along with various cyborgs and mutants.

The novel is not only generically derivative: it also explicitly refers to and borrows from a number of other texts, many of which 'Pony' subsequently lent us. As we have argued, reading can be seen as a process of dialogue, which inevitably involves intertextual references. In making sense of a given text, we inevitably compare it with other texts that we have read, both historically and contemporaneously — that is, in terms of both our own 'reading profiles' and our own 'reading histories'. In the case of the writing of *Plaz Investigations,* this process is quite conscious and explicit. 'Pony' was motivated to write the novel in the first place because, as he put it: 'I was watching *Escape from New York,* yeah, and I thought the guy, yeah, that was in there . . . Kurt Russell yeah, I thought he was a very good character.' He then went on to list the other major influences behind the story:

> There's, er, *Death's Head, Dragon's Claw,* um, *Blade Runner,* all the *Star Wars* trilogy, um, *Terminator* sometimes. I didn't use that much of *Terminator,* just about the war and the computers taking over and all that and, er, what else? All those futuristic films . . . Suppose I'd better mention *Robocop.* Uh, I got *Action Force,* some of the comic *Action Force,* like, some of the Ninja stuff.

Some of these references are just in the form of borrowed names: for example, Plaz visits the 'dagerba system' (from *The Empire Strikes Back*) but doesn't use any other themes or qualities from the *Star Wars* context. Other references are direct quotes, such as the mechanised/electronic arm from *Robocop* or the phrase 'freelance peace keeping agent' from the Marvel comic *Death's Head,* and these carry a broader ideological significance. Also, there are the borrowings of narrative structures, and of character types such as the hero being used by a corrupt police force to carry out 'real' law enforcement — as found (again) in *Robocop.*

This wealth of references from a range of media output indicates an intense involvement in certain kinds of fantasy. By choosing to identify with certain kinds of hero, and by selecting key moments and actions from his favourite films and comics, 'Pony' is revealing the most significant elements of his media use and consumption. As we have already indicated, these can primarily be defined in terms of gender and age — as adolescent boys' culture. While there are obvious points of continuity, we believe this should be differentiated from generalisations about forms of adult masculinity, just as in Chapter 2 our observations about girls and 'girls' magazines' exemplifies similarly ambiguous claims about consciousness and identity in relation to femininity.

In the analysis of *Plaz Investigations* which follows, we want to concentrate on the ways in which 'Pony' negotiates his own adolescent masculinity in relation to the texts on which his writing draws — both the texts he identifies above, as well as others like the 'new' Batman stories *The Killing Joke,* or *Wolverine* which he lent us to further the study.

'Ready to Take Them On'

One of the first tensions in the narrative is that between description and action. Indeed, compared to the almost continuous battles of 'Pony's' earlier work, *Plaz* is a model of restraint. As in the case of its 'sources', *Action Force, Wolverine* and *The Sleeze Brothers,* a large proportion of the narrative is dedicated to establishing the parameters of the fantasy world rather than describing the actual events of the fantasy. Much greater attention is given over to 'getting ready' than to actually acting out the investigations or fights.

This skewing of the narrative seems to have two distinct functions. First, the story takes the way in which we enter fantasy extremely seriously. There is lot of pleasure in setting up situations, such as the mechanisms of time travel:

> 'listen, me and my friend Danual came here from the future 7026 yrs in the future, wait let me finnish, In our time we that is earth found this crystal which opens doors through time when you pas an electrial current through it,'

and an enormous amount of sheer descriptive detail:

> It has been one year since Plaz Hunter came to this time. (8963 ad) Plaz has become a private investigator and he owns a craft a set of guns which consist of an normal handgun which never leaves Plaz's side two daggers which are always atthe sides of his boots a fusion canon and one puls rifal with an under carage pump ~~at~~ ction grenade luncher and he's only 15years old. , Plaz is also a 8th levelblack b~~l~~elt at 12 differerent martial arts such as karate, Te quan do, Ninjitsoo and tichee. Plaz has to deal with the most dangerous ~~peo~~ kind of people like police don't have to deal with like gangs such as the mafe~~ar~~ but in this time the mafear does not exist but we do have gangs much r more dangerous like THE KOO — VAKS MOB, TheNOMEAGO and The ~~Empire~~ Force

Finding the right names for the right enemies and listing the various elements in his arsenal all seem to contribute to the credibility of the story. What this second extract also demonstrates is that this preparedness is a form of empowerment, that the 'skilling' in martial arts and the detail of the weaponry enables the hero to be ready for anything. As 'Pony' writes later in the story, after Plaz has lost his arm in a fight:

> At the hospital they replacd Plaz's arm with a robot arm which has a built in ardour cuff a compter, weapons system and also anything Plaz could ever need and more.

The phrase 'anything Plaz could ever need and more' is revealing. It indicates an underlying anxiety that however prepared Plaz might be, 'Pony' might not be able to predict the kinds of eventualities that he might have to face. This exposes a kind of paranoia at the heart of the adventurer or warrior, that however invincible he might be, there remains the possibility that somewhere, somehow, there might be a greater power.

This possibility is bound to be ever-present in a futuristic world where the human imagination, by definition, cannot know probable outcomes.[3] Yet it is certainly more likely in the world of an adolescent boy, where the recourse to fantasies of power and violence derives from an underlying acknowledgment of powerlessness, at least in relationship to adults. Thus, Plaz reveals his fears in the same moment that he purports to be all-powerful. The more these fears are acknowledged, the more exaggerated and violent the fantasies become: as John Fiske argues, 'masculinity becomes almost a definition of the superhuman, so that it becomes that which can never be achieved.'[4] However socially unacceptable such fantasies may be to middle-class teachers like ourselves, we do not feel that it is helpful simply to dismiss the perspectives of the boys for whom they are so important. While on one level, these fantasies could be seen as reflecting the impoverished emotional universe of many adolescent boys, it is crucially important to avoid taking them literally, or to read them at face value.

This exaggerated need to allay anxiety is 'Pony's' rationale for Plaz's eclectic martial-arts training: 'Plaz is also a 8th levelblack b~~l~~elt at 12 differerent martial arts such as karate, Te quan do, Ninjitsoo and tichee.' The enormous popularity of 'Eastern' fighting skills, with their associated magical and mystical powers, has a long tradition within masculine genres, and they exercise an extraordinary hold over the adolescent imagination. (For those in the know, the inclusion of 'tichee' — or rather 'Tai Chi' — may seem bizarre, but it adds narrative colour, and, as 'Pony' explained, it's what his Maths teacher does in an evening class.) *Action Force, Bad Company* or *Wolverine* show similar periods of preparation; and the advertisements and 'profile' pages in these comics often carry information about such skills. *Plaz* stresses the mental control that such skills confer, to the extent of compensating for physical weakness. It indicates the reassuring capacity of external forces, in this case, training rather than military hardware to supplement and redress various material and historical power relationships. As Plaz explains to the obtuse and ignorant police officer Browning towards the end of the novel:

> 'He's a' browning stopped to think, he atarted to clik his fingers
> 'Nineja or Nin something away'
> 'Ninja' ~~Plaz correctedg~~ said Plaz correting browning.
> 'Yeh thats it Ninja, anyway he's a ninja warrier, I think its one of those ~~unarm~~ unarmed combat things'
> 'Its an anchent Martal art, it gives you the abilaty to
> defend yours self agenst almost any weapon' Plaz said.

The idea that being a Ninja can make one more powerful than almost any weapon reveals its psychological attraction. The Ninja way of life initiates the powerless into a position of 'superpowerfulness' or 'hypermasculinity' through a ritualistic transformation of almost transcendent power.[5]

'His Little Gadget Thing'

The other traditional form of empowerment is of course weaponry. Fiske, for example, refers to guns and vehicles as 'penile extenders',[6] suggesting that they provide a way of closing the gap between the imaginary (the phallus) and the real (the penis). Thus, guns, forms of transport and robotic arms all function as ways of extending Plaz's control of his environment. And, as we have already seen, *Plaz* has its fair share of weapon fetishism and gadget adoration.[7]

Yet, if we end up merely satirising *Plaz* for its explosive arsenal and 'willy waving' technology, we run the risk of ignoring the ways that boys construct themselves as masculine. 'Pony's' own explanation for his interest in gadgets does in fact move the emphasis away from the psychoanalytic to the social. He explains why he likes James Bond:

> 'PB': He had a suitcase and it had a plane inside it, have you seen that? It's good that.
> JSG: Why is it good?
> 'PB': . . . 'cos what his stuff is like disguised into normal day things like a pen and all stuff and he has a wristwatch and things like that.
> JSG: So would you like to have a wristwatch that was really a laser?
> 'PB': Wouldn't mind really 'cos that way yeh, say you get captured by people right and they search you for guns and all that stuff right

and they take them offa you, right, but if you've got it disguised like a watch, yeh, then they won't take the watch off you will they?
JSG: True — how often have you been stopped and searched?
'PB': I have been stopped a few times by the Old Bill [The Police].
JSG: But is that what you meant by being stopped and searched?
'PB': No I meant the hero, being captured by the enemy.
JSG: Like you being stopped by the Old Bill?
'PB': No, like say James Bond yeah, he's got his little gadget thing yeh, he always seems to get captured, taken prisoner and they take away his gun and all that stuff right, but they always seem to leave his little gadgety thing and then he just escapes and saves the world.

The idea of powerful weapons being disguised as 'normal day things' is intriguing, not so much because of 'Pony's' professed explanation that it will help him to get past the police but more because it reveals a desire to endow the mundane and everyday with the abnormal and heroic. Similarly, at the beginning of the novel, the schoolboy Plaz is just trying to get to a class registration on time while being distracted by having to save the damsel in distress. There is a great willingness to transform the normal into the exciting, and although the ironic tone at the end of this extract shows that 'Pony' is aware of the unlikelihood of 'saving the world' through the use of guns and gadgets, he cannot help fantasising about the possibility of such transformations. He also recognises, however, that he isn't James Bond, and that being stopped by the Old Bill is not the same as being a super hero. For all these reasons, therefore, the level of explanation that he initially offers about the usefulness of concealed weapons should not be taken at face value.

Gadgets offer a way of escaping the regulation of authority, and seem to allow a way for fantasy to evade external reality. Rather than interpreting gadgets merely as forms of phallic power, it also makes sense to interpret them, within the contexts that 'Pony' proposes: as a way of overcoming his fears about those who are more powerful than himself. This would be supported by Lynne Segal's neat summation of the contradictory nature of masculinity: 'The more it asserts itself, the more it calls itself into question'.[8] In expressing his desire to exert power, 'Pony' simultaneously articulates his vulnerabilities and weaknesses.

'Some Sort of Trouble with a Form of Othoroty'

'Pony's' expression of anxiety about being stopped and searched also reflects his concerns both about his position in relation to authority and (more broadly) about the relation of the individual to society at large. As we have seen, 'Pony' has to create an 'other' in order to articulate his own sense of identity: '. . . say you get captured by people, right, and they search you for guns and all that stuff, right, and they take them offa you, right . . .' Yet why is one likely to get captured in the first place, and who would be the 'they' constricting and imprisoning the protagonist? The emphasis falls on secret and hidden powers, as the external forces control and restrict. This is most evident in 'Pony's' attitude towards the police. Indeed, part of his motivation for writing the story in the first place stemmed from his enjoyment of *Escape from New York* (1981, directed by John Carpenter) and his identification with the attitude of its hero Snake Plisskin, played by Kurt Russell, towards the police and towards criminality: 'Well maybe I just like the character, the way he doesn't like the police and, um, he was a soldier and he was the best and then he turned criminal and all that.' Likewise in *Plaz,* the hero is employed by an impotent and corrupt police force to carry out *real* law enforcement.

Significantly, the first group of 'baddies' that Plaz has to deal with are the FBI. They are after Sam to get her 'to open a door way to our time so they can come though'. The FBI are nameless and unindividuated. They seem to shoot indiscriminately, so much so that Plaz has to escape back with Sam to the future. Just before departing, he asks her:

> 'What's it like where you come from?'
> 'Well, theres more crime than ever and there's police agencys as well as the normal police you can now hire a cop, we don't have cars just hover~~s~~ crafts but with these you can fly realy high, almost everyone has one of those energy cuts for pretetion'

The choice of policing, crime and transport as the salient characteristics of the future are ideologically revealing, although they do also serve a narrative function, directing the reader towards the immediate concerns of Plaz's impending career. When he gets to the future, he sets up as a detective, and in the major case that he solves he is employed by the 'LEA (Law Enforcement Agents (new FBI))' to 'go after and kill the leader of the Nomeago gang'. The following conversation takes place:

> "Why? Why don't you do it youself?"
> "Think about it Plaz"
> "Oh yeh your the athoritis aren't you and because its murder . it would make you lot look bad"
> "No .No. Not murder, Questor has ~~comited a lot of crimeshe.~~ murdered more inocent people then you could ever imagin, so you see you'll be doing everyone a favour"

Towards the end of the story, Plaz is hired by another cop who is described as 'the kind of cop who hides behind a desk taking credit for other peoples work'. He is asked to capture a gang who have broken out of a high-security prison: the police have already lost an army in the pursuit of these criminals. However, Plaz is 'different from everyone': he is 'the best', and therefore more likely to succeed. This idea is directly borrowed from the plot line of *Escape from New York,* except that in this film the protagonist is ideologically compromised by already being a war hero turned criminal. In *Death's Head, The Sleeze Brothers, Batman* and virtually all of 'Pony's' own sources, the forces of Law and Authority are effectively impotent and their functions are carried out by independent individuals.

There are several contradictions implicit in 'Pony's' borrowing and adaptation of this theme, which, as Jim Collins points out is a characteristic feature of many contemporary popular texts.[9] First, there is the notion of institutional corruption and weakness, set against the pure embodiment of justice in the shape of Plaz. Plaz is, of course, individualised, as opposed to the FBI organisation. Again, there is a tension between the weak forces of society, opposed to the strength of the one man. The authorities are constrained by being accountable to public scrutiny, while the hero is only answerable to himself. There is an ambiguous conflict between the values of pro-social behaviour and violent anti-social activity, and an ironic sense of the torn fabric of society being *sustained* by those forces which that society appears to marginalise: the violent, the individual, the independent and the free.

Yet, the key question here is why 'Pony' adopts the role of justice in a society that appears to devalue it. Whatever kind of psychological purpose might be fulfilled by acting as an agent of murder and physical force, or whatever the thrill might be in having a robotic arm, Plaz's actions are moral. This attitude partly stems from an ideological framework which equates masculinity with the individualistic. Thus, as Fiske argues, the striving for achievement which characterises male genres is part of the way in which a capitalist patriarchy motivates men to work in order to prove themselves.[10] To prove oneself, one must necessarily oppose the mass: rebelling against authority becomes a way of defining oneself. It therefore becomes necessary that the symbols of authority are emasculated, and that the virility of the various police forces that Plaz encounters is open to question. Their weakness defines him. However, why, then, does Plaz implicitly *support* the weak social structure through his actions?

This seems to be yet another contradiction in the role of the hero of these genres. Society is left vulnerable, and comes under threat from antisocial elements; yet those elements can only be defeated by a more powerful force, and that force is similar in kind to the antisocial elements in question. In other words, masculinity is torn between asserting itself in relation to the larger whole and, in doing so, destroying it. Society can only be protected by a privileged version of its antisocial impulses, on that takes the form of the hero. This is why Plaz is outside the law. He becomes, in 'Pony's' favourite phrase borrowed from *Death's Head,* 'a freelance peace keeping agent' — or 'bounty hunter', as the uninitiated would describe it. The heavy irony in this phrase embodies the ideological contradictions caught up in this role, and gives some insight into the way that the character of the hero is fraught with anxiety, doubt and multiple identities.

'At Least I'll Die Knowing I Tryed to be Someone OK'

'Trying to be someone' underpins the whole story: but the salient question to ask, given the uncertainties surrounding the person of the hero, is who that someone might be. In the previous section, we looked at how 'Pony' defined himself in relationship to the social body. But he also defines himself internally, in relation to the contradictory tensions within the masculine persona. In his analysis of *The A Team,* Fiske describes the four characters in terms of the separate elements that combine to form the contradictory whole of the masculine identity.[11] The relationships between Mr T, Face, Murdock and Hannibal thus bring into play 'a structure of masculinity' that gives the programme its ideological meanings. There is an absence of other characters in *Plaz Investigations* which might allow us to discern an equivalent 'structure'. However, Plaz does define himself in relation to his enemies and allies, and, equally importantly, in relation to his previous incarnations as 'Pony'.

In virtually all the sources of *Plaz,* a common feature emerges: that of an opposition either between the different aspects of the split personality or between the protagonist and his enemy. In *Wolverine,* the hero Logan is transformed into a beast with an adamantium skeleton through the intervention of either 'Lady Deathstrike', the daughter of a Japanese scientist, or the Canadian government. Either way, the hero leads a schizophrenic life as a 'super-soldier', combating his bestial impulses in order to serve as part of a superhero team, many of whose members, like 'the Hulk' (in reality Paul Cartier, victim of a supernatural curse), also embody this dual identity. In discussion, 'Pony' talked in particular about the Berserker (a Marvel modification of the Anglo-Saxon personality category for an Adventure game book), and how he cannot be controlled when 'nutty'; and he also described himself as possessing a similar uncontrollable essence which often breaks out of his disciplined social identity.

In the new *Batman* stories, in particular *Batman: The Killing Joke,* Batman becomes increasingly aware that the Joker is not so much an independent criminal force as his (Batman's) alter ego. As the story progresses, the similarities between Batman and the Joker become more and more obvious: they are both mutated (through dress, self-discipline and, in the Joker's case, acid) and are both outside society; both experience anti-social impulses, that Batman is forced to repress for the social good. Batman seems to decline into a kind of existentialist introspection as he realises that what appears to be a moral struggle is more a question of rationalising transcendent meaning in a postmodern world.[12]

There are various manifestations of this narrative structure as *Plaz* proceeds. Primarily, masculine difference is established in relation to the feminine and in particular by the traditional absence of women from male stories. However, there are two female characters in *Plaz*: Sam, 'the brewnet' whom Plaz rescues at the beginning of the story, and Kim, a girl 'he use to like a lot', who is kidnapped as a hostage to trap Plaz on his return to Tottenham, and who rescues him at a vital moment — before he has to leave her in tears as he returns to the future.

Both fulfil passive roles, both have to be rescued and both are described in terms of physical attributes. However, although Sam may begin the novel as an irritatingly needy female, she changes as the novel progresses — perhaps having an 'ungendered' name gives the game away. She becomes Plaz's assistant, the person he asks advice from as he embarks on his adventures, and she alternates between maternal rebuke and giving him the choice in various matters — although he tends to walk out on her as his way of ending debate. She also plays a physical role in some of the adventures, and as long as she is subordinated to his prowess, she can also fight and kill. In a sense, she is necessary as a measure of his ability: a male assistant would be too threatening. Her most vociferous attempt to dissuade Plaz from taking on dangerous work occurs when she says: '"Why are you always trying to be that stupide comic book charter Deaths head, You'll never be him you will always be Plaz Hunter no one els"'. Her commonsensical plea to 'grow up' and stop pretending that you live in a fantasy world allies qualities of adultness to the feminine; and again, the fact that he proves her wrong by succeeding in his fantasy role seems to point to the fiction acting as a form of transformation, showing that 'Pony' can assert himself against a commonsense female viewpoint and thus define himself. By choosing Sam as the embodiment of those qualities that 'Pony' despises, and by allowing the narrative to recuperate her, 'Pony' uses Plaz as way of proving grown-ups (is it too fanciful to say Mum here?) wrong and thus confirming his own status.

Kim, the other woman in the story, is far less problematic. She is introduced as 'a girl Plaz use to like a lot', and she was upset at his disappearance into the future. She is used as a conventional romantic heroine. When she rescues Plaz at a crucial moment, she breaks down in tears and has to be held in his arms. She even blows him a kiss as he departs and Plaz realises th ıt 'sheεmust really like him'. She functions as a fictional way for 'Pony' to live out what is probably a specific fantasy. What is noticeable about his identity in relation to her is that he can infer her interest in him without exposing any vulnerability on his part: he can disappear back to the future having solved the romantic conundrum, but without having to commit himself. He is the better for having saved her, and the fact that she breaks down because she has to kill in order to save him only serves to intensify his invulnerability.

In *Batman* and *Escape from New York*, the hero is measured against the villain, respectively the Joker and 'the Duke'. Similarly, in *Plaz* the main adventure involves the destruction of a gang, 'flaming fist', whose main leaders, Questor and Kelgor, are not described in any detail. (At the end of the novel, where Plaz is employed to catch a gang of escapees, these villains are endowed with a variety of specific characteristics, such as Ninja skills, physical strength and so on — more in keeping with the classic 'Manichean' binary oppositions of the genre.) However, the actual moment of victory in the deaths of both Questor and Kelgor is notable for the roles played by the cyborgs and troopers that guard their leaders. This is perhaps a surprising shift in 'Pony's' reading of his primary material, and a curious re-working of the binary opposition between hero and villain. First of all, the actual description of Questor is balanced by that of his bodyguard:

> A great big guy said obveusly the leader Questor he had a scare on the right side of his face and a silver glove with spikes on the left hand on~~d~~ his left stood a great big 6ft ~~s~~ cyborg who had muccel on his mucsel and sword on his back and two miny rockets on his left cuf. and a double barrol lazer gun on the ~~right~~ other.

It is the cyborg who blows Plaz's arm off (which leads to its mechanised replacement); and when Plaz kills Questor, it is, according to the conventions of the genre, an impersonal act (blowing up his spaceship). However, this leads into a duel with the cyborg, because although Plaz expected the cyborg to stop serving Questor when Questor was killed, Questor's legacy was to endow the cyborg with a mind of its own after it had killed whoever killed its master. (This is symmetrically balanced by the troopers' response after Kelgor's death: they feel that they are no longer bound to serve him now that he has been killed.)

The cyborg's independence is pertinent for two reasons. First, it implies that a relatively democratic status is bestowed on master and servant (in terms of narrative importance, at least), which may reflect 'Pony's' awareness that battles between lesser social actors are more relevant to his future. Secondly, and more importantly, there is the narrative function of the unstoppable and literally 'mindless' opponent. By contrast, it is important to the hero's self-esteem that he is self-motivated, and existentially responsible for his actions. Similarly, on at least two occasions, Death's Head is caught up in duels with either mechanical or animal opposites: Plaguedog and Iron Man. In both cases, he wins out due to the application of human cunning, often ironically expressed, referring at one stage to 'behaviour that gets us mechanoids a bad name'. Clearly, the greater drama and fear implied by the unstoppable and impersonal destructive force makes it central to the masculine narrative. This is partly explained by 'Pony's' earlier references to 'berserkers' and to the immutable forces within the male psyche. It also articulates a contradiction, that Death's Head and Plaz are themselves partly de-humanised and machine-like, and yet they possess enough significant human qualities to overcome such weaknesses. In this sense, strength and vulnerability are almost confused: physical power is only really powerful when allied to human weakness, which may explain the significance of overcoming the indestructible. Plaz is thus defeating the cyborg within himself as much as outside his character.[13] The focus on subservient characters elevated to the position of opposites thus indicates an attempt to dramatise conflicting desires within the male identity that 'Pony' is creating for himself.

The final 'other' identity here is the persona of Plaz himself, and the fictional characters of Death's Head and Snake Plisskin (the hero of *Escape from New York*). There are several points in the novel where Plaz reflects upon who he is in relation to his heroic role models. These moments offer an insight into the author's conflicts over modality status, as well as a sense of what 'Pony' takes from his heroes.[14] We have already encountered Plaz's first reflexive moment when he is criticised by Sam:

> "Why are you always trying to be that stupide comic book charter Deaths head, Youll never be him you will always be Plaz Hunter no one els"

It is significant that this threat to his self image brings forth an explicit acknowledgement of the weakness of fantasy identity and a simultaneous avowal of its strength.

> "look maybe I'm not lik you, I need something to keep me going.o.k.
> I know I'll probobly never be Deaths head but if I die tomorrow then at least I'll die
> Knowing I tryed to be someone OK"

Later in the story, Sam again accuses Plaz of behaving like a star-struck child:

> "look I know you like Deaths head alot but you will never be him, he's a comic book charter this the real world you can't take on both of them at the same time".
> "I'm going to and if you want you can help"

There is a level of irony and wit at play here which it is well not to ignore. We cannot seriously believe that Plaz thinks that he is living in the real world, if only because Plaz is not a real character. Yet the novel persists in this fiction. It often refers to Plaz's reputation and character as if he were a real person and, even more confusingly, Plaz also refers to 'Pony' as if *he too* were real:

> "Hi who are . . . wait a minute Pony (Plaz's name which he used ~~fr~~ from the book the outsiders)

"Yep you remember"
"of course I remember my best friend, come in" Ray said dragging Plaz in.
"I've changed my name again its Plaz Hunter now"

In theory, if 'Pony' is real, Plaz is too. But despite the episode which follows with Kim and the more naturalistic setting of the school in Tottenham, which is obviously modelled on a specific fantasy, it is difficult to take the story at face value. If anything, the more the novel appears to claim to be 'realistic' rather than fantastic, the more it offers itself as something in between. According to the extracts above, Plaz is real because he was once 'Pony' (whom we know *is* real because he is named as the author), yet Plaz's grip on reality is insecure because he is always trying to pretend that he can measure up to comic-book characters. On the one hand, we have an attempt to build a fictional and fantasy world, and on the other, the undermining of that fantasy even as 'Pony' is building it.

Who, then, is Plaz — and what might it mean to ask and answer such a question? Ultimately, Plaz is an amalgam of social and psychological contradictions that make up the persona of the male superhero: he makes choices, he is in control, and he is in a position of power over women. Plaz is the mode through which 'Pony' reconciles the contradictions and tensions of his fantasy with his real life situation and experiences — that is, the relative powerlessness of 'Pony's' material situation as an adolescent schoolboy carrying the expectations of being a man.

Plaz is also a dramatisation of his self-image as a reader, an image which, as we have noted, derives from a retrospective construction of his 'reading history' — the part of 'Pony' who is so immersed in the experience of generic fiction. The character of Plaz reveals the emotional investment that 'Pony' has made in his reading, and it combines a personal, biographical response with a web of intertextual connections. It also represents his attempt to locate himself within a narrow range of masculine subject positions. On the one hand, he is a fantasy figure re-enacting 'Pony's' readings of masculine genres; and on the other, he embodies the rationale for that fantasy by exposing the fraught ambiguities that led 'Pony' towards fantasy in the first place.

'If You Like Killing, Imagine How That Would be Like in a War?'

Throughout Julian's discussions with 'Pony', there was a thread of 'violence' which would only seem to reflect the deeply psychotic readings that he was making from these fictions and to bear out the destructive effects of fantasy:

JSG: Do you enjoy fighting?
'PB': Um . . . It's an enjoyable sport.
JSG: What do you enjoy about it?
'PB': Inflicting pain on others . . . the thrill of winning.

However, there are numerous reasons why we should be cautious about these avowals of pleasure, and about how we interpret the significance of the violent action of *Plaz.* Not the least of these is 'Pony's' use of irony and excess. Ultimately, the meaning of 'violence' is mediated by the ways in which the fantasy worlds of 'Pony's' fictions and of *Plaz* construct themselves as real.

Comics, and in particular the Marvel comics favoured by 'Pony', appear to adopt a specific approach to representing violent moments. 'Pony' described how a comic 'freeze frames' action, allowing for a particular kind of concentration on selected highlights within what is inevitably a stylised and fragmented mode of representation:

JSG: . . . What do you like about this picture?
'PB': I like the fact he's pulled a man through a windscreen.
JSG: So its the actual kind of action bit?
'PB': Yeah, I just look at the pictures, yeah, right, then say I see a good bit, yeah, like that, where the man is crawling up the stairs . . . when Death's Head is crawling up the stairs. I'd probably start reading it there . . . and flick to that page where Death's Head is crawling up — 'cos it's like the same, innit, 'cos Death's Head is doing the hunting here, right, and later on he's crawling up the stairs being hunted by some other guy — and then I'd just basically read the whole thing from beginning to the end.

Of course, we have to be sceptical about statements like 'I like the fact he's pulled a man through a windscreen', or 'Pony's' claims that he enjoys inflicting pain on others. What such comments represent is not so much a straightforward reflection of the male psyche but more a discursive attempt to claim a masculine identity. This is reinforced by 'Pony's' descriptions of going to specialist comic shops and circulating comics with his peers. Choosing one's favourite moments, or boasting about the pleasures that one derives from witnessing the destruction of others can offer a way of asserting one's identification with a larger group identity.[15]

As we have argued, we need to read such statements in terms both of the social functions that they might serve and of the social context in which they are produced. Throughout these discussions, there was a strong sense in which 'Pony' was trying to push Julian (as the teacher) towards condemning his pleasures — which of course, would only go towards asserting his masculine identity, through exclusion from the social mass. There were numerous occasions when he purported to enjoy sadism, disembowelling and so on. Yet what is also revealing about the pleasure that he appeared to take in the image of the man crawling up the stairs is that he immediately sees that image in the context of a larger narrative pattern, in that it is balanced against the later picture of Death's Head crawling up the stairs. So the apparent sadistic pleasures that he wants to acknowledge in order to appear 'hard' are in fact mediated by other more 'innocent' pleasures, such as his interest in reading the whole story. His skill in grasping this narrative structure is part of the game that he is playing with the producers of *Death's Head.*

To be sure, *Plaz* does contain its fair share of deaths and gory violence. There is one moment where Plaz shoots off the limbs of an opponent before 'blowing him away', and 'Pony' proudly recalled this moment in discussions. 'Pony' was all too aware that the graphic element of comics and films could not be reproduced in his text, and this absence suggests yet another reason why the text is so interesting: it's clearly already a substitute in its own terms, and more likely to reveal its motives because of this. Indeed, there is a superfluity of such violent action within the text:

> Plaz didn't know what to do fight of run, so he done both, he pulled out hand gun and shot ~~s~~ five guards he couldn't shoot Questor because the cyborg stepped in the way. Plaz then picked up his fusion canon and blew a ~~hole~~ along in the wall along with a few guards. Plaz then began to run but the cyborg shot one of his rockets at ~~p~~ Plaz and blew Plaz's left arm up to the shoulder off.

Nevertheless, the absence of detailed description, which hinders the creation of any atmosphere of sadism or violence, is not just attributable to the author's lack of 'literary skill'. It shows that the moments of violent action fulfil different kinds of narrative function. The sequence quoted subordinates an interest in action to the narrative of Plaz's achievements: to be heroic, he has to kill so ma ıy guards and cyborgs, and this is meaningful in terms of the narrative tropes analysed above. The sheer lack of impact that losing his arm has on Plaz (other than having to go to a hospital, which he doesn't particularly like) shows a curious lack of engagement with the story. While this could be read as evidence of male desensitisation to violence, we would argue that, deep down, 'Pony' himself doesn't take the story that seriously. He knows that it's following the requisite generic conventions and that these do not necessarily reflect real social situations. Thus, fantasy violence might allow men to express an anti-social identity, and to enjoy forbidden pleasures, within a 'safe' psychological arena. It does not necessarily imply an enjoyment of *real* 'violence' — although, of course, it may also serve to confirm established positions and inequalities that are based on gender differences.

This sense of not taking the violence that seriously is also borne out by 'Pony's' use of humour and the comic pleasures afforded by his reading of the source material. He was particularly struck by the deep irony found in

Death's Head. This is emphasised in *Plaz* where, as we have seen, Plaz himself wants to be like Death's Head. In the opening episode of *Death's Head,* the protagonist uses a heavily underscored official discourse to rationalise his shady and semi-criminal activities. Yet the laugh here is on polite society for believing the value of keeping up pretences. Thus 'a freelance peace keeping agent' is preferred to 'bounty hunter'. Time after time, we see Death's Head dupe unsuspecting victims, and he is consistently motivated by self-interest: 'A fellow bounty hunter, er, freelance peace keeping agent once gave me some valuable advice "Always remember you're a *businessman*" he said . . . "never kill for free, and never turn down the contract — *whoever* the target is!" I thanked him for his advice and put a bullet through his forehead.'

'Pony' couldn't quite manage this level of wit in *Plaz,* although many of the exchanges in our discussions were conducted in a similar spirit. 'Pony' said of the above extract from *Death's Head* that he liked it because it shows 'he really doesn't care, he hasn't got that much emotions. He's got a job to do and he does it right.' On the surface, this is a worrying comment — indeed, it's like a parody of what's wrong with men — but again we would be sceptical about taking this comment at face value. Just as Death's Head is trying to stand outside human and social norms and use his wit to criticise those values, 'Pony's' preference for doing a job, suppressing one's emotions and not caring contain within them an ironic acknowledgment of the opposite. What *Death's Head* offers is the opportunity to mock, rather heavy-handedly, those values that 'Pony' is anxious about and keen to suppress.

Thus, in the generic use of 'violence' (whatever that might mean), excess and irony serve to undermine the realism of the story, and its pretence to be taken at face value. 'Pony's' sources and indeed most masculine genres undercut themselves in this way. What this means is that, far from being escapist dreams or ideological wish-fulfilment fantasies, these narratives constantly play on the tensions between fantasy and real life. They are powerful in as much as they offer ritualised ways of negotiating a gendered identity under pressure. Above all, they illustrate how the adolescent masculine self perceives itself to be at variance with the dominant discourses of adult responsibility and social purpose. Of course, the power of irony derives from the fact that it enables one to be 'serious' and 'not serious' at the same time: yet in this respect, the ironic play with those values only articulates the unused and excessive 'advantages' of being a man.

We have implicitly seen masculinity here as something that has to be socially and discursively achieved, rather than something that is simply given. This is to regard masculinity, in David Morgan's terms, 'not as a quality attached to individuals but a kind of cultural resource . . . a set of potentialities which may be realised and shaped in particular contexts'.[16] Popular culture represents one of the most significant of these 'resources', albeit one which (as we have shown) is profoundly ambiguous.[17]

The problem with an analysis of this kind, however, is that concentrating on the psychological or generic insecurities of such resources side-steps the material dimensions of male power. With 'Plaz', there is a sense that, as Morgan argues, studying men whose masculinity becomes problematic has the effect of 'denaturalising' masculinity. But for whom does that denaturalisation occur, and whose interests does it serve? Ours, as academics and teachers, or those of 'Pony' and other adolescent boys? Are we merely attempting to recuperate 'unacceptable' male fantasies in a vain endeavour to establish our credentials as 'new men'? Is the irony that we have identified ours or 'Pony's'? We will return to these questions in the second half of the book, particularly in Chapter 10, where we will consider girls' relationships to dominant discourses of femininity in a similar way, and discuss how media teachers might intervene to effect political change.

Writing Masculinity

> In children's writing we need to look for what the writing does for the writer, not what the writer does to it, nor what it does for us.[18]

In her study *The Tidy House,* Carolyn Steedman is rightly critical of the ways in which adult readers patronise children's writing on the grounds of style and spelling. She draws attention to the differing uses that adults and children make of writing of this kind. At the same time, we would want to refine her formulation, quoted here, about the relationship of children's writing to its authors. We are not sure if 'Pony' is strictly a child in the way Steedman's writers are, although he is very much a child writer within the context of the school, both in terms of his writing skills and in terms of the way that his writing implicitly positions him as a powerless boy.

Let us deal first with issues of spelling and grammar. Adult readers of *Plaz* have been entertained by its naiveté and 'directness'. It automatically puts us in a position of power and authority over the writer. This reinforces our rejection of its sexism and silliness. Thus, for example, the opening page when Plaz rescues a 'brewnet' stands for all that is laughable about boys. 'Pony' is himself bilingual, and as such his control of written English is, in conventional terms, weak; and although he obviously enjoys producing stories, he doesn't really like writing. It mirrors his social powerlessness: just as he is invited to take up a position of power as a man, and simultaneously to have that power circumscribed, so his control of formal literacy is something that he can't quite master. In this respect, it remains surprising that he actually spent all the effort on *Plaz,* given how unsatisfying it must have been to write. Not least because it is not a film or a comic, it is bound to fail to reproduce the textual pleasures that are so meaningful for him.

In fact, 'Pony' rationalised the effort spent on *Plaz* in economic terms, by suggesting that it was the plot for a film, which he could sell to a Hollywood studio in order to raise money to emigrate to America. The limits of such cultural production as a means to material empowerment are probably fairly obvious: when we last saw him, 'Pony' was working shifts at Burger King for minimum wages. This throws into perspective our much grander argument for such writing as a form of *psychological* empowerment — the notion that it acts as a way of negotiating gender identity, and dealing with the insecurities that this entails.

Our reading of 'Pony's' anxieties and dilemmas has inevitably reflected our own intellectual agendas and personal experiences, although our position here is massively privileged: to say the least, there is a significant material disparity between our lives and his. What motivates our sympathetic reading of 'Pony' and his story, however, is not some kind of vicarious identification with the fantasies of adolescent boys. If anything, it is because we feel sorry for 'Pony' — although of course this is no less problematic. Nevertheless, as teachers, we think it is vital that we do not merely reject 'Pony's' perspective as hopelessly irredeemable and politically incorrect. Rather than merely seeking to police masculine pleasures, or to romanticise them as forms of progressive 'resistance', we need to identify positive opportunities for change.

Our analysis of *Plaz* has followed Steedman's argument in that we have been looking at what the writing does for the *writer*. What we have not considered yet is what the whole act of production has done for 'Pony', as opposed to what the individual readings of moments and incidents might be achieving for him. The simple answer is that the writing of *Plaz* puts 'Pony' in a position of control over his material. In this respect, there is a qualitative difference between being a reader (or 'consumer') of popular culture and being a writer of it. In effect, the process of production gives 'Pony' the control that he may feel he lacks in social terms. The main difference between reading and writing, in these terms is that the writing forces the author to deal with the un-pleasures, as it were, of his reading. *Plaz* explicitly reveals the very uncertainties and fears that it appears to redress: the act of writing is a kind of magic that helps the writer to 'deal with' the anxieties of becoming a man.[19] How explicit this process is to 'Pony', and whether one would argue that the story fulfils therapeutic rather than 'educational' aims, are issues that we cannot resolve at this stage. However, we will return to these broader questions about 'empowerment' in later chapters.

Steedman's argument thus makes a vital shift of emphasis; but it may also be unnecessarily restrictive. In 'Pony's' case, the writing also seems to enable him to do something to his own reading. By offering control over the process of narration, and the possibility of ironic 'distance', the writing enables him to manipulate and to extend the 'reading positions' that are offered by those texts from which his story draws; *Plaz*, thus becomes a kind of snapshot of 'Pony's' 'reading profile' at this moment in time. In a sense, we have been using 'Pony's' story primarily as a way of gaining insights into his reading — in effect, as a form of 'audience research'. Yet the very act of writing almost inevitably enables him to assume a much more powerful position as a reader.

In terms of teaching about popular culture, this would suggest that 'writing' (or the production of texts) may in fact have much greater potential than is often assumed. Far from serving merely as a form of training in technical skills, or as a means of illustrating predetermined theoretical insights, practical production may offer students the potential for a much more genuinely active and playful relationship with popular culture than can be achieved through analytical critique. The case studies in the following two chapters will provide further examples of this process in relation to quite different media forms.

Notes

1. Sarland (1991).
2. See, for example, Batsleer *et al.* (1985) and Doyle (1989).
3. This may be one explanation for the preference for this kind of setting: that it articulates masculine paranoia.
4. Fiske (1987a).
5. See Segal (1990) for a discussion of the concept of hypermasculinity. Marsha Kinder (1991) also considers this issue in her discussion of the ways in which young viewers read *Teenage Mutant Ninja Turtles* as a psychological quest for empowerment.
6. Fiske (1987a).
7. For a somewhat determinist account of the relationship between weaponry and phallic power, see Miedzian (1992). As Lynne Segal, *ibid*, points out, reducing male power to the phallic does run the risk of essentialising masculinity.
8. Segal, *ibid.*
9. Collins (1989).
10. Fiske (1987a).
11. Fiske, *ibid.*
12. See various contributions in Pearson, R. and Uricchio, W. (1991).
13. See Haraway (1991) for a feminist interpretation of the cyborg metaphor.
14. These kinds of reflexive moments are plentiful in 'Pony's' sources. As Collins (1991) suggests, they may reflect the postmodernist angst of the contemporary comic and graphic novel.
15. See Buckingham (1993b, Ch. 5) for an account of how boys 'do' masculinity in the context of peer-group discussions of television . . .
16. See Morgan (1992).
17. For a more extended discussion of the advantages and limitations of this approach, see Sefton-Green (1993).
18. Steedman (1982).
19. Cf. Moss's (1989) account of boys' writing.

Chapter 4

Hardcore Rappin': Popular Music, Identity and Critical Discourse

Plaz Investigations was a story written — and intended to be read — outside school. For its author, one of its primary aims was to offer a means of access to the world of work, albeit the largely mythologised world of Hollywood. Yet, as we have shown, the story is marked by a tension between the demands of the popular genres on which it draws and the rather different generic requirements of the 'school story'.

In this chapter and the next, we move on to consider some texts produced by students in the context of their school work. These texts — magazines, photographs and popular music — were produced primarily to satisfy our requirements as teachers, and those of the examination syllabuses within which we were working. Yet while the teaching context to some extent determined what students produced, these texts need to be seen as part of a wider social process.

As we have argued, 'Pony Boy's' story cannot be seen simply as the personal expression of an individual creative consciousness. On the contrary, it emerges from a series of social *dialogues* with other texts, with other 'authors' and with a range of real or imagined readers. This is equally true of the media texts that we will be considering here. In encouraging students to use and adapt existing forms and genres, rather than merely to 'express themselves', we were explicitly positioning them as participants in these dialogues. As teachers, we were not their only audience, nor even necessarily the primary one. The texts that they produced were also partly designed for 'real' audiences: the specific audience of peers and other students, but also more hypothetical audiences beyond the school community. And in requiring the students to work collaboratively, we were attempting to make these dialogues a salient part of the production process.

Thus, while we will be raising questions about teaching and learning, our main emphasis here is on the texts themselves, and on the social functions that they appear to serve. As in the case of *Plaz Investigations,* the concerns that they address, the cultural investments that they reflect and the language that they use are inevitably only partly accessible to us.

Teaching Pop: An A-Level Unit

The texts that we will be analysing in this chapter were produced by year-12 students as part of a unit on popular music, which formed the Basic Production module of the Cambridge B A-level syllabus in Media Studies. As its title implies, the module was undertaken at an early stage in the course, and was primarily practical. However, the students were expected to demonstrate both implicit and explicit knowledge of a range of theoretical 'media debates', both in the products themselves and in the writing which was to accompany them.[1] What was clearly required, and indeed what we would regard as a central aim of media teaching, was an integration of 'theory' and 'practice' — although, as we shall argue in later chapters, this is something that has proven extremely difficult to identify and to achieve.

In this case, we sought to accomplish this integration in two main ways. Rather than offering free choice, we established a shared focus for the unit and spent some time on critical study before proceeding to the practical work. In addition, we encouraged the students to produce 'secondary texts'[2] aimed at specific audiences — that is texts *about* music, rather than music itself. In both ways, we sought to create a space for critical reflection, which we hoped would be extended in the accompanying piece of writing.

The whole module lasted 11 weeks, of which seven were spent on the practical production itself. We began with a two-week introduction, aimed to enable students to share and reflect upon their existing knowledge of popular music. In the first week, we included a 'blindfold test' in which we listened to and discussed examples drawn from a broad range of popular-music genres; some work on publicity images taken from the music press; and some discussion and analysis of music videos, again reflecting a broad range of styles, from Kylie Minogue and Jason Donovan to the avant-garde approach of New Order and the very different anti-realism of Hindi film music. In the following week, the students were asked to present and discuss music of their choice, along with related videos and album covers. Here again, we attempted to encourage diversity, and the material presented ranged from hardcore rap and techno to mainstream white soul and even Turkish belly-dancing music.

The brief for the practical project required students to choose between four different media. One group chose to produce a video to accompany a Soul II Soul song, taken from a selection that we had provided. A number of students worked in pairs producing album and cassette covers, again based on a selection of music that we had provided, ranging from African pop to white independent ('indie') music. Three groups chose to produce music magazines aimed at a specific target audience of their choice, using basic DTP (desktop-publishing) technology if they wished. Finally, a pair of girls produced a sequence from a radio programme, again aimed at a specific audience, which included a rap that was written and performed by one of them.

In the final two weeks of the unit — which we will not be considering here — we looked at academic and popular debates about Madonna, using her videos as well as the films *Desperately Seeking Susan* and *In Bed With Madonna.* Madonna was a predictable choice, but one which we felt would provide a reasonably painless way of coming to grips with academic writing on the media — although, not for the first time, we found ourselves having to 'translate' the convoluted prose of Media Studies academics into intelligible English. Interestingly, Madonna had been the only specific name mentioned in the previous year's examination paper, which perhaps reflects her meteoric rise to academic canonisation.

Talking Pop: Taste, Identity and Critical Discourse

Our broader aim in this unit of work was to find a way of teaching about popular music which enabled students to engage with, and to reflect upon, its *cultural* status. Existing Media Studies teaching materials tend to focus primarily on pop as an industrial product, and on issues such as marketing, promotion and distribution.[3] In the process, the music itself and the meanings and pleasures that students derive from it seem to be at risk of disappearing from view.[4]

Perhaps inevitably, this was an uncomfortable process. One of the major difficulties of teaching about popular music — and the reason why we suspect many teachers avoid it — is that it highlights the tensions between teachers' and students' perspectives. While this is to some extent the case with most areas of teaching about popular culture, it is particularly acute here. The music that we like is almost certainly going to be different from the music that our students like. We can (and indeed should) seek to inform ourselves about 'their' tastes, but any attempt to profess superior knowledge — to bluff our way in hardcore — is almost bound to fail. Indeed, much of the pleasure of popular music for young people lies in the sense that it 'belongs' to its listeners, that it is precisely 'theirs' and not 'ours'. There are then real dangers of imagining that there is no gap between ourselves and our students or, conversely, of romanticising them as the 'Other', as a way of crossing over what can be an awkward divide in the classroom.

In the context of Media Studies teaching — particularly at A level — this difficulty is compounded by the emphasis on academic discourse. Students are expected not merely to talk about what they like but also to analyse it critically. How to achieve this without 'colonising' or merely invalidating students' pleasures remains one of the central problems of teaching about popular culture.

These issues of taste and critical discourse were raised very clearly in the discussions with which the unit began. The central aim of our 'blindfold test' was to encourage the students to think about *genre*. Our basic question — What type of music is this, and how do you know? — proved to be a useful means of enabling students to reflect on their existing knowledge, and to make their critical categories explicit. Attempting to define why a particular piece of music would be classified as 'soul' or 'country and western' involved paying close attention to the basic elements of the music itself — harmony, rhythm, melody, lyrics, instrumentation, vocal style, production, and so on. In the process, we were attempting to teach a set of analytical terms that would enable students to define these categories much more precisely.

This emphasis on *genre* reflects our argument that texts are 'read' in the context of their relationships with other texts, and against the background of what we have termed individual and collective 'reading profiles' and 'reading histories'. In identifying genre, it is as important to know what the text is *not*, as it is to know what it *is*. At the same time, it was clear that these generic categories were not fixed, and that more was at stake in categorisation than simply an objective description (as Steve Neale argues in relation to film genre[5]). Defining the boundaries between genres was a flexible process, which inevitably entailed broader questions of taste and identity.

On a basic level, it was quite hard to encourage the students to listen to music that they didn't like. Rather like the complaints that often surface in relation to black-and-white films, 'old' music was initially dismissed outright. Persistence on our part eventually led to the recognition that — as Nicky said — 'this isn't just about what you like', but this clearly involved an accommodation to the teacher's perspective. On the other hand, dismissing music that we had brought in seemed to be much easier than condemning fellow students' tastes. One student who brought in a tape of Wet Wet Wet — a white pop/soul group who would have been rejected by many of the other students not merely on the grounds of taste but also for 'political' reasons — had a comparatively easy ride, largely because the others didn't want to offend her. By contrast, attacking what were perceived (sometimes inaccurately) to be teacher's tastes was a safe and enjoyable spectator sport.

At the same time, it was not necessarily any easier to get the students to discuss music that they liked and had chosen to bring in. To some extent, the act of playing loud popular music in a classroom (particularly one positioned next door to the staff room) was one which already seemed replete with subversive meaning — not least for us as teachers. Analysing the music and rationalising why you liked it was bound to detract from this, recuperating it back into an official educational framework. Our attempt to encourage the students to talk about the music in an objective, analytical way was thus bound to be an uphill struggle. Young people may have a great deal of 'investment' in what they like, and may actively resist attempts to question or appropriate this.

Yet, as we have argued, taste is much more than an individual matter. In classifying cultural phenomena, we are simultaneously classifying ourselves. In making distinctions between what we consider to be good and bad taste, we are also distinguishing ourselves from others who do not share those tastes. In Pierre Bourdieu's analysis of French society in the 1970s, this process was primarily a function of social class: the unequal distribution of economic capital was partly reflected in the uneven distribution of 'cultural capital'. However, as we have shown, this analysis can be extended to include distinctions in terms of age, gender and ethnicity.[6]

To claim particular tastes in popular music is thus to claim a particular social identity — or, in some cases, *multiple* identities. As Simon Frith[7] argues, young people use music as a means of locating themselves socially, historically and politically. Music may provide access to a more complex system of symbolic meaning than that which is available locally, in the peer group or the family. In this way, it can provide a means of claiming a positive status for identities that are rejected or undervalued; of rejecting the official identities proposed by the family, school or workplace; and of negotiating or aspiring to new identities beyond those that seem to be on offer.

Furthermore, part of the function both of discourse about popular music and of the artefacts associated with it (clothes and posters, for example) is to do with establishing 'expertise', and thus sustaining group membership. In making distinctions between musical genres, or between examples of the same genre, for example, one is simultaneously defining oneself as one of these people who possesses the competence to make such distinctions. Distinctions that may be important to 'insiders' — for example, between house and techno, or techno and hardcore techno — may be irrelevant to, or may not even be perceived by, 'outsiders'. Within the peer group, talk about popular music thus acts as a form of 'symbolic communication'[8] which maintains the boundaries of the group and acts as a marker of status within it.

Black music — and primarily black American rap music — appeared to offer this possibility for a number of our students. For black British students, this had obvious benefits, as we shall see in considering Nicky's work below. While the students' relationship with black America was often tenuous or confused, rap music offered these students a positive definition of black identity that provided self-esteem and status within the peer group, as well as a consciously political critique of white racism which transcended (and indeed implicitly challenged) notions of national identity.

Yet some white students also attempted to buy into this identity, albeit with ambiguous consequences.[9] Harry, for example, a Greek Cypriot student whose work we shall also consider below, consistently sought to align himself with 'hardcore' black music — a fact which led Nicky to accuse him of 'wanting to be black'. While Harry's position was actually more complex than this, it was clear that becoming 'Hardcore Harry' — as we came to call him — was much more than simply a matter of choosing to listen to a particular type of music. Like Pony Boy and other Greek Cypriot students that we have known, Harry was attempting to disavow or at least renegotiate his own ethnicity, in this case through proclaiming musical taste.

In categorising the music that we listened to, and in staking out their musical tastes, the students were also employing a relatively consistent series of critical terms and concepts — albeit ones which were applied in a variety of ways. The notion of 'hardcore' itself, for example, has been applied to punk, rap and (most recently) techno and house music. Yet the boundaries of hardcore are difficult to define, since the term itself is a relative one, whose meaning shifts historically and socially.

Yet the distinction between hardcore and 'commercial' music was merely one example of the critical terms which recurred throughout our discussions, often in the form of binary pairs. Further examples included 'pop' versus 'rock', 'independent' (or 'indie') versus 'mainstream', and 'sell out' or 'commercial' versus 'serious'. While these categories were partly aligned with generic distinctions, they also provided a means of making broader judgments both within and across genres.

These judgments appeared to function on a number of levels simultaneously. On one level, they were a matter of form, or of the *aesthetics* of music. Thus, (MC) Hammer was deemed to have 'sold out' on the grounds of his increasing alignment with mainstream soul music: his more recent records give more prominence to melodic 'hooks', and play down the spoken rap content, while also using slower and less abrasive rhythms. On another level, they are to do with *economics*. For example, as Stephen pointed out, 'indie' bands are defined not simply by their musical style but also in terms of their appearance on smaller independent record labels — although, as he acknowledged, this distinction has become increasingly blurred as major labels have now started to sign 'indie' bands and established 'independent' subsidiaries. *Audience* was another significant factor here; although whether or not a band can be defined as 'commercial' depends not merely on how many people buy your records but also on who those people are. Thus, Nicky argued that Public Enemy were as popular as Hammer in chart terms but that they appealed to a more specifically black audience, and had not alienated their 'true fans'.

Finally, the presence of an explicit *politics* was also at stake here. While this factor applied to some of the white 'indie' bands, it was also a key distinction between 'commercial' rap artists such as Hammer and bands such as NWA (Niggers With Attitude) or Public Enemy, who espouse a revolutionary separatist black politics. For Nicky and others, this was partly a matter of being 'honest' to the experience of inner-city ghetto life, and of raising issues such as poverty and drug abuse. However, it was also intimately connected with the issue of *ethnicity*. At a number of points in the discussion, students referred to the ways in which white artists such as Lisa Stansfield have appropriated 'black' musical forms — although the accusation of 'sell out' levelled at black artists like Hammer or Salt 'n' Pepa was also based on their apparent abandonment of a specifically black audience.

Underlying these distinctions is a notion which is probably the central validating criterion in critical discourse about popular music, that of *authenticity*. As numerous writers have argued[10], pop criticism is often based on a romantic distinction between 'art' and 'commerce'. Thus, on the one hand, we have a 'genuine' folk culture, which is seen as honest and spontaneous, and is produced collectively 'by the people'; while on the other, we have a 'false', mass-produced popular culture, which is seen as synthetic and commodified, and which is produced '*for* the people' by corrupt and manipulative outsiders. In a sense, the foundation myths of pop — both of musicians and of critics — are based on this elemental paradigmatic opposition between 'nature' and 'culture'; and the syntagmatic narrative of 'sell out', of genuine creative expression emerging spontaneously 'on the streets' and then rapidly being incorporated and neutralised by the capitalist industrial machine, is largely responsible for regenerating the myths and keeping the business going.

We will return to these broader arguments about 'mass culture' in Chapter 7. What is important to note at this point is the way in which these everyday critical discourses about popular music connect with debates in academic theory and research. As we have indicated, these debates about who has or has not 'sold out', or who is or is not truly 'hardcore', in fact reflect much broader conceptual understandings, particularly about the relationships between media institutions and their audiences.

In terms of the A-level Media Studies syllabus, these students' discussions touched on many of the major 'media debates' — for example, about independent and mainstream media production, about cultural imperialism and about ideology and popular culture. At the same time, they also pointed to some of their limitations. For example, the notion of 'independence', which the syllabus carries over from 1970s film theory, is actually a rather misleading way of understanding the music industry, as Stephen's comments on 'indie' bands indicated.

Our role as teachers in these discussions was primarily to encourage the students to make the reasons for these distinctions explicit, and to draw connections with the theoretical debates. As an introduction, this seemed to make sense. Yet, how we interpret the work that the students went on to produce — let alone how we evaluate it — raises many questions about these students' relationships with popular music and our aims in teaching about it.

Writing Pop: Forms of Critical Discourse

We want to move on now to consider three magazines produced by different groups for the practical section of the unit. The students' brief was to produce a magazine designed for a specific target market of their choice. They were required to produce between 16 and 24 pages, which could include a range of material, including feature articles, interviews, reviews, news, and advertisements. The covers of these magazines are reproduced below.

Crossover, produced by Stephen and Andy, identifies itself as 'an alternative magazine for alternative people' (see p. 68). According to Stephen's written account:

> The market audience of our magazine is young adults ranging from 18 to 30 years of age to which most chart music does not appeal. Our audience is looking to widen their listening taste outside of the very commercial pop music associated with radio stations like Radio One or Capital Radio and television programmes like Top of the Pops. The type of person who would buy our 'alternative' magazine would probably watch television programmes such as the 'Jonathan Ross Show' or 'The Word' and buy already existing music magazines 'Vox', 'Select', and towards the older end of the market 'Q'.

Crossover contains articles on 'punk 'n' funk' band The Red Hot Chili Peppers, the politics of Irish music, an interview with British rapper Rebel MC (who had been invited in to speak to the class), a 'Guide to Thrash', three pages of upcoming concert dates and album reviews — including John Lee Hooker, Nirvana and REM reviews.

The Click, produced by Harry, Anthony and Ka Wai, is essentially a hardcore fanzine (see p. 68). In his written account, Harry defines the audience for the magazine as 'people aged between fifteen and twenty years old', arguing that 'race, sex or religion' were irrelevant. He claims that the magazine speaks for 'our generation', and notes with some pleasure that his teachers were 'excluded' from this. The magazine 'visions our generation with much energy and it shows that our generation just want to have a good time as seen on the cover'.

At the same time, Harry asserts that:

> . . . we are a hardcore magazine as opposed to a commercial magazine such as smash hits. We opted to make the magazine as hardcore as possible because we believe that the majority of our generation enjoys hardcore and because we believe that the commercial artists such as Kylie are in the music business for the money where as most hardcore groups such as THE PRODIGY make tracks for the fun of being known and they make tracks that will be enjoyed by many people.

Figure 4.1 Magazine Covers

Despite these claims to universal appeal, the magazine seems to be aimed primarily at those who attend 'raves'. While the record reviews are divided into sections for hip-hop, 'commercial', soul and hardcore, the rest of the magazine includes an illustrated two-page 'rave report' (based on a rave Harry had organised himself), a specialist dance chart and two pages of information about clubs and raves. The text is also interspersed with advertisements for raves, specialist dance record shops, and hire companies specialising in sound and lighting gear.

Finally, *Reaction*, produced by Angela, Aylin and Mei King, appears to be aimed at a rather more diverse audience, although this is not immediately apparent from the cover. In her written account, Angela appears to echo Harry's claim for universal appeal, although there is some ambiguity here:

> This magazine is not manipulating a labelled or stereotyped audience which it should appeal to by saying it is a 'black', 'hardcore', 'rock' or musicians music magazine, because I believe that by doing that you are automatically narrowing the audience and reducing the number of sales... The place where we failed *not* to exclude was on the front page, where the type setting [i.e. design] tended to have the same genre as 'SMASH HITS' or 'Just Seventeen'; this automatically write off people who see themselves as serious readers and view Smash Hits as a comic book or something to wipe your feet on . . . the original type setting appealed more to someone who views themselves as more worldly and mature than your average Smash Hits or Just Seventeen reader.

In terms of its content, *Reaction* is probably the most diverse of the three magazines. It includes a gossip column, an article on 'The Death of Vinyl', a profile of Nuno Battencourt from the band Extreme, charts, club news, a report on the Reggae Superfest, a critical piece on Madonna, a page of illustrations with 'cheeky' captions and an interview with 'MC Rheality' (also known as Nicky), a student in the class, whose work we will consider below.

As we have noted, the brief that the students were given for this activity required the magazines to be aimed at a 'specific target audience', although this could obviously include themselves and their peer group. In our experience, however, the notion of audience — which recurs as a 'key concept' throughout media education syllabuses — is in practice one of the hardest for students to grasp, not least because it requires a kind of 'de-centering'. The logs that accompany practical media productions often include bland assertions that they are aimed at 'young people aged 16–25', but rarely offer more detail than that.

As the above quotations begin to suggest, the students have interpreted this requirement in different ways. Harry appears to have had the greatest difficulty here. To begin with, he incorrectly he claims that his magazine has universal appeal by making the patently false assertion that 'the majority of our generation enjoys hardcore' — although it is worth noting that this rhetoric of generational unity is an important aspect of rave culture. And at other times, his written account appears to refuse the notion of a target audience completely, asserting that 'we aimed the magazine at no one in particular'.

By contrast, Stephen is much more calculating, and indeed even cynical. He argues that *Crossover* would cater for the same audience as other magazines such as *Vox* and *Select* 'but on a smaller scale making the buyer feel they had bought a "non-commercial" or "independent" magazine' — and thus offers what he terms '"indie" credibility'. While Stephen is himself a fan of 'indie' bands, such as Carter USM (the Unstoppable Sex Machine), he also indicates some of the contradictions here:

> Part of the male teenage sub-culture is to rebel against the systems of society and this is something 'indie' bands like Carter USM promote strongly and something which has been adopted as part of the definition of 'independent' music generally. However, the overall message carried by 'indie' bands is to rebel against the 'system' *through* the 'system' . . . 'indie' music is the result of consumer culture being given some sort of political meaning which is designed to appeal to people with socialist politics who have the money in their pockets to buy records and additional merchandise (many of the 'indie' bands rely on T-shirt sales as their main income).

While some of these arguments arose from our discussions with Stephen, the formulation is very much his own. What is particularly striking here is his ability to distance himself from an audience of which he himself is a member, and to turn the 'independent' critique of the music business against itself. The inverted commas here serve as markers of that distance: as Stephen himself points out, 'questions can be asked like: what is working outside the "system"? and what is the "system"?'

While Angela's notion of her audience is less precise than Stephen's, it is notable that she too places a distance between herself and her readers — the 'people who *see themselves as* serious readers' and 'who *view themselves as* more worldly and mature' (our italics).

These different stances towards the reader are particularly manifest in the styles of critical discourse that the magazines adopt. Like that of its models *Vox* and *Select,* the style of *Crossover* combines an apparently 'personal' informality with language that verges on the academic. The record reviews, for example, employ an elaborate system of generic distinctions, ranging from 'classic rock' to 'techno-punk', 'punk/thrash' and 'hard thrashy rock'. Technical terms like 'tempo' and 'rhythm', and praise for the musicians' 'versatility' and 'subtlety', are set alongside reflections on the meaning of 'sell out' and admiration for the political directness of Stiff Little Fingers. For example, the article on the Red Hot Chili Peppers employs an elaborate, almost technical style:

> On paper the Red Hot Chili Peppers new double album 'Blood, Sugar, Sex, Magic' uses the same formula of all previous Chili's albums but the amazing thing is everything they tried to achieve i.e. the rapping/singing style of singer Antwan, the hard funk bass of Flea, together with the rock guitar sound of Johnny has finally cohered, resulting in a double serving of classic funk rock containing the originality the Chilis have always strived for.

The feature articles also attempt to set the music within a wider political and cultural context. Andy's article on Irish music situates the work of contemporary bands both in a tradition of 'rebel songs' dating back to the 1916 rebellion and in the current context of Republican opposition to British rule (Andy is himself from Northern Ireland, and has since returned there). Similarly, in writing up the interview with Rebel MC, Stephen emphasises both his political views and his explicit anti-racism, while also questioning his position within the mainstream music business. At the same time, Stephen draws ironic attention to his own role as interviewer, in autobiographical 'New Journalism' mode:

> It's 1.45 on a Tuesday afternoon and I am waiting patiently to interview Michael West a.k.a. the REBEL MC. He adopts the tradition of most popsters these days and arrives late. To everyone's surprise with him are fellow Tottenham rappers the DEMON BOYS who take a seat either side of the REBEL in a bodyguard like fashion.

The overall stance of the articles combines enthusiastic fandom with ironic distance and sociological observation (not to mention some geographical uncertainties) — as in Andy's account of the origins of 'thrash':

> Spawning from the merging of rock and punk, thrash has carved a niche for itself in modern society... Along the south coast of America (Florida, Miami and Seattle in particular) young, white, middle-class men picked up their instruments and headed for garages. The result, in my opinion, was pure genius.

In his written account, Stephen explicitly acknowledges the aim to offer a 'grown up' approach, and also comments on the under-representation of women — which, he argues, reflects the situation in the business as a whole.

While *The Click* shares this rejection of the mainstream music industry, its politics are much less explicit. The magazine is very much concerned with policing the boundaries between hardcore and other musical genres that it deems 'commercial', and (despite Harry's claims to universal appeal) between 'serious' hardcore fans and others. This is particularly apparent in the 'commercial section' of the record reviews. Harry's review of 'Give Me Just a Little More Time' by Kylie Minogue is representative of his direct prose style:

> This tune is just totally poor, and even though i may sound unfair because i'm a hardcore nutter i seriously don't give a f**k [*sic*]. I never thought i would come across a tune that was too commercial for the human eardrums but Kylie has done it. The poor vocals and the typical Stockaitken and Waterman backing tune earns the skinny roach from Oz: -3/10. (YES THAT IS MINUS THREE)

These distinctions become more acute as they get closer to home. Significantly, the record that earns the lowest marks, and the full weight of Harry's scorn, is by KLF, a band who use many elements of hardcore but who are ultimately damned as 'commercial'. When it comes to the 'hardcore section', this need to distinguish between the authentic and the fake becomes paramount. The compilation *Hardcore Essential,* for example, is described as 'the latest contribution in the move to take hardcore into the world of mainstream music', and the inclusion of 'tracks that are straight off 'TOP OF THE POPS'' earns it 'a measly 4/10'.

However, within the specialist hardcore reviews, different mixes are compared, and ratings allocated. The criteria on which these judgments are based are typically just *asserted* rather than argued in detail: records are described positively as 'mental', 'WICKED' or 'bloody brilliant', and 'originality' is a key term which recurs in a number of reviews. The reviews also strongly emphasise the social uses of music. For example, Mariah Carey's 'Can't Let Go' 'is especially made for when you are alone with your girl or when you want to ask a girl to dance', while the Fushnikens 12″ includes a remix 'which has bass that nearly cracked my windows'.

In comparison with *Crossover,* the critical discourse of *The Click* appears much less elaborate and sophisticated — although to a certain extent this reflects the different status of the two products. While Harry's assertion of his musical preferences might appear to be merely arrogant, he also claims to speak on behalf of a specific subcultural group whose tastes and critical criteria do not need further justification: 'because i'm a hardcore nutter i seriously don't give a f**k.' Music is not, as it is to some extent for Stephen and Andy (and indeed for the writers of *Vox* and *Select*), an object of intellectual and political debate, or a pretext for the somewhat narcissistic display of the writer's critical expertise.

These differences are also apparent in the design of the two magazines. *Crossover* was produced using a combination of DTP software and cut-and-paste methods. The pages are laid out in columns, and while the text is interspersed with images, there is an overall symmetry which is almost formal, even compared with the relatively conservative approach of its models *Vox* and *Select* (although this may have been encouraged by the limitations of the software itself). By contrast, the design of *The Click* is haphazard and lacking in symmetry. The text has been word-processed, but advertisements have been stuck on seemingly at random in order to fill gaps around the edges. As Harry argues in his written account, this reflects the overall lack of formality, which is also apparent in the writing:

> . . . we set out to make the magazine as 'no holds barred' as possible and we were not going to let the layout change our way of thinking. It may sound like we did not really think about the layout, but we believe the teenagers interested about raves and the rest of it do not care what order the magazine is in, as long as it is there to read.

Despite Harry's assertion, in his written account, that 'race, class and gender are three topics we did not consider when producing the articles', these issues *are* undoubtedly raised in the magazine itself. We have already noted Nicky's accusation that Harry 'wanted to be black'; and there is undoubtedly some ambiguity here in his contributions to the magazine. For example, his review of The Fushnikens includes the line 'the whitest person in the world could listen to this tune and would have to move to it' — a comment which clearly (or ironically?) draws on racist notions of 'essential rhythm', while also appearing to speak from an implicitly 'black' perspective. Furthermore, in his photo-report on the rave that he organised, Harry quotes a number of Greek participants' complaining about the presence of 'too many Greeks' — views which are partly endorsed by his editorial comments, and which may well relate to the kind of disavowal of ethnicity mentioned above.

Finally, *The Click* also appears to speak from a specifically male perspective — although in a rather different way from *Crossover*. Harry's review of Mariah Carey (quoted above) is a case in point, although again the more explicit aspects of this bias come from the mouths of others — for example, in the form of a quote from a male 'raver' who comments enthusiastically on the presence of 'so much pu**y' [*sic*].

In comparison, the agenda of *Reaction* is much more obviously female — although it represents a more assertive form of sexuality than the submissiveness that young women's magazines are often accused of promoting. Unlike the boys' magazines, *Reaction* does not include record reviews, although its general articles — for example 'The Death of Vinyl' — are as well-informed as those in *Crossover*. In general, however, the music itself takes a lower profile here. What distinguishes *Reaction* is its emphasis on the personal (and particularly sexual) lives of the artists. This is certainly apparent in the gossip page, which includes speculation about Madonna and AIDS and a particularly tasty morsel about Jodie Foster and a 'nude body stocking'. Likewise, 'Ten Extremely Interesting Facts' about Nuno

Battencourt and his new album PORNOGRAFFITTI culminates with Angela's considered opinion:

> 10. Nuno is the sexiest looking man in the history of Rock Music. Need I say more.

Furthermore, compared with the other magazines, more thought has been given to the design of *Reaction,* and more space is given to visual material, including drawings, photographs and blocks of bright colour. This may partly reflect the magazine's address to a younger target audience: indeed, in her written account, Angela describes how the younger students to whom she showed the magazine were primarily interested in the pictures, which she took as evidence of the 'short attention spans' of 'young minds'. However, the emphasis on visual material may also reflect the less discursive, abstract nature of these young women's use of popular music.

In fact, where the music itself is addressed, the writing is much more straightforwardly 'personal' than the distanced approach of *Crossover.* Angela's account of the Reggae Superfest, for example, is far from uncritical, but focuses primarily on emotional response:

> Next to take the mic, Jamaica's best vocalist of 1991 Beres Hammond. The hits EMPTINESS INSIDE, STEP ASIDE and RESPECT TO YOU sent the temperature soaring with excitement, then came the showstopper. BERES wished the NICELY DRESSED SWEET SMELLING LADIES a Happy Valentines and proceeded to throw roses into the crowd. The place erupted with the opening bars of TEMPTED TO TOUCH. Beres trade mark impassioned voice drew in the crowd which clearly empathised with the agonised lover.

Unlike the critics of *Crossover,* Angela does not take up the position of a disinterested, ironic observer; nor does she seek to explain the event in sociological or political terms for the benefit of outsiders. On the contrary, she identifies directly with the audience — the 'crowd' — of which she is a member, and speaks primarily of her emotional and sexual responses as a fan. While the boys' affective investments and bodily participation in the music *are* certainly apparent — most clearly, if somewhat abruptly, in *The Click* — they are conveyed much more directly in Angela's account.

Perhaps the major problem facing us as teachers here — and it is one that we shall be considering in greater length in the second half of the book — is that of evaluation. While we can read these texts as subcultural products, tracing the different ways in which they 'position' their writers and readers, evaluation obliges us to make a rather different kind of comparison.

Part of the problem here lies in the relationships between these texts and the 'models' on which they have drawn. While *Reaction* and *Crossover* are consciously based on original texts or genres with which we are familiar —

even if they go on to do rather different things with them — we are much less familiar with the 'original version' of *The Click.* As far as we can tell, *The Click* is not a pastiche or a 'critical' version of a fanzine: it actually *is* a fanzine. Of course, 'as far as we can tell' is where the problem lies. It may be that Harry's identification with the rave subculture is partly vicarious or imaginary, although we doubt it. Is Harry an 'authentic' hardcore fan, and if he isn't, then who is? And how would we know anyway?

At the same time, in contrast to *Plaz,* these magazines were obviously produced as part of a school project, and for the purposes of assessment. Yet apart from the self-censorship of Harry's asterisks, it is hard to know how this inflected or determined them. In terms of assessment, we would have to look for evidence of students' learning, not in the texts themselves, but in the process of production and in the written account which accompanies them. In particular, we would look for the students' ability to employ a critical academic discourse — to talk about genre, representation, institution and audience, for example. Both in the magazine itself and in the accompanying writing, Stephen clearly does this much more effectively than either Harry or Angela.

Yet there are several problems here, as we shall see in more detail in later chapters. In this case, for example, it is clear that the genre and the narcissistic style characteristic of 'new wave' pop journalism, which Andy and Stephen have chosen to work in is one in which this kind of academic critical discourse — or at least a version of it — serves as a key marker of critical sophistication. For the writers of *Reaction* and *The Click,* however, this is not the case: academic analysis in their context would be seen as irrelevant, if not pretentious, and would certainly result in a loss of subcultural credibility. At the same time, as we have tried to show, these writers are making some quite precise critical judgments; and much broader cultural and ideological investments are at stake here, even if they are not made explicit. Indeed much of the social function and power of these discourses lies in their remaining implicit, and as such only perceptible to 'insiders'. In uncovering them for the critical gaze, and in privileging academic discourse, we may inevitably undermine their meaning and pleasure, and hence much of their power.

Finding a Voice: Rapping with the Female Force

The difficult question of 'authenticity' raised in our discussion of *The Click* is also at stake in the final text that we would like to consider in this chapter. This is a 15-minute segment of a radio show for an imaginary pirate radio station 'Finesse FM', produced by two black Afro-Caribbean girls, Nicky and Karen, using a four-track sound mixer.

The tape consists of a sequence of rap, hardcore and hip-hop tracks introduced by 'DJ KC' (Karen) and interspersed with jingles and advertisements for raves sung and spoken by the two girls. Our analysis here will centre on an interview between DJ KC and 'up-and-coming female artiste MC Rheality' (Nicky), and on Nicky's rap 'The Female Force' which follows it.

According to Nicky's written account, the music and style of Finesse FM is based on the approach of pirate station Rush FM, as well as on the hardcore and hip-hop shows of more mainstream stations like Capital and Kiss. However:

> The only way I would say that Finesse differs from the mentioned stations, is that it would have all female DJ's. I don't feel that this would put boys off from listening, it's just a matter of females getting an equal slice of the cake that the male DJ's always seem to be dishing out.

Nevertheless, Nicky maintains that Finesse is 'not particularly aimed at females but at the youth', at 'teenagers' in general — although she is also aware that the programme has an 'inner city' feel. As she points out, the 'female' concept is only emphasised in a few of the jingles, which promote the station as being 'for all the females in the house'.

Nicky's rap combines the familiar self-assertion of rap with an anti-authoritarian stance, as the following extracts indicate:

The Female Force

Giving them my all or nothing
I don't believe in bluffing
When it comes to me there'll be pushing and shoving
Just to see us crossing our way on the British stage
At such a young age
I don't mean to brag and boast
But I'm a-making toast
For myself
I put my feet up on the shelf
And I quote
'There's never been a female MC so dope'

I'll hold to do the things I do
and say the things I want to
Let the trumpets sound
Huh! Cause I can prove it to you pound for pound
That I can go on and on and on and on and on
While the other suckers are dropping bombs
'Cause I can flow on
I got lyrics to go on

This is Rheality
Local versatility
This is Rheality

Go! Go! Go!

But my rhyme won't slacken to the answer
I listen to no queen and no master
Say it to my face 'cause I say it to yours
It's not a criminal offence
But I'm prone to breaking laws
Cynical
Snapping like a crocodile
This ain't no faith
This is worthwhile
Rhyming like a sinner
And standing like an enemy

Pump your fist get ready
'Cause here I come
I'm in neutral
So come and get some — hard!
And my lyrics and I'm living large
No more 'yes ma'am' and 'no sarge'
People wanna compete
I say hell no
'Cause when I get on the mic I can't let go
So less group, but I can go solo
Plus I got philosophy
And bam! hey presto
Rhymes in the air in no time at all

Versatility
Yeah
Rheality's in the house
With versatility
Yeah
Peace!

In her interview, MC Rheality gives a brief account of how she began rapping, and moves on to some more general reflections on the politics of rap, as shown in the following extracts:

KC: OK. Do you believe that rappers and groups such as Public Enemy use too much abusive language to bring their points across?

MC Rheality: No. I really think it depends on where you're coming from. I mean, if you come from East Coast of America, or something, or West Coast, then you'll use lyrics to your suitability. I mean, if you take it like Ice-T comes from somewhere where he had to grow up selling drugs or shooting and everything, he does it his way. Whereas Public Enemy have a message to get across, they're not going to go into the charts like MC Hammer. They prefer to do it their way, and they're not going to sell out for anybody.

KC: Does this make their audience like them for what they're singing and what they're saying?

MC Rheality: Yeah. They get much more respect from a black audience. I don't really think they're out to please anyone, they just want to get their point across, you know, talking about what we've gone through, what our ancestors have gone through and what we should know about our past, and they're just trying to recap their audience on what they feel they should know.

KC: OK. Do you feel you get more response from your audience due to the fact that you're a black female artist? I emphasise the word female.

MC Rheality: Yes, I believe that. There's many females out there who's got talent, and they're wasting it on singing. There's a majority of singers out there are female, and I think it's different if a female's gonna go on stage and rap. She should do something more constructive, and um, like for example, when I went up on stage one time, a lot of the audience thought I was going to sing, but they was amazed when I started rapping, and I got a lot of, um, applause for it.

KC: So, as you said before that Public Enemy use abusive language to come across to their audience, do you do any sort of way to make your audience like you? Like a certain style, or certain lyrics or things that you say?

MC Rheality: Well, when I was starting off, you know, I'd write about myself and things like that, but, I mean, the more you grow up, you go through certain stages, you're influenced by a lot more rappers, so you rap how you feel, the situations you're going through in life, and you find you have more to rap about, and you get more respect that way, and you're not always focusing your raps on yourself, or, you know, just to make money.

While Nicky's rap sounds to our (relatively ignorant) ears at least as authentic — if not as professionally polished — as the models on which she has drawn, there is clearly a certain artificiality about this exercise. Karen's contributions in particular have the hesitancy of a school student attempting to appear grown up, reading out her prepared questions and playing at her DJ role: 'Well, we're running out of time, so I'd like to thank MC Rheality for coming into the studio.' (This is much like 'Pony' the schoolboy playing at Plaz the hero, returning to rescue his sweetheart Kim from the middle of a boring lesson.)

The implicit and explicit references to the United States are also significant here. Nicky's rap is delivered in a strong American accent, and her references are all to American rap artists — although, as in the piece on 'garage rock' in *Crossover*, her geography is a little imprecise. At the same time, her rap emphasises *'local* versatility', and refers both to the 'British stage' and (in a section omitted here) to the 'London masses' whom she presumably sees as her potential audience. The line about 'making toast' refers to the Caribbean reggae tradition of 'toasting', which could be seen as a local precursor of rap.

Nevertheless, Nicky's claim to authenticity — embodied in her chosen name 'Rheality' — is a central factor. Her rap is explicitly concerned with 'finding a voice', with developing the self-confidence and authority to speak: 'feeling no fear, standing tall . . . continuing with the rhymes *I* choose to.' Finding this voice simultaneously requires and permits a rejection of established authority, both in general terms — 'I listen to no queen and no master' — and more specifically, of the police and, perhaps also, of teachers — 'No more "yes ma'am" and "no sarge".' The voice is also established competitively, in opposition to other rappers — the 'other suckers' who will be reduced to silence while she is able to continue, to 'flow on', without faltering or 'slackening'.

The rapper's voice is seen as honest and direct, without pretence or compromise: it is not about 'bluffing' but about 'Giving them my all or nothing', being 'cynical' rather than promoting a false 'faith'. She is an adversary, a 'sinner' and an 'enemy', but one who is needed because she speaks the truth. And while the voice is clearly 'hard' and aggressive, its honesty requires honesty in return: 'Say it to my face 'cause I say it to yours.'

While this might be dismissed as merely the generic self-aggrandisement of rap, the exercise clearly does enable Nicky to articulate an explicitly 'female' black politics, albeit one that she does not herself refer to as 'feminist' (indeed, we strongly suspect that this is a term she would refuse). While this is only partly explicit in the rap — she refers at one point to becoming 'the next female MC . . . sitting in a gold chair with a black crown' — it is undoubtedly a central aspect of the 'philosophy' which she claims to promote, and which she defines more fully in the interview. Thus, what Nicky praises in her favourite rap artists is both their honesty to the realities of inner-city life and their sense of black history. There is, furthermore, an inherent significance in being a female rapper in that it subverts stereotyped expectations. Rapping, as Nicky defines it, is 'constructive' and 'worthwhile'

Figure 4.2 Record Sleeve: MC Rheality

— it is about having 'a message to get across' — whereas 'singing', a word that we infer that she associates with the romance of Soul, is a waste of women's talent. In describing her own development in the interview, Nicky defines this in terms of maturity, abandoning a self-centred (and self-aggrandising) style in favour of a broader, and implicitly more political, approach.

The relationship with the audience is central to these broader political aims. Yet this is not merely a matter of fame or public acclaim for its own sake (as referred to in the first verse of the rap). As Nicky says later in the interview, 'selling out' or moving towards 'commercial mainstream music' means forgetting 'the true meaning' and will lose you the respect of your fans. Respect will only be won by integrity, by 'doing it your way', and by attempting to 'get your point across' rather than merely seeking to please. And while the audience is potentially diverse, the respect that counts is that which is won from a specifically black audience.

'Finding a voice' is thus much more than an individual, personal process. On the contrary, it is a matter of moving beyond the personal and defining your position in social and political terms, which may involve a rejection of authority and a consciously oppositional stance. Furthermore, it involves a social dialogue with your chosen audience. The claim to honesty and authenticity — which, as Nicky's account suggests, is an explicitly *ideological* claim — is central to this relationship. Defining 'rheality' is thus bound to involve a struggle for power and control.

In this respect, perhaps one the most interesting aspects of Nicky's written account for us, as teachers, is her 'rap review'. Here, she takes apart an article about 'feminist rap' written by a white academic, Beverley Skeggs, which we had provided.[11] Nicky refutes what she sees as Skeggs' attempt to present male rappers as (in her words) 'loud, thoughtless, cold-hearted and inconsiderate' and female rap as solely a matter of 'competitive dissing' and 'threatening' of other women. She quotes numerous exceptions to these arguments, arguing that rap is 'simply a form of expression' that reflects people's 'different positions in society', and also referring to rappers who emphasise female solidarity. She concludes with a list of female rappers and their 'messages', quoting herself (in the third person) as an example:

> What many people don't seem to understand is that the lyrics of female rappers isn't always just about 'Bitch this, Bitch that'. MC Rheality deals with her rapping style and goes on to more serious topics like drugs, government issues etc.
> 'They tell me looks are deceiving, while I stand in my militant pose
> They'd rather see me pushing base [cocaine] and working with hoes [whores]
> But I'm no playgirl take heed of what I say girl
> Cos I got more rhymes to make your mind curl.'
> It is basically revolving around realism in the state of the world, whatever you go through, is as much influence as you need. Beverley Skeggs does not seem to understand this, as she seems to be judging the context of the lyrics in such a way as to ask is this feminine/non-feminine?

Nicky seems to us to confuse Skeggs' positions with those that she is attacking (for example, the notion of fixed definitions of 'femininity'); and, despite her comments, she is not above a certain amount of 'dissing' herself. Yet the accuracy of her arguments here is less important than the way in which she effectively rejects the attempt of a white academic to speak on her behalf (Nicky had specifically asked us whether the author was white). Thus, she argues that Skeggs 'speaks without enough knowledge' and suggests that she should 'read a book or two before trying to associate herself with rap or females at that!' In addition, she again makes claims for the authenticity of her music, arguing that it is not concerned with 'looks' but with 'realism in the state of the world, whatever you go through'. In this respect at least, she seems to argue, 'feminist' criteria are simply an inappropriate basis for such judgeents.

Conclusion

In this chapter, we have considered a number of examples of students' writing which both use and critique existing media forms. As in the case of *Plaz Investigations,* these texts are part of an ongoing dialogue, not merely with other readers and writers but also with the media themselves. As we have shown, a great deal may be at stake in this process. In adopting 'critical' positions in discourse, in staking out their tastes and identities, and in intervening directly in popular cultural forms, these writers are actively defining themselves in relation to wider social, cultural and ideological forces. Although, as we have argued, 'reading' the media is also a dialogical process, 'writing' media texts brings this dialogue into the open, and thus potentially opens it up for critical reflection and analysis. It is for this reason that we regard it as a central and indispensable part of teaching about popular culture.

In the following chapter, we will develop and broaden this notion of 'writing' by considering visual texts — in this case, photographic images — produced by students. To an even greater extent than the texts we have considered thus far, these images relate directly to a popular cultural practice in which 'ordinary people' are not merely consumers but also producers. Yet, as we shall argue, the visual representation of the 'self' is far from being a matter of individual 'self-expression'. On the contrary, it is a process which raises much more fundamental questions about cultural and social power.

Notes

1. In the 1991 A-level syllabus, the areas for these 'debates' included the following subjects: realism, ideology or popular culture, media systems in different cultures, media and cultural imperialism, new media technologies, regulation and deregulation, public-service broadcasting, film and video workshops and film theory.
2. This term derives from the work of John Fiske (1987a).
3. For example, Blanchard, Greenleaf and Sefton-Green (1989), Ferrari and James (1989).
4. See the reviews of the above packs by Bell in *English and Media Magazine*, Nos 24 and 25.
5. Neale (1980).

6. Bourdieu (1984). For a useful critique, see Mander (1987). The related notion of 'taste cultures' proposed by the US sociologist Herbert Gans has been applied to popular music in the work of Lewis (1987).
7. See Frith (1983, 1992) and the work of Keith Roe (e.g. 1987) on the relationship between musical taste and academic capital.
8. See Lull (1987).
9. For a detailed ethnographic study of this issue, see Jones (1988); and for related studies of this issue, see Hewitt (1986) and Gilroy (1987).
10. Middleton (1990) considers this process in relation to folk music. See also Frith (1988) and Redhead (1990).
11. Skeggs (1991a and b).

Chapter 5

'The "Me" in the Picture is *Not* Me': Photography as Writing

In Chapter 3, we looked at a generically conventional piece of story writing as a way of examining how mainstream media might be read and given meaning by an adolescent boy. In the last chapter, we used the practical production work of A-level students in order to raise questions about subculture and taste which indirectly challenge the role and purpose of media teaching within the school curriculum. This chapter is based on an extensive photography exercise carried out with year-10 students in the first year of their GCSE Media Studies course, and it develops one of the central concerns arising from these earlier enquiries: the extent to which young people already possess the competencies to 'write' in contemporary media forms, and the kinds of knowledge such writing mobilises.

The use of writing as a metaphor for media production work is not without its theoretical problems,[1] although in many ways it seems a productive one. The processes by which students produce photographs that reflect their perspectives and concerns are strongly reminiscent of the expressive purposes of creative writing. The strategic construction of images has many parallels with the ways in which we invite students to consider the effect of voice and register on potential readers and audiences. And the talk that surrounds the photographs is very similar to that which accompanies the drafting and redrafting of written texts. In all these respects, we are implicitly regarding writing as an active, social process, whose meaning is located in specific social settings and relationships.

To a greater extent than the media discussed in the previous two chapters, photography is a genuinely popular medium, in which ordinary people are not merely 'consumers' but also producers. As we indicated in Chapter 2, all the students in our survey either owned or had access to at least one camera, and all were likely to have had experience of taking their own photographs. The cultural significance of popular photography in the construction of our own histories and identities — particularly through the medium of the 'family album' — has been well documented.[2]

While it acknowledges this popular usage, photography in the context of formal education has often had an ambiguous relationship with it. The most relevant work in terms of our concerns here is that of feminist practitioners, like Jo Spence,[3] and of the Cockpit, in London, which developed an influential approach to using photography with working-class youths. Early work in this field tended to regard photography somewhat uncritically, almost as a way of enabling the oppressed to represent themselves — and thereby achieve status and a mysterious form of 'deep' knowledge. However, Andrew Dewdney and Martin Lister's reflective account of the Cockpit's work begins to problematise these arguments about the radical potential of the medium: in particular, it questions the extent to which allowing young people to celebrate and articulate their sub-cultural identities can in fact be seen as 'empowering'.[4] Yet despite its limitations, this approach represents a powerful alternative to the highly theoretical, 'deconstructionist' approach to Media Studies which was prevalent at the time, not least because it attempts to connect with the material experiences and 'structures of feeling' of working-class youths.

Ultimately, however, there is bound to remain a tension between the motivated 'artistic' or 'critical' uses of photography within education and the popular recreational uses of students' out-of-school experience. What has proven so difficult to achieve is to bring such a popular cultural practice into the field of education, while at the same time preserving its popular nature. In a way, this paradox goes to the heart of our concerns in this book: can we bring popular culture into the classroom without merely incorporating it into the framework of yet another academic discipline?

The Photography Assignment

Bearing this dilemma in mind, we tried to design a practical activity that would allow students to reflect on their home and personal use of photography as well as giving them an opportunity to create popular narratives. The students were given a choice of two activities, to be carried out in groups. The first involved the production of a photostory, in a maximum of 24 shots. The brief asked students to imagine that the story would be published in a teenage magazine, but one aimed at a slightly older audience than *Jackie* or *My Guy*. The story could be either complete or the first episode of a serial, and was not required to be a romance or to have a happy ending. The second activity was an 'identity portrait': a photographic collage showing 'different aspects of yourself'. The brief also asked students to consider the way in which individuals display a variety of identities or images in different contexts, and to consider how these can be conveyed by using different clothing, poses and gestures. The task also included a written reflection on the whole exercise. For a follow-up activity, the students were asked to collect some pictures of themselves, taken from their personal or family albums, and to reflect upon how they were defined and represented in these pictures.

It was significant that only five of the 50 or so students who completed this exercise chose to make the identity portraits. This was partly because the activity was more individualistic, whereas the photostory immediately lent itself to co-operative group work. In fact, the 'identity' students quickly decided to work together and developed a common format and language to structure the activity. These students were worried about the self-centred focus of the activity — as compared with that of the photostory groups, who described the process as 'acting'. We also felt that the photostory was a recognised cultural practice, whereas the idea of 'representing identity', at least as we defined it, seemed to have a less obvious connection to the students' previous experience of photography.[5]

However, when the students began designing their photostories, it quickly became clear that their concept of the photostory itself depended on the reading histories of different students. Those girls who had read photostories in teenage magazines (usually, it should be pointed out, when they were a couple of years younger) were much more sensitive to the conventions of the genre. On the other hand, many of the boys seemed to view the exercise as a form of comic-making, and the graphic style of several of their productions reflects this.[6]

Ultimately, however, we suspect that most students chose the photostory not because it was more familiar or more pertinent but because it offered opportunities for indulging in other kinds of narrative — especially those that involved possibilities for play and ironic comment both on the students' own personal stories and on their place within school. It was this mix of the personal and the generic that most intrigued us.

Popular Narratives

We ended up with nine photostories, four by groups of boys, four by girls and only one by a mixed group. (The 'identity' group, interestingly enough, comprised four girls and one boy.) At first glance, these stories appear to divide along gender lines, into romances, school stories and thrillers. However, a closer examination of the narratives reveals a complex web of parody and intertextual references. Most of the stories mix genres, to the extent that it becomes almost impossible to assign any one story to a recognisable generic category.[7] Thus, for example, *The Rude Boy Serial Killings* is ostensibly a thriller, in which a mysterious mass murderer wipes out a group of friends when they stay late one night; but it is also set in school and involves brushes with teachers and a romantic sub-plot. Setting the story in school was not just a logical use of available resources: none of the stories by the other three boys' groups (*The Bank Robbery, The Squat* and *The Drug Dealers*) did this. In those three narratives there is an identifiable thriller plot acted out by the boys, although *The Squat* cannot quite sustain the social realism, and eventually it wittily disintegrates into self-parody.

These different generic choices also had implications in terms of form. The boys clearly interpreted the task as that of making a 'still film', and sought to maximise the visual impact. As Costas wrote: 'We wanted to create scenes of poverty, violence and the effects of robbery . . .', which reads more like a description of a film. The girls, on the other hand, referred to the conventions of photostories as something that they explicitly wanted to avoid, and to show their superior knowledge of. This was a reflection of their desire to distance themselves from forms of presentation that they associated with a younger age group. Manivone, for example, described her group's motives in a sophisticated and analytical fashion:

> . . . it was quite difficult making up a story that didn't have any romance because most photostories have something to do with love . . . In our photostory we wanted to create the effect of peer group pressure and alcoholism, it took us forever to take one picture because we wanted to get the footing and body positions right and real looking facial expressions.

Several of the other girls also made explicit comparisons with the conventions of the photostory, chiefly to assert their individuality by contrast, as in Zoe's disparaging comment: '. . . It was different because they all had love stories . . . and other things that people think of when they hear "photo story".' On the other hand, Emily used the same term as Manivone and Costas to describe the credibility of her work:

> We wanted the shots to look realistic and the murder scene dramatic . . . We tried different shapes for the pictures i.e. hearts, ovals, and a jagged edge for the murder shot. I was pleased with the finished product. Some shots looked very realistic, like professional ones . . .

Realism here, however, is not an aesthetic judgment but rather an index of professionalism. The work is real if it is like real photostories, as opposed to Costas's and Manivone's 'real life'.

If the girls' superior knowledge of the generic conventions of photostories is shown in their reflective comments on the finished products, it is also evident in the kinds of narratives that they produced. *The Unbelievable Theif* (*sic*) and *The New Girl* are typical stories of how a new pupil is socially isolated and driven to deviance: in the first case, to thieving, and in the second, to drink, drugs, (possible) prostitution and death. In these cases, the 'real life' school story is translated into their own environment. By contrast, in *So Sweet But So Sour,* the elements of the school story are combined with the teenage romance (a standard combination), but are then given a macabre twist by a love-crazed (or possibly feminist) murder.

Part of the problem with the photostory format is that these girls see themselves as too old to take it seriously and are vigorously critical of cultural forms aimed at a less adult audience. Thus, they are keen both to show off their control of the form and to distance themselves from it. This results in one of the oddest photostories, *Jill & Meg's Excellent Adventure.* Closely modelled on *Bill and Ted's Excellent Adventure,* the girls' story is an improbable time-travelling fantasy. In a way, it is closest to the boys' thriller-type filmic productions *The Bank Robbery, The Squat* or *The Drug Dealers.* However, it is perhaps the most reliant on dialogue of all the productions and seems to owe most to the idea of the creative story derived from English. Indeed, its sense of character, thought and motivation, and its static, rather illustrative pictures seem to derive more from an imaginary, pre-extant written story.

The Codes of Narration

1. Controlling Conventions

If the narrative structures of the photostories reveal an eclectic variety of popular sources, the range of codes and conventions employed by the students in order to tell the stories and to construct the individual shots also show how they located the task within their readings of popular culture.

The most conventional production, in terms of closeness to the photostory genre of teenage magazines, is *So Sweet But So Sour,* in which classic narrative conventions are demonstrated in profusion. As Emily wrote: 'We tried different shapes for the pictures i.e. hearts, ovals, and a jagged edge for the murder shot.' At one stage, the group realised that one of their pictures, featuring a conversation between two characters, had broken the convention whereby we read from left to right (see Figure 5.2). This explicit understanding of what is effectively the 'grammar' of these kinds of narrative shows a deliberate control of the form which clearly derives from a personal reading history. Indeed, Emily brought in one photostory magazine, *Sweet 16,* to demonstrate to the others in her group the variety of shapes and imaginative graphic techniques available. The little hearts floating above the heroine's head in Figure 5.1, or the jagged inter-cut picture (again Figure 5.1)

Figure 5.1 So Sweet But So Sour

showing simultaneous narration are examples of this control. This latter shot was not, as one might imagine, composed of two images sewn together but was actually taken as a single shot (which was an exceptionally economic use of the available film).

Figure 5.2 So Sweet But So Sour

It might appear from this that the narration (on the level of the movement between images) was constructed after the pictures were taken. However, this group did actually produce a storyboard which looked like a magazine page in conception, and which differed only in slight detail from the finished product. Again, this indicates that these students were able to exert a high level of control over the exercise.

Different groups approached the various stages of the exercise (planning the story, storyboarding, and producing the final graphic presentation) in different ways. As we have just seen, the *So Sweet But So Sour* group attempted to plan the project in a holistic fashion, which was not the case with the other groups. Indeed, we were struck by the enthusiasm with which the boys' groups approached the task, significantly because of the way they enjoyed making up criminal scenarios as a form of fantasy. What some of these groups failed to do was to conceptualise their stories as images, or to think through to the final stage about how these narratives would communicate on paper, and they all needed direction and questioning at each stage of the process. Yet the way in which each group conceptualised the various stages of the production process also depended crucially on how they related the task to a real cultural practice.

This point becomes even more obvious when we contrast the narrative depth of the single pictures from a number of stories. In *So Sweet But So Sour*, an enormous amount of thought went into the narrative possibilities of each picture. Thus, for example, the bottom shots in Figure 5.1 make deliberate use of foreground, middleground and background, as well as leaving space for speech bubbles. The first image is symmetrically balanced against the next image, showing an alternative point of view, in the 'shot-reverse shot' mode of classical Hollywood narration. By contrast, in *The Squatters*, for example, each image is used as a kind of 'freeze frame' of the action. Thus, we see the characters running or engaged in single acts of narration, such as being on the phone. This is primarily because of the different ways in which the groups conceptualised the activity and imagined the potential of the medium.

In the second half of the book we will look in more detail at how students talk and write about practical work. We cannot help but be struck by the way in which the deliberation and control of the *So Sweet But So Sour* group was reflected in their writing. Cheryl, another member of the group, wrote of the final product:

> We wanted to create an effect that you could read the expression on the people's faces. The other effect we wanted to create was a close up of someone and see someone not focused in the background . . . I have also learnt how spaces and expressions mean sometime in photographs.

The last comment, in particular, is a remarkably concise reflection on the relationship between form and meaning. Clearly, the invitation to work in a form that was so familiar to the group resulted in a very self-conscious command of formal conventions. In this respect, it is noticeable that the only other comments which begin to match this level of control come from the other 'classic' photostory *The New Girl*, also produced by an all-girls group.

2. *From Movies to Photostories*

In many respects, *So Sweet But So Sour* is the most conventional of these productions — although this is not necessarily to imply that it is in any way better, or that it demonstrates a greater level of learning, than the others. Rather, it simply demonstrates the successful accommodation and use of standard narrative conventions. There are, of course, no rules for this kind of writing, in the sense that we might correct the spelling or syntactic structure of a written text. What does happen, though, in the necessary absence of narrow constraints is that the students start producing their *own* genres through a process of assimilation and mutation. What was also evident, but is difficult to convey here, was the fact that the process of working in groups and producing work for an audience of peers meant that these 'new' genres gained currency and meaning through the ways in which they were received and interpreted in class.

Figure 5.3 Jill and Meg's Fantastic Adventure

Inevitably, some of these cross-overs also failed. We have already described how students incorporated filmic elements into their narratives — although ironically, the photostory that most explicitly derives from a film, *Jill & Meg's Excellent Adventure,* does this least successfully. We will return to this particular photostory later when we examine the role of fantasy in these productions, but for the moment we would like to focus on Figure 5.3, which shows 'Jill and Meg travelling back in time'. It patently doesn't: but what is interesting is why its authors think it might. Georgina wrote:

> When we had finished the story it looked like a real story, really professional, except that it is very big and colourful, a bit like a child's book.

Indeed, the layout is childish, and the colourful squiggles around the images remind one of younger pupils' work. (Figure 5.3, with its stuck-on silver lightning flashes, attempts to find an appropriate form to narrate time travel.) However, as in the large chunks of written text that the story employs, the attempt to translate film into photostory clearly becomes untenable. Georgina's comments above reveal a split between loyalty to the group and honest evaluation.

It is *The Rude Boy Serial Killings* which most successfully adapts and transforms filmic and comic conventions. Like the producers of *So Sweet But So Sour,* this group impressed us with the way that they visualised the final product right from the beginning. The students in this group approached the task by first writing a conventional story, then producing a detailed storyboard and then going on location. Even more than with *So Sweet But So Sour,* one can trace the finished product back to its initial conception. The use of graphic styles derived both from hip-hop graffiti and, to a lesser extent, from boys' comics are clearly mutations of form — as, for example, with the 'oooo!' in the fourth picture on the first page (Figure 5.4), with its visual representation of verbal intonation and the way that it dramatically spills out of the frame; or the way that the 'blood' from the word 'killings' (in the title) sits on one of the photographs.

Obviously, this whole piece is heavily inflected by race, not just in its black cast but also in its extensive references to 'rude boy' dress and speech. It is also heavily influenced by contemporary films. The urban black culture of *Boyz 'n the Hood* and *New Jack City* pervades the *mise en scène.* Whereas *So Sweet But So Sour* used a kind of narrative depth within each image to communicate relationships and interactions between the characters, *The Rude Boy Serial Killings* uses the conventions of filmic realism. There are a number of shots at the end of the story (see the bottom of Figure 5.4) where the meaning is created through manipulating the point of view of the camera, or where the use of light and shadow create suspense and special effects.

Yet if film is the dominant narrative mode, the accompanying text tends to underscore this with an ironic distancing tone. Thus, phrases like 'crazy kid, he is our last hope' or 'The killer refuses to make friends with Scott' are spoken as if from a voice-over, allowing the authors to parody both themselves and the realist conventions that they appear to adopt. This double narrative voice is remarkably similar to the way that young children's books use a narrator to comment on the action, setting up a tension between verbal and visual forms of narration.[8] Many of the films and comics discussed in Chapter 3 also utilise this ironic mode.

3. Finding a Voice

As we have indicated, the students' different conceptions of the photostory genre gave them a starting point from which they could modify and develop their own narratives. The students who chose to make identity portraits had no such common ground, and were therefore forced to construct an appropriate narrative in which to communicate their sense of themselves. Nandai described the process that the group went through to select images to be photographed as follows:

> . . . for example if we thought our careers were important we talked about our dreams and what we want to be . . . we wanted to create an image of different angles of our lives.

Figure 5.4 The Rude Boy Serial Killing

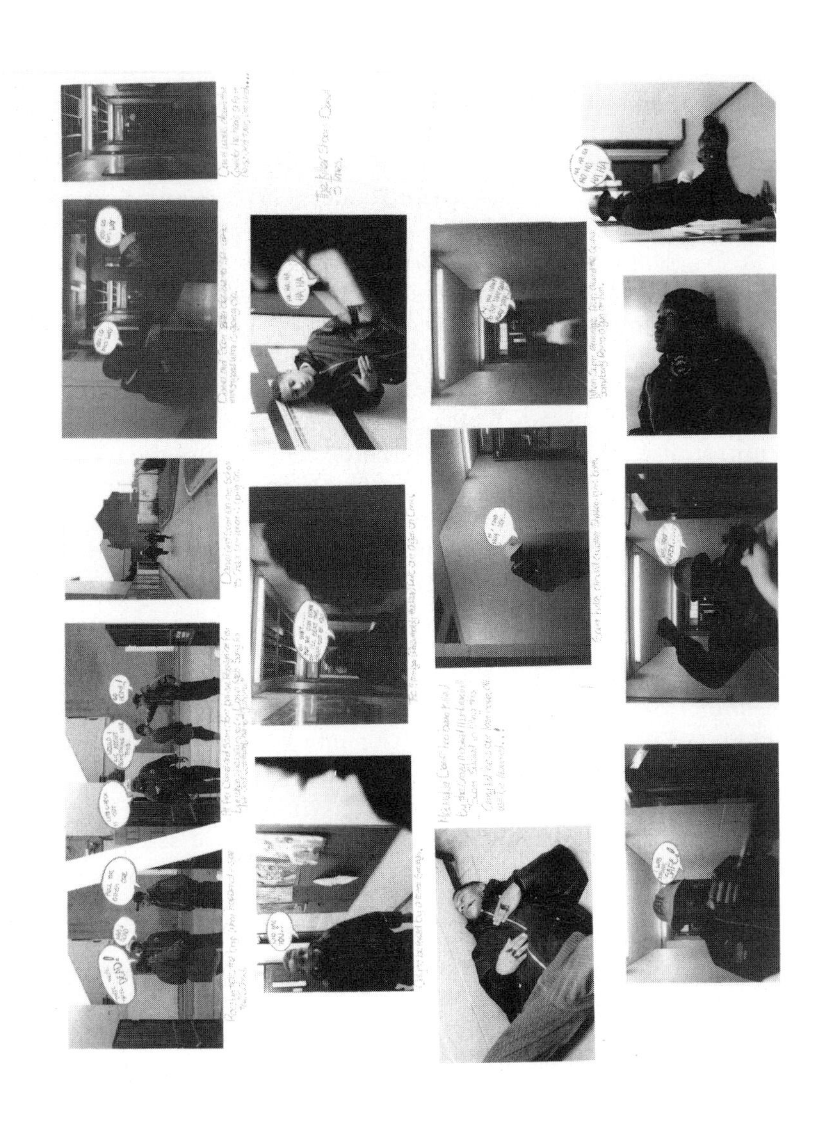

Figure 5.4 The Rude Boy Serial Killing

We are not quite sure whether all the students ended up with similar 'angles' for logistical or strategic reasons. Either way, each of these productions is made up of posed shots of the individual: as a pupil, going out, in the kitchen and at work, as well as less specific portraits. When evaluating the work, they all commented on the technical aspects of the project; for example: 'I think I have learnt all about different ways of taking pictures such as lighting and shadows. Things like that.' However, they did not comment on whether the project 'taught' them about themselves and their image. There could, of course, be many explanations for this, although we would argue that the comparative distance between this activity and the students' prior experience of photography did not allow for the kind of explicit control that is apparent in the work discussed above.

However much we scrutinise the finished products, it is difficult to find a coherent narrative. Only Jeremy's poster (Figure 5.5), which balances poses across the diagonals, and which has two pictures of him looking at himself in a mirror plus the head shot at the centre, actually uses the layout as a way of making connections between the images. In the other cases, the pictures seem stuck down with a rather superficial or unfocused design sense — although we would argue that this is because the idea of using images of oneself to tell a story is not a familiar cultural form, rather than because there is no story to tell.

Significantly, the actual pictures themselves are all framed in a similar fashion. With the exception of Jeremy's head shot, the subjects are all in medium close-up. In our experience, students at this age (or at least with this amount of photography experience) tend to avoid close-ups in self-portraits — despite our injunctions in the brief to 'get *close* enough so that you get only what you want in the picture'. While this might be put down to adolescent embarrassment, or to a gendered lack of self-confidence, it also reflects the fact that most domestic photographs also frame the subject in this way.[9]

The most significant characteristic of this group's work was in fact the pleasure that they took in dressing up for the photographs. Indeed, the other students' interest in this group's project stemmed from their tendency to disappear into the stock cupboard for periods of time and reappear clothed in an un-school-like way. It would seem as if the social process of dressing up and posing was the most significant way that the students had of exploring their identities within the school context, and that the act of transferring the pose to film was secondary to the real moment of exploration. This was reinforced by our experience of watching the students going about their work. Posing for the photos, 'cussing down' the comments of passers-by, and colonising the Headteacher's office for the 'at work' pictures were all significant acts of self-assertion. The actual photographs themselves seemed almost redundant. This focus on the process of photography rather than the product has also been commented on by previous studies.[10]

Figure 5.5 'Jeremy' Myself

It does seem ironic to us, however, that the project we imagined would concentrate students on questions of subjectivity and identity only achieved this in an oblique way. Ultimately, this reinforces one of our central premises: that unless there is a dynamic cultural and social practice in which students can situate themselves, they are unlikely to produce expressive writing.

This is not to denigrate the work of this group. In some ways, the pictures are a study of gender roles, even if the students were not explicit about this fact in their writing. This is particularly true of the shots of hassled domestic labour, and in the way in which Cherie and Rosslyn identify themselves as 'Ms.' when at work in the office — a title that is still comparatively rare in working-class communities, and one that signals a complex set of social aspirations. Tia's label for a similar picture reads 'Talking to boyfriend on the phone at work', which may indicate a fantasy reformulation of conventional power relations. By contrast, Jeremy's vain posturing is classic image-conscious posing.

Yet, the fact that these students decided to work as a group, and devise, as it were, identity genres (or a series of appropriate codes and conventions) into which they could position themselves, provides an interesting indication of how we inscribe the 'self' into different forms of writing and of how we use writing to create different forms of ourselves.

'The "Me" in the Picture is *Not* Me': Self and Play

On the face of it, the above assertion by Georgina about the picture of herself in an old holiday snap is absurd. Yet she is articulating a view that we have all held at some time or another. Indeed, part of the pleasure of photography is the play that it allows between fixity and flux between changing aspects of ourselves and the notion of an immutable identity. As we have already suggested, the actual process of taking these photographs in the intense, socially aware atmosphere of a school significantly inflected their meaning, both for the authors and for their audience. In many ways, the social process of production allowed for fantasy and 'play' with the social selves that these students were interested in projecting.

By far the most hilarious photostory, *The Chippendales* was a riotous production from start to finish. The story concerns a group of girls who are seen fantasising about a group of scantily clad male dancers, the Chippendales. They proceed to encourage a group of boys in the school to undress and act out their fantasies — although they eventually reject them in favour of the initial fantasy.

The girls who produced this story set out to create as much subversion as possible. For example, when they were planning the exercise, they wanted to set up an audition to evaluate the boys' physical defects, and this immediately triggered off various anxieties within the group of boys who were working on *The Rude Boy Serial Killings.* This was humorously indicated in the following exchange:

Daniel: I'd like to be Incredible Hulk.
Andrea: No man, you should just be yourself.

The girls also wanted to bring in a doctor to do blood tests on prospective home-grown Chippendales, and at one stage thought they would construct their narrative around teacher Chippendales! In the end, they used popular boys from the year above to pose for them. The logistics of filming this group created a maximum disturbance in the school: Julian had to beg for some of these hunks to be released from their normal lessons. Somehow, the act of photographing this photostory involved large groups of students prominently enjoying themselves when they ought to have been somewhere else. As most of the actors and actresses involved were students with unruly reputations, the whole process of producing *The Chippendales* clearly subverted the 'official' pedagogic dimensions of the activity.

The most obvious point to consider here is the way that the activity of production and the narrative itself place the girls in positions of power. Their desire is the motor of the story; and they also assert their independence by eventually crushing the vanity of the boys, who in the normal conditions of school are seen to 'rule the roost'. The boys' plaintive comment 'What's wrong? Ain't we good enough for you?' has a particular resonance within the wider social relations of the school and within these pupils' lives.

This point would also hold true for many of the other stories. The boy who plays the hero (or villain) of *So Sweet But So Sour,* and who is killed because he two-times the heroine, is also being set up. The girls in this group specifically wanted to use a boy who 'fancied himself', and who had annoyed them (as opposed to other boys in the class who also fancied themselves but who weren't in the authors' social circle). The narrative allowed the girls to kill off this boy, and contributed in no small way to the pleasure of this story and to the response it received when shown to students beyond the Media Studies class.

Although the conditions of the photostory's production thus inflect the meaning of *The Chippendales,* it should also be read in terms of its generic conventions. Thus, the girls play with the language of fantasy, which is part of the discourse surrounding the Chippendales and similar acts. The 'naughty' puns — 'I wish I can workout with the Chippendales', 'I wish I could be in the Chippendales' dressing room', and so on — both allow for the expression of the girls' sexuality and at the same time contain it within the comparatively 'respectable' activity of gawping at the Chippendales. Just as they laugh at the boys trying to pretend that they are sex objects, so the girls mock their own ventures into this territory of fantasy and desire.

However, we need also to read this playfulness as operating in the other direction; that is, in terms of the way that the girls themselves are positioned within conventional notions of heterosexuality. For example, Deniz wrote:

> We went through many different ideas and we ended up choosing the story about the 'Chippendales'. It sounded like a good idea because to meet the Chippendales is like every teenage girls fantasy . . . we wanted to make our story look real like the ones in the magazines . . . I wanted to create a meaning to our story. Something that girls could read and look at and think 'I wish that could happen to me too, or say feel the same about it too'.

Deniz appears to take the fantasy at face value rather than (as we have argued above) on the level of parody and irony. The very serious faces on the final sheet of the story, and the curious photomontage of the male breast at the centre, might lend credence to her. We would not want to discount the way that this exercise might have facilitated a serious engagement with issues of sexuality, although we would argue that the whole process was much more ambiguous — even if that ambiguity could not be articulated.

The narrative structure of the whole story is notable for its use of symmetry and balance. The first and last sheets use the same visual structure of four photographs surrounding a montage of magazine images, while the bottom two central pictures on the second sheet balance each other. It may well be that this use of duality in the narrative reflects the way in which the exercise pulls the students in contradictory directions: towards the expression and containment of desire; towards an engagement with their peers and a move away from reality into the safer world of fantasy.

Furthermore, the fantasy itself also engages with the dimension of race. We mentioned above that these students had reputations of being unruly; and it is also evident that they are mainly black (certainly all the substitute Chippendales are).[11] Apparently, there are some real black Chippendales, but the use of black boys within the fantasy is also clearly suggestive of a wider social purpose. Although the girls knew what they were doing in contrasting black boys with white Chippendales, they never made such a comparison explicit to us, and we are therefore unable to tell whether they made it explicit to themselves. There is certainly the possibility that the girls were using the project as a way of expressing their own desires for the exhibition of black flesh, which would represent a kind of transgression. For the black girls involved, this might serve as a criticism of dominant images of white sexuality — even if the best that they can get is silly boys. However, for the white girls, the project allows them an opportunity to express the socially forbidden desire for black boys — forbidden, that is, by their Turkish parents, as well as, to an extent, by the interracial policing of mixed race relationships that went on in the school. This reading takes us into a complex and contentious interpretation of the project. It raises questions about what kind of licence the playful nature of the activity offers; and clearly, the different participants, black and white girls, black boys and white teachers, all have a different kinds of investment in such a reading.

The issue of racial identity also surfaced in *The Rude Boy Serial Killings*, and Damien, one of the authors of this story, did write about the matter. In the original draft for the story, the murderer was to have been played by Mark, but the photographs of Mark committing the deeds did not come out. The final version uses another boy, Steven, who was the only actor that the group could come up with at short notice once we allowed them two more shots. Damien's account of the significance of this recasting is worth quoting at length:

> In the original pictures the murderer has been a small white boy (excuse the expression) going around killing everyone, also, this person was not very popular in our school (this would have made the play more humorous to the reader to find out it was him). But as I said earlier the pictures of this murderer did not come out, so we had to use someone else. At the time we couldn't find anyone else to use, Sir said he would play the part, but nobody knew how to use his camera because it was different to the ones we were used to using. So Sir couldn't play the part. We looked around us and saw Steven Seymour (a popular strong black person) doing nothing. We asked him to be in the play and he agreed. Now (looking at the pictures) the play is not as funny as it should have been because Stephen is well known in the school (as mentioned earlier) and him being the murderer would not be quite as shocking to the reader as it would to the quite unpopular Mark (the original killer). Also Steven being the murderer sets up a typical stereotype of black people being killers, muggers, thieves, etc.

This is an extremely interesting account on a number of levels. In fact, Damien needed a fair amount of persuasion to write down his thoughts. Initially he was, understandably enough, reluctant even to name the colour difference between the two boys. As we have noted in Chapter 2, students often seem unwilling to identify racial differences, at least in the presence of white teachers: apart from anything else, they are accustomed to a school ethos which appears to value all as equals and yet seeks to deny differences. Indeed, as the next chapter will show, they often seem to have difficulty finding an appropriate language in which to raise the topic. Damien does not want to allow himself to be open to the accusation of racism; yet the facts of racial difference are of course plain to see, and play a crucial part in students' progress through school. In conversation with Julian and with Leon (his co-author on the project), Damien said that he did not 'want people to think we're racist or something', and again tried to pre-empt the accusation that he was just setting Mark up to fail: 'People will think we are racist getting a little white boy to do all the killing 'cause we're going to be strong.' In the extract quoted, he actually apologises for using the words 'small white' — which we might view as a dismal reflection on the way white teachers would use the words 'large black'.

However, the element of caution found in the piece that Damien wrote for his white teachers should not divert us from the more radical and political play with power that suffused the original intention of the project. Damien's account explicitly recognises how the meaning of the photostory will depend upon the meanings that his potential audience is likely to bring to the text. He acknowledges that his readers will measure the fictitious drama of the 'play' against the school personae that the actors 'naturally' possess. These personae are partly determined by the larger social categories of race, which are themselves inflected by social acceptability, or (in Damien's terms) 'popularity'. The written account thus reflects upon the polysemic nature of the text, and shows that the control of multiple narrative voices and the play on differential audience readings is highly calculated.

If *The Chippendales* implicitly raises racial identity as a determinant of subjectivity, *The Rude Boy Serial Killings* (at least in the original version) uses the category of 'race' — as lived by Tottenham school children — as an explicit and socially manifest bearer of meaning and identity. In other words, Damien knows how to use 'race' as a signifying category within the kinds of meanings that are available to his readers, and he uses it ironically. Many teachers would be content with his final remarks about the 'typical stereotype of black people being killers, muggers, thieves etc.' But for us, Damien has moved beyond the limitations of this debate about 'positive images' (see Chapter 10) and into the realm of 'syncretic culture'[12], in which he is able to deconstruct and then play with the categories of identity itself.

'Every Teenage Girl's Fantasy . . .'

The Rude Boy Serial Killings to some extent subverted the acceptable conventions of school activities and allowed for a 'resistant' appropriation of the task by the students — for example, smuggling the weapons/props past a deputy head and into the Media Studies class. Yet the reflectiveness of Damien's writing, and the co-operative way in which the group worked made such 'resistance' acceptable within the social conditions of the classroom. We now want to return briefly to *Jill & Meg's Excellent Adventure* to explore a rather different kind of resistance, in this case through fantasy. As we have shown, the narrative of *The Chippendales* is also centrally concerned with fantasy, yet it situates this within a broader tension between wish-fulfilment and reality. The fantasy is a realist one in the sense that it is set within the established surroundings of the school; and it is also socially shared, for example in the way that it plays on the 'real' personal connotations of the individual actors. By contrast, the fantasy of *Jill & Meg's Excellent Adventure* operates on a more implicit, almost unconscious level. Yet albeit in a different way, it also signals a level of shared meaning and mutual understanding between its four authors and reveals the different ways in which they read and appropriate cultural forms.

In some ways, the story follows Valerie Walkerdine's description of the typical narrative structure of young girls' comics.[13] She suggests that:

> Girls' comics, because they engage with the production of girls' conscious and unconscious desires, prepare for and proffer a 'happy ever after' situation in which the finding of the prince . . . comes to seem like a solution of a set of overwhelming desires and problems.

Although *Jill & Meg* doesn't even remotely rely on a male hero to solve the problems of Meg's inheritance, it does use fantasy in the form of time travelling as a way of getting Meg's grandmother to change her will and thus cut out the evil Olivia Weston in favour of Meg (Jill is Meg's best friend). What is perhaps most striking about the piece is its cheerful heartlessness and self-interest. Nobody cares about granny at all, and the dialogue and thought bubbles are full of comments like 'stupid bitch', 'old bag' and 'hurry up and change your mind'. The long piece of written text at the end of the story gives a good flavour of the tone and 'humour' of the piece:

> Jill & Meg got their money and were very happy but were also sad at the loss of granny.
> Olivia Weston went on to make more and more money, but soon enough she went bankrupt.
> The years went by and Jill & Meg lost contact. Meg got married to a guy called Atay and had 3 kids, 2 boys, 1 girl. She named the girl after Jill. Meanwhile Jill travelled the world, she finally came back to London. At the age of 35 she met up with Meg on *Surprise, Surprise* with Cilla Black. From then on they kept in contact for as long as they can Remember.
> **THE END!**

There is much here which should now be familiar: the use of a peer (Atay) to marry off Meg (which humorously mocks the girl who played Meg, and thus gives the story a particular resonance for the class); and the wry play with dominant culture in the form of Cilla Black's *Surprise, Surprise.* What we also find striking is the way that the whole piece subverts conventional expectations of gendered behaviour. It is pertinent to add that this group was comprised of high-academic-ability, well-motivated pupils, which makes their choice of genre all the more interesting. It would seem, following Walkerdine, that the students adopt a characteristically female approach for their piece, using fantasy as a form of resolution, and attempting to construct an ideal future for the girls. However, this approach is undercut by the 'uncaring' ruthlessness of the characters (granny excepted, though she is patently shown as too stupid to tell good from bad), the parody of traditional endings and the implied contempt for programmes like *Surprise, Surprise,* which are targeted at a female audience.

Like *The Rude Boy Serial Killings,* the story effectively resists a larger ideological formation than is implied by the constraints of the task — although, like *The Chippendales,* it sits uneasily between fantasy and common sense. The authors clearly share a level of unconscious understanding: their pleasure in fantasy stems from those desires which Walkerdine sees as central to the production of gendered subjectivity. Yet, in contrast to the emphasis on selflessness that Walkerdine detects in girls' comics, the authors of *Jill & Meg* in fact use the fantasy as a way of allowing themselves to act selfishly and get what they want. In this sense, *Jill & Meg* might be seen as a critique of such notions of gendered subjectivity. Furthermore, these students are able to distance themselves from the fantasy sufficiently to satirise themselves as 'good girls'. Here again, the *social* nature of the production has enabled the girls to perform a kind of critique of their reading. Although *Jill & Meg* is not as witty as *The Rude Boy Serial Killings,* and certainly was not received with the same sardonic humour, it also changes the power relationship between reader and writer and allows broader ideological concerns to be articulated and explored in the classroom.

In discussing these students' work, we have sought to demonstrate how the creative use of photography has allowed them to insert images of themselves into popular narratives. In the process, they have been able to manipulate the meanings both of the 'self' and of the narratives in which the self is located. In particular, the collaborative nature of the exercise highlights the *social* production of identity and reveals the differing ways in which cultural forms can articulate — and perhaps 'express' — aspects of ourselves. We have shown the sophisticated control readers of popular genres can exert over the writing of such pieces but also the ways in which the process of writing can reflect back upon, and potentially change, the process of reading.

In doing so, we have extended the metaphor of media literacy to the full. We have defined writing as both a mechanical and a social process. The control of 'film grammar', picture composition and *mise en scène* could all be compared with the control of narrative, character and dialogue that characterises print literacy. Clearly, some of the photostories are more effective forms of communication than others in terms of these 'literate' competencies. At the same time, we have also emphasised the social nature of the process of composition and reception. Conventional approaches to English teaching tend to stress the invisible and internalised nature of the writing process, whereas 'writing photography', we have argued, is a highly reflexive and self-aware process. In these respects, our students' conscious uses of generic formulae, conventions and explicitly public or social forms of communication reflect the emphasis on 'genre' within some recent research on children's writing development.[14]

The broader theoretical implications of the ways that the students approached the process of writing will be considered in more detail in the second half of the book. As we shall argue, extending the metaphor of 'media literacy' in this way may well lead us to reconceptualise print literacy itself.

'That Picture is False of my True Self'

Perhaps inevitably, we have 'spoken for' the differing voices, as we have found them in the classroom, in the images or in the written text. To end this chapter, we would like briefly to consider some of the follow-up work, which invited the students to reflect on the various images of themselves that they found in their personal or family albums. Although not many students completed this activity, mainly because of time factors, those that did all produced deeply anxious and self-critical accounts. To an extent, this may be an inevitable response to the demands of the task: being asked to pay close attention to past pictures of ourselves is perhaps bound to produce doubt and intensive self-analysis, particularly for adolescents.

We were struck by the way that different students seemed 'hung up' on the same issues. Thus Cheryl needed to reinforce in her writing that she was not what she thought she seemed:

> Photographs of me now show me as being snobby . . . In the picture I come across as being very vain. I look like a real poser. I am not vain or a poser, so that picture is false of my true self . . . In picture number 3 I am sitting near a flower bed. I think I look very posh. Once again I come across as being a snob. But I know I'm not a snob.

Emily conveyed similar worries: 'Here I was on holiday, pony trekking. I think this picture makes me look snobby, for some reason.'

Being perceived as 'someone else' led these pupils in two contradictory directions. On the one hand, they wanted to confirm their essential individuality; while on the other, they stressed the ways in which they might seem the same as other people. Thus, Ben wrote: 'I don't think I was a stereotypical kind of person'; by contrast Emily constantly attempted to bolster herself:

> I used to love horses, which I think is typical of many young girls. The horse's name was Chip . . . This was my last year in Junior school. I look kind of happy and I was. I can't think of much to say about this picture, except it portrays me looking happy. (God knows why, I'm a miserable so and so!!!)
>
> This was taken Xmas 1991 (looking at myself now, I've changed a lot in a year) My hair was permed, which is sort of typical of teenage girls.

> In the last few years I don't think I've changed too much, except my hairstyle. It was funny looking back at the way I was, ~~I wish I never~~

Each statement of individuality here is undermined by the reference to a wider generality or typicality. On the other hand, we have comments like Georgina's assertion of a rampant individuality:

> The me in the picture is *not* me. When I go on holiday I feel like a different woman. Going on holiday is to relax and enjoy yourself. When your (sic) not on holiday you have many responsibilities like homework for one.

Of course, we might be tempted to read this as an *aspiration* towards an individuality which she has yet to attain — as a 'woman' on holiday, not a schoolgirl. Georgina can still only assert her true self by negation: 'The me in the picture is *not* me.' In that sense, Emily is right to comment that she can't say who she is, only what she has changed from: 'It was funny looking back at the way I was.' These brief extracts point to a classic dilemma inherent in the way in which we talk about images of ourselves.[15] The students seem almost trapped in the formulations of individuality and stereotypicality available to them.

This question of the relationship between the subjective and the social, and of how we might talk about either, raises much broader theoretical questions which are central to our concerns in this book. As we have shown in this chapter, photography can provide important opportunities for students to explore these issues in a concrete and accessible way. Its effectiveness in doing so seems to us to depend crucially on the collaborative, social nature of the activity, and on the students' ability to use and to manipulate existing popular cultural forms. Photography can allow for a distinctive kind of dialogic play between the subjective self, and the social self.[16] In educational terms, it is crucial that students learn both to reflect upon this dialogic process and to make explicit the tensions between the individual and the stereotypical. This question of how young people conceive of their relationship with the larger social formation will be discussed in more detail in the following chapter.

Notes

1. For a detailed discussion of the problems of the 'literacy metaphor', see Buckingham (1989).
2. See, for example, Sontag (1979), Bezencenet and Corrigan (1986), Spence and Holland (1991) and Kenyon (1992).

3. Spence (1986).
4. Dewdney and Lister (1988). See also Cohen (1990).
5. The exception here would be the bedroom wall or 'fashion book' put together by aspirant models.
6. Kenyon (1992) describes how it is possible to buy stick-on speech bubbles and other graphic conventions of comic narration to add to photographs. It is possible that the adoption of the comic form for this exercise derives from this practice.
7. This is what one might expect, given the extremely slippery nature of generic definitions: see Neale (1980).
8. See Meek (1988).
9. Of course, this would be difficult to prove, although it was certainly true of the pictures brought in by most of the students in these classes.
10. See Sontag (1979).
11. We note the obvious connection between race and a reputation for unruliness. Our point would be that the activity of writing *The Chippendales* allows for the articulation of this aspect of institutional racism from a positive and strong perspective, even if it doesn't directly engage with it.
12. This phrase is taken from Gilroy (1987).
13. Walkerdine (1984).
14. See Kress (1993).
15. See Billig *et al* (1988).
16. See Sontag (1979).

Chapter 6

Reading Audiences: The Subjective and the Social

In the first half of this book, we have focused primarily on students as 'readers' and 'writers' of popular culture. In doing so, we have sought to move beyond traditional views of young people as passive victims of media influence. Thus, while questions of ideology and social power have been central to our analysis — particularly in terms of gender and ethnicity — we have challenged the idea that young people are simply 'slotted in' to existing social categories and ideologies as part of some inexorable process of socialisation. On the contrary, we have emphasised the diverse ways in which young people actively create and define their own social identities through their relationships both with their peer group and within their school. In the process, we have adopted a view of subjectivity not as unitary and stable, but on the contrary as diverse and changeable.

Popular culture is, in our view, a central aspect of this process: it offers a heterogeneous range of 'symbolic resources' which young people use in making sense of their lives and of their positions in the world. To be sure, the range of those resources is limited; but, as we have shown, young people actively select and negotiate — and in some cases resist — the positions that are available to them. 'Reading' and 'writing' popular culture are thus inherently social processes, which can only be understood in terms of the social contexts and social relationships in which they are situated.

This account is, we would argue, very different from the celebratory approach to popular culture which has emerged in some recent writing.[1] We would certainly want to reject the traditional élitism of the Left, which regards the critic as somehow immune from the ideological indoctrination that so captivates the masses. Yet the notion that popular culture speaks directly to people's needs and desires appears equally simplistic. In both cases, there is a sense in which people's relationship with popular culture is seen much too readily in terms of its immediate political consequences. We have resisted the implication (which is apparent in a great deal of work on youth culture) that the alternative fantasy identities that are made available by the media automatically represent forms of 'resistance' to dominant ideologies, or that they are necessarily 'empowering' in real life. The positions made available, for example, by 'Pony Boy's' 'masculine' texts, or indeed by Nicky's appropriation of rap music, cannot be seen either as merely reactionary or as inherently 'progressive'. The fact that these debates continue to be conducted in such narrow, either/or terms, and at such a general level, says a great deal about the political limitations of academic Cultural Studies, and about the ways in which it is being institutionalised.

In some ways, we have used students' 'writing' here as a means of informing ourselves about their 'reading' — in effect, as an alternative form of audience research. We believe that this approach has considerable potential as a means of supplementing and extending the insights provided by the more traditional qualitative and quantitative approaches used in Chapter 2. At the same time, we have drawn attention to some important differences between 'reading' and 'writing'. We have argued that writing in popular genres — in however artificial or technically simple a form — provides opportunities for students to exercise control over those genres, to make their meanings and their pleasures in them explicit, and (potentially) to manipulate and change them. Writing, as we have defined it, thus involves much more than the unthinking imitation of dominant forms, or an unquestioning 'celebration' of the ideologies and pleasures that they make available. It provides a vital opportunity for students to reflect upon their experience of popular culture — a process that we would regard as a central aspect of learning.

Thus far, these pedagogic dimensions have only been raised in passing: we will be addressing them much more explicitly in the second half of the book. In moving towards these issues in this transitional chapter, we want to focus on some of the ways in which students can reflect upon their own 'reading', by briefly examining some audience-research studies produced by students themselves. These studies are diverse both in kind and in quality, but they all derive from our attempts to encourage students to analyse their own and others' use of popular culture.

In discussing these studies, we want to emphasise two further general points which we would see as essential elements of the kind of education about popular culture that we are advocating. Firstly, following our conclusions in the previous chapter, we want to argue that this kind of work can offer important opportunities for students to reflect upon the relationship between the subjective and the social — or, in effect, to learn to see themselves in social terms. This is, we would argue, an essentially *political* process, although it is not one that seeks simply to confine or relocate students in positions that we find acceptable.

Secondly, we want to emphasise the importance of students themselves becoming researchers, and reflecting on the process of research. In that sense, we want to set this kind of work by students against our own work as we have presented it in this book. Researching the reading or writing of young people inevitably places us in a position of power. These young people are constituted as the objects of our enquiry, and indeed of our surveillance. We take upon ourselves the right to ask them questions, yet we rarely expect them to do so in return. And in presenting their words and their productions, we inevitably select and interpret the data in the light of our own perspectives and commitments. By contrast, in this chapter, we want to consider the effects of enabling young people to do research on their *own* behalf.[2]

Doing Research

'Audience' is a key area of study in both GCSE and A-level Media Studies syllabuses, and most courses are likely to include a component that requires students to design and carry out their own research. The concept of research suggests an impersonal mode of writing, one of a more sociological variety, in which the researcher's voice is subsumed in the objective presentation of evidence. Yet this need not necessarily be the case, as we shall argue. In practice, getting young people to carry out research can establish a rather different agenda.

Clearly, such research has immediate pedagogic purposes. The framing of any research enquiry immediately raises questions of epistemology, in that students have to make decisions both about what will count as evidence and about how that evidence will be used in reaching conclusions. In the process, they often begin to realise how received knowledge has been constructed and circulated, and as a result they may often come to question it. For example, in considering the way in which television-viewing figures or chart ratings in the record industry are calculated, students often come to challenge the authority of such apparently objective statistics. Furthermore, by placing students in positions of control over their research, this kind of activity can give them a different kind of authority in the classroom: in certain respects, they take on equal status to the teacher, as bearers of specialist knowledge. Perhaps the most challenging aspect of this work, however, is that it often forces students to conceptualise both the audience *and themselves as part of that audience* in a manner that is simultaneously very personal and comparatively distanced. Having to establish an appropriate framework for enquiry, to collect and collate 'evidence' and to interpret data almost inevitably forces one to question one's own presuppositions, as well as one's own position in the process. Such dilemmas are not merely the prerogative of academic researchers.[3]

The work that we want to describe highlights this double focus. It allows the students to reflect on their own position not merely as 'consumers' — that is, as members of the audience that they set out to explore — but also as researchers. The written 'results' of their work articulate their understanding both of the topic itself and of the method that they have used to investigate it. In many instances, the writing provides them with an opportunity to reflect on their own tastes and preferences in a manner which is much more direct and 'engaged' than the apparently objective mode of academic theory.

This sense of engagement can be clearly identified in the extended research projects undertaken by two British-Turkish girls at the end of the first year of their A-level course (year 12). Zerrin set out to examine the media tastes of what she termed 'educated and non-educated' women living in Turkey. The work was conducted in both English and Turkish and was a mixture of interview and survey work, partly conducted during her summer holiday in Turkey. Although the topic under consideration was ostensibly that of media usage, her work was really about the media users themselves. As Zerrin recognised (and as we have argued), the attempt to separate media use from the broader context of the social practices and relationships in which it is situated is bound to result in a reductive account. The research represented an opportunity for Zerrin to reflect upon aspects of her life that we suspect would have been much harder for her to address through the more intrusive form of autobiographical writing. As she wrote: 'As I am a young English-Turkish woman my interest in this topic was already there from a long time ago.'

Zerrin's distinction between educated and non-educated women drew on her knowledge of the Turkish educational system, and especially on her awareness of the limited opportunities available to women in a society that she regarded as more oppressive than her own. Cynically perhaps, we might be tempted to view the topic as one that was designed to show off her 'culturally superior' knowledge of Western media to friends and relatives in Turkey. Yet the broader issues that were raised also have a personal significance for her. As she wrote, in justifying the research process:

> As I wrote before me just being a young Turkish woman is the most important issue here. It's the biggest advantage to any person in this situation could have. Me being there when things happen observing the behaviour of women I know and even strangers helps to be in it before you start gives you a lead. All this entitles me to my views . . .

In fact, although she might not realise it, Zerrin's rationale is very much in the tradition of feminist ethnography:[4] the research is grounded in personal experience, and derives its *validity* from her relationship with her subjects. Indeed, as her account of the research progresses, it appears to tell her more about herself and the research process than about its apparent aims. Thus, she describes: how her subjects perceived both the Western practice of market research and the experience of being interviewed or surveyed as unusual kinds of activity; how the notion of a school student's carrying out work of this nature was also beyond their received notions of a secondary curriculum; and finally, how they saw the notion of there being a school subject like Media Studies. She moved between rural and urban areas while on holiday with her family, and as the project's narrative unfolds, it tells us more and more about the particular histories of the women she interviewed, as well as about their reception of her as a researcher to the extent that this begins to obscure her initial object of study.

Aylin, another British-Turkish student in this group, chose to examine video usage amongst different generations of Turkish families living in North London. In particular, she wanted to explore the viewing of Turkish and American films amongst first and second generation immigrant families, as well as the ways in which Turkish films were used as a form of cultural maintenance and home-language education.[5] Although this project did not explicitly raise questions about method or about schooling, it did act as a way of reflecting on the relationships between gender and taste from a strongly personal perspective. Indeed, Aylin effectively used the research as a way of writing about gender and power in her community:

> In the Turkish society there was no equal opportunities between men and women in my parents time. It's just recently that its been accepted that its allright for women to have a say in what they want.

Researching media tastes thus became a means for exploring larger social issues (as it inevitably is for academics too):

> I expected the women would go for the romantic, musical and comedy types of film. I expected the men would go for the horror, war and science fiction types of film.

Likewise, there are significant 'asides' about viewing films in Turkish which in fact relate to arguments about bilingualism and cultural identity in second generation families. As the project gathers momentum, it reflects further on this personal agenda: 'I think it is very hard to grow up in England as a Turkish female . . . it is . . . very much the opposite for boys. Our family and most other families are sexist.' Indeed, Aylin concludes by saying that, were she to carry out further research, she 'would ask a bit more personal questions'.

Adopting the position of researcher gave both Aylin and Zerrin a sense of power over their material and an authoritative position from which they could reflect upon the range of social roles available to them. While the quality of the research may not live up to expectations — inasmuch as the actual design and interpretation do not really support the kinds of conclusions that we have drawn — the process of becoming a researcher and writing the research was a significant one in itself for these two young women. Ultimately though, as with most academic and professional research, the initial agenda effectively pre-empts the conclusions. The kinds of comments that we have quoted derive from prior positions taken up in respect to gender or ethnicity; and the capacity to construct the research in the first place is, indeed, dependent on those positions.

Defining the Social

By contrast, the year-10 students with whom we have attempted similar projects seem to need to use the process of research as a means of conceptualising these more abstract issues and of coming to form a position on them. This is most apparent in the way that these students find it problematic to verbalise and to define sociological categories such as race and class. This is not necessarily to say, however, that they are unable to conceptualise those categories. In the last chapter, for example, we argued that two of the students' photostories, *The Rude Boy Serial Killings* and *The Chippendales,* questioned representations of race and gender both implicitly and, in some cases, explicitly. Obviously, this questioning was based on students' existing understandings of these categories, not as biologically given, but as socially constructed. However, when we asked those same students to construct surveys of peer-group tastes or media usage (much like our own work described in Chapter 2), they found it difficult to translate their sophisticated understanding of social categories into the language of academic research. This is not to suggest that their understanding was somehow merely intuitive, or a kind of 'felt knowledge': as the photostories themselves (and particularly Damien's written account) clearly demonstrated, these understandings were also embedded in particular kinds of narratives and discourses, albeit of the popular rather than the academic variety. This discussion leads us into much broader questions about the relationship between discourse and learning that we will be addressing in the second half of the book.

The research that these students carried out formed the basis of their introductory unit in GCSE Media Studies. Following an introduction to a range of research methods, they were asked to construct and carry out a piece of quantitative or qualitative research, and then to evaluate their findings. A number of different research projects were constructed as a result of this brief, many of which reflected students' existing specialist interests in the media. We list a sample below to give an indication of the range of interests and methods:

- a detailed study of television-viewing habits and tastes;
- a study of the pattern of music sales in local shops;
- a study of music tastes in the school, with particular emphasis on differences of gender and race;

- small group interviews on media usage;
- filmed interviews on media usage;
- a study of the reading of magazines and comics;
- a comparison between staff's and students' newspaper reading.

There was a considerable amount of overlap and reduplication of topics between the students, and, of necessity, most also focused on the peer group. The range of sample sizes and methods was quite broad — from taped and filmed interviews with individuals and small groups to questionnaires administered to over 200 people. The results were painstakingly collated in a number of ways, from graphs to transcripts, which often led to rueful comments about the nature of samples and methods:

> One of the biggest problems with our survey was, as I have said, too many open questions and uneven numbers with different age groups and the possibility that some were duds. There was too much information which made it very difficult.

The students were then asked to write a 'media autobiography' in which they reflected personally on their media usage and tastes, as well as on the ways in which these might have changed or developed over time. In effect, we wanted the students to write their own 'reading histories'. The broad aim of this unit of work, therefore, was to develop students' *conceptual* understandings of 'the audience'. In particular, we wanted to encourage them to consider the ways in which they themselves could be regarded as members of broader audiences, defined and placed by wider social and economic forces.

For many students, the initial problem that they faced in constructing the research was one of labelling their 'subjects'. In some cases, this appeared comparatively straightforward. At least as biological categories, age and gender were easy to define — although obviously this is to equate gender with sexual difference. It is worth mentioning, however, that many students divided the respondents to their questionnaires into very uneven age bands, with some extremely fine distinctions between 11 and 21, often followed by a single category for anybody above the age of 24.

Perhaps predictably, the categories of race and class proved much harder to define. While they may be comprehended on the level of lived experience, having to use a public language to describe this seemed to cause the students some difficulty — although for a variety of reasons. The concept of social class is perhaps the most problematic of all since it does not directly relate to even the most superficial of physical characteristics. Furthermore, defining the class position of children in terms of that of their parents — as social researchers often tend to do — is problematic. In practice, like many adults, these students used the terms 'working' and 'lower' interchangeably.

Yet particularly with regard to race, students found it almost impossible to know how to describe themselves and their peers. It was this problem that sparked the discussion about black and white musical tastes, considered in Chapter 2. Damien and Leon were clearly anxious, not just about acknowledging the complex relationships between ethnicity and taste, but also about naming racial difference in the first place. As Damien eventually wrote:

> We had found that the majority of black people listened to ragga and hardcore. Also the majority of white people listened to ragga and hardcore. I found this shocking because I thought that most white would listen to music like rock and pop music, but I never knew that ragga would be top of the list.

Despite the 'equal opportunities' policies prevalent both in the school and in the borough, and despite the fact that they would probably have filled in numerous ethnic monitoring documents, most students were even more wary of using the words 'black' or 'white' than Damien is here. They frequently used terms like 'nationality', 'religion', 'culture' or 'background' rather than the kind of language preferred by the 'politically correct' white middle class. Only one other pupil explicitly acknowledged the influence of racial differences in the construction of taste, and she used heavily coded, symbolic terms: 'someone with completely opposite media tastes to me would not know much about *roots or culture*' (our emphasis). Far more common was the kind of confusion (or evasion) exemplified by another black boy, Darrell:

> The boys in my class [are] mostly of the same culture. Black-English, Turkish, Greek and pure English. Some girls even watch mostly the same things I do.

The confusion here may partly stem from the way that gender — which is clearly the most important element for this boy — seems to level down racial difference. But it is also the case that he does not want to acknowledge racial difference in this context. As we noted in Chapter 2, the claiming of specifically 'black' tastes is a process that is often fraught with difficulties and contradictions. This kind of embarrassment extended to all students, and even led to the use of the term 'coloured' by both blacks and whites — a term which in the UK is largely confined to white racist discourse. Meanwhile, mixed race students or Mauritian Asians, who did not like being called black, were never satisfactorily labelled and were entered into an intermediate category in students' final accounts of media usage.

Of course, this is more than an issue of terminology, or indeed of the students' level of conceptual development. It reflects much broader social and political concerns which are the subject of studies in their own right.[6] Obviously, the classroom is not a neutral space in this respect, however many equal opportunities statements may be displayed on the walls. The ways in which students acknowledge or avoid articulating racial difference will crucially depend upon what is to be gained or lost in doing so — and this will in turn depend upon the context in which it occurs, and on the power relationships that obtain in that context.

From our perspective, however, this tension between a formal public language of description and the implicit or unconscious understandings derived from lived experience has a crucial educational significance. These concerns about terminology point to a deeper anxiety about the ways in which we can and do describe (and thus conceptualise) both 'the audience' and the social world more broadly.

In general, the students were much happier to refer to their implicit understandings (for example, of taste) than to employ the official language of social classification:

> My opposite listens to opera and classical music. They watch very little TV and when they do it is to see documentaries. They wouldn't be seen dead at the cinema . . . The radio is never on in their house.

It is the implicit meaning of the details that is important here: Emily's wit and humour may say more to *her* readers than the dry language of academic description. More rarely, this process could spill over into explicit descriptions, as in Elizabeth's case:

> My favourite media is TV as I can't live with out soap operas and the 'Big Breakfast Show' and 'The Word' and Blossom and Bottom and 'Fresh Prince' and Desmonds etc. etc. . . . I'd describe the opposite of me as being upper class, rich, reads 'The Sun' and 'Sunday Times', thinks that the ozone layer is a children's programme and believes in corporal punishment.

However, this overt reference to class is unusual. Far more common is the use of *gender* as a marker of taste; for example, in Madeka's account:

> The media tastes of someone completely different opposite would be described as follows: hates reading, watches TV all day, frequently plays computer games and strictly likes one sort of music. In my eyes that person would be very different to me and would be a stereotypical view of a boy!!

What is also important about all these remarks is the way that these young women define themselves and their tastes by imagining a hypothetical opposite. This was partially in response to our guidelines for this piece of work, which invited students to compare their own tastes with those of their peers — and, in effect, to define their own 'reading profiles'. Yet as well as providing a comparatively accessible method of getting students to reflect upon the construction of audiences, this process of differentiation also seemed to connect with the ways in which they imagined their place within the wider social world. For example, Nandai wrote:

> I think I am similar to people of my age in a lot of ways, excuse me if I sound stereotypical but most girls I know watch 'Home and Away', 'Neighbours' and 'EastEnders'. I know a lot of boys do too they just won't admit to it. Most of my friends watch the same programmes because we have the same tastes.

This notion of shared tastes was most often articulated in terms of gender, perhaps more acutely by girls rather than boys. Yet, on the other hand, the use here of the word 'stereotypical' reflects Nandai's caution about the dangers of taking an unduly generalised (or indeed determinist) approach.

What was also evident, however, was a form of self-description that sought to assert individuality. On one level, this discourse reflects the popular adage that 'there's no accounting for taste'; although it might also be seen to reflect notions of individual identity that fit awkwardly with the pleasures of 'mass' culture.[7] Deniz adopted this position in her account:

> I don't think I'm similar, typical to my age, sex or culture. I don't think that's got anything to do with it. Each person has got their own taste and that's all I can say. Since this is near enough the same I'll say again age, sex and culture has got nothing to do with anything. If you like something you do, and if you don't, you don't.

Yet this disavowal of social identity in favour of a rampant individualism was in fact the only example of such a position found among these pieces of writing. For most of the students, the process of research and reflection seemed to have developed their understanding of the ways in which, as individuals, they are constructed by larger social forces. Ultimately, their difficulties in articulating this understanding may simply reflect the complexity of the issues involved.

From Reading to Learning

This chapter has begun to move on from our earlier concern with 'reading' and 'writing' to the more directly educational issues that we shall be addressing in the second half of the book. In our view, any educational process has to begin by acknowledging what students already know. As we have tried to show, young people are far from being the 'dupes' of popular culture so often condemned by critics of both Right and Left. To begin, as teaching in this area often does, by assuming that students are passive and that we need to make them active — or that they are uncritical, and that we need to make them critical — is to ignore the diversity and complexity of their existing knowledge.

Of course, this is not to suggest that there are not gaps and limitations in their understanding. Nor is it to imply that we should seek simply to celebrate what students already know — to position them as 'experts', and ourselves as mere apprentices. As teachers, we want to do more than just leave students where they already are. Of course, we have to respect and validate their existing knowledge, but we also want to enable them to extend that knowledge and to move beyond it.

The activities that we have described in this chapter begin to suggest the kinds of learning that we would see as important, as well as some of the ways in which it might be achieved. Our intention here was to enable students to become researchers in their own right — to develop their own hypotheses, to devise methods for investigating them, and to generate new knowledge that would reflect back on their existing interests and concerns. In the process, we also raised fundamental epistemological questions about what 'counts' as evidence and about the ways in which knowledge is determined by the tools and concepts that are used to establish it. These questions about the relationship between language and conceptual understanding — raised most clearly here in relation to the students' difficulties in 'labelling' themselves and their peers — are fundamental to our consideration of the learning process in media education, and will be addressed in much more detail in Chapters 8 and 9.

Nevertheless, the basic principles of our approach should already be apparent. It begins not with a body of 'critical' academic knowledge but with the understandings, and with the emotional and cultural investments, that students bring to the classroom. Yet it also seeks to enable them to make those aspects explicit, to reflect upon them, and to question them. In the process, it encourages students to examine the complex relationships between both the subjective and the social and between the concrete particulars of lived experience and the powerful generalities of theory.

Notes

1. For example, Fiske (1989) and Willis (1990).
2. We are aware that there is a sleight of hand being practised here in that this is still our account of these students' research — although it is hard to see how this might be avoided.
3. See Walkerdine (1986) and Ang (1989) for notable examples of this kind of questioning of the researcher's role.
4. See Stanley (1990).

5. See Gillespie (1994, forthcoming) for a parallel account of South Asian families.
6. See in particular the studies of racism and discourse by Van Dijk (1987) and Wetherell and Potter (1992).
7. See Ang (1985).

Part Two

Teaching and Learning

Chapter 7

Intervening in Culture: Media Studies, English and the Response to 'Mass' Culture

The first part of this book has been centrally concerned with the ways in which students 'read' and 'write' popular cultural forms. Although we have discussed the role of teaching — and indeed much of the material that we have considered has come from projects carried out in lessons — we have not so far paid much attention to our aims and our role in the teaching process. Indeed, to some extent, the position that we have adopted might be seen to question the whole necessity of teaching about popular culture in the first place. If young people are already as active and sophisticated as we are suggesting, why should we *bother* to teach them?

However, we do believe that teaching about popular culture makes a difference, and that this difference is important and worth making. Yet, as we shall indicate in this chapter, we do not regard this as a matter of defending or protecting children from harm. We do not view teachers as missionaries whose role is to rescue children from ideological manipulation, or indeed from cultural deprivation. Such arguments, in our view, place both teachers and students in impossible positions, and lead to teaching strategies which are ultimately ineffective.

The aim, therefore, of the second part of the book is to point towards a more constructive approach to teaching about popular culture. Again, we want to develop 'theoretical' arguments through accounts of our own classroom research. Chapters 8, 9 and 10 offer extended case studies of teaching and learning, concentrating in considerable detail on individual students' work. This chapter, however, is rather more 'theoretical' — although it also includes some empirical data which will illustrate and develop the arguments.

Our focus here is on the broad aims of teaching about popular culture, and on the various ways in which they have been defined by academics, teachers and students themselves. We look back to some key moments in the evolution of the field, and seek to draw broad distinctions between various approaches and traditions. Our primary aim here is to *situate* our own arguments, rather than to offer an exhaustive historical account or a detailed critique of alternative perspectives.

This inevitably involves paying some attention to the role of English as the school subject which has traditionally been concerned with preserving and renewing cultural values. As we have indicated, teaching about popular culture has often entailed opposition to the dominant values of English, and in particular to the 'cultural heritage' approach currently being reasserted in the proposals for revising the National Curriculum. Yet we are not simply offering a familiar critique of English. We also want to indicate some of the problems and limitations that are found in dominant approaches to media education. We will argue that media education has largely been preoccupied with *teaching* at the expense of *learning* — with defining 'ideologically correct' positions, which students are expected simply to occupy, without paying sufficient attention to what they already know, and how that connects with what we might want to teach. This chapter outlines our critique of this approach, while those that follow it represent our attempt to construct an alternative.

Leavis and the Left: Preaching Against Popular Culture

English teachers of all political persuasions have consistently resisted any reduction of the subject to instrumental notions of 'basic skills'. As we have noted, English is centrally concerned not just with the acquisition of 'functional literacy' but with a much broader form of 'cultural literacy' — although of course this has itself been defined in some very different ways. Traditional versions of English teaching have been informed by an almost overpowering sense of moral and political duty. The fundamental task of English — and the reason for its central place in the curriculum — is seen to be nothing less than the preservation of our common language — and with it, our cultural heritage. English teaching, it is argued, is the ultimate guarantee of the moral and spiritual health both of the individual and of the nation. Yet this process is not merely 'conservative': it also entails an active opposition to forces which are seen to be undermining that culture from without. In this account, English becomes the first — and, for many writers, the only — line of defence against the ravages of an increasingly commercial and industrial society.

The book which is often identified as the starting point of teaching about popular culture in schools was in fact written by two of the most celebrated advocates of this approach to English. *Culture and Environment: The Training of Critical Awareness* by F. R. Leavis and Denys Thompson was first published in 1933, and remained the most influential book in the field for more than three decades.

While Leavis and his acolytes were fond of presenting themselves as an embattled minority, their work can usefully be seen in the context of broader contemporary debates both about culture and society and about the development of industrial capitalism — debates in which the Left also participated. For Leavis, like others before and since, arguments about the effects of the mass media served to condense a whole series of broader frustrations and anxieties about cultural decline, about the threat of social unrest and about the erosion of respect for traditional authority. *Culture and Environment* represents a call to arms for English teachers, an appeal to defend the national culture and the national language, to 'maintain continuity' against the encroachment of commercial popular culture — which is seen as largely American in origin.

The nature of Leavis's concerns, and the desperation of his rhetoric, are probably too familiar to require further elaboration here.[1] What is worth noting, however, is the central role that Leavis and Thompson assign to English teachers in schools. They are to function as missionaries — or, in Matthew Arnold's terms, as a 'secular priesthood' — in a crusade against the 'illusory values' and the 'cheap mechanical responses' of mass culture. This struggle is to be waged not merely against 'the multitudinous counter-influences' of the media but also against *'the whole world outside the classroom'* (our emphasis). Rather than seeking simply to develop an appreciation of the literary canon, teachers must go on the offensive. By extending the techniques of 'practical criticism' to advertisements, 'journalese' and popular fiction, teachers will enable their students to cast aside their 'immediate pleasures'. Students, it is argued, must be trained *against* their environment, 'trained to discriminate and to resist'.

The contradictions and limitations of this perspective have been widely discussed, not least by advocates of media education. For example, Len Masterman offers an extensive critique of its central notion of 'discrimination'.[2] This approach, he argues, has been essentially paternalistic: it has sought to impose middle-class tastes and values under the apparently neutral guise of a concern with artistic 'quality'. The application of such criteria to media texts has been a largely negative exercise, which has inevitably been perceived as an attack on the personal preferences of students — and to this extent, Masterman argues, it has generated little by way of lasting or effective practice.

These (and other) criticisms of Leavisism have been echoed by many recent writers, and would probably be shared by the majority of 'progressive' English teachers. Contemporary definitions of English teaching are diverse and often mutually contradictory; and yet there are probably few English teachers today who would see their role in such explicitly missionary terms. Nevertheless, we would argue that a broadly *defensive* approach to popular culture still has considerable currency among English teachers, even if the motivations that inform it may be more diverse.

In fact, there are significant continuities between Leavisism and the more left-wing approaches which might appear superficially to oppose it. Indeed, the similarities between the arguments of Leavis and his colleagues and those of some of their Marxist contemporaries at the Frankfurt School have been frequently noted.[3] In many respects, they represent parallel responses to effectively the same set of historical developments: the rapid growth of cities, extensive changes in the division of labour and the increasing efficiency of mass production. Both are informed by a kind of nostalgia for a pre-industrial 'golden age' — for what Leavis terms 'the organic community' — that existed before the capitalist system of commodity production 'invaded' the cultural sphere. Both offer an impassioned critique of the products of 'mass culture', which are seen as standardised and homogenous: they offer nothing but 'crude emotional falsity' and 'aesthetic barbarity'. Both perspectives regard the consumers of mass culture as essentially duped and manipulated, and easy prey to irrational emotions and fantasies. And in both cases, this leads directly to a form of aesthetic or political élitism according to which a vanguard group of artists and critical intellectuals is seen to hold the key to cultural survival.[4]

While their rhetoric now appears unfashionable, we would argue that these arguments do represent a type of 'common-sense wisdom' which continues to inform most educational responses to popular culture — not merely those of Conservative policy-makers, described in our introduction, but also those of more progressive or radical educationalists. Whether explicitly or implicitly, most teaching about popular culture seeks to wean children off things that are seen as essentially bad for them, and thereby lead them on to things that are seen as politically or aesthetically 'better'. The attempt to counteract the ideological effects of the media is outwardly very different from the call to preserve the cultural heritage; and yet it positions teachers and students in similar ways. Essentially, it is the teacher who is seen to be in possession of a 'truth' which is invisible to the students. By disabusing students of their false emotional responses, and by developing their rational, critical faculties, the teacher will liberate them not merely from their compulsive desire to consume popular culture but also from its debilitating effects. This notion of teaching about popular culture as a matter of 'inoculation' persists largely because it provides teachers with an attractive and positive justification of their own power — albeit one which, in our view, drastically overestimates that power.

From Discrimination to Demystification

Despite the anxieties which it has recently provoked, teaching popular culture in schools has a long history.[5] The approach outlined by *Culture and*

Environment in the early 1930s was steadily developed and disseminated to schools in subsequent decades, particularly through the journals *English in Schools* and *The Use of English,* both edited by Denys Thompson. The central aims of English teaching, as defined by these journals, continued to involve a crusade against the 'dehumanisation' and 'impoverishment of spirit' wrought by the 'dummy life' of American popular culture.[6] However, as English teaching entered the 1960s, a less strident and more egalitarian perspective began to emerge.

The early work of Raymond Williams and Richard Hoggart,[7] both former students of Leavis, offered the possibility of a broader definition of culture, which extended beyond the narrow concern with an approved canon of 'art' and 'literature'. In terms of English teaching, the emphasis began to shift away from literary appreciation to include a (limited) range of 'new' media and a wider range of books, including those produced specifically for young people themselves.[8]

Nevertheless, there was a sense in which these approaches still represented only a partial revision of Leavisism. In terms of texts, the emphasis here was on 'discriminating *within*' the mass media rather than simply *against* them. Yet, as Len Masterman has shown,[9] the criteria for evaluation continued to derive from those of 'high culture'. So, for example, film could be regarded as a serious 'art form', although genuinely popular films were seen to be lacking in the requisite aesthetic qualities. By the same token, most (if not all) television was simply beyond the pale. Likewise, in terms of culture in the broader sense, the aim was to devise criteria which enabled students to distinguish the 'processed' from the 'living', or the 'good and worthwhile' from the 'shoddy and debased'. In the work of Richard Hoggart, for example, this entailed a validation of what he saw as 'authentic' working-class culture as distinct from the 'mass-produced' commercial culture which again originated primarily from America. While the Leavisite 'organic community' had been relocated, many of the fundamental assumptions of the 'mass society' theory remained in place.

These and subsequent developments in English teaching deserve much more detailed consideration than we can give here.[10] Our interest at this stage is primarily in the way in which different 'versions' of English have defined the *aims* of teaching about popular culture. Stephen Ball, Alex Kenny and David Gardiner[11] make a useful broad distinction between the 'progressive' and 'radical' versions of English teaching which have developed since the 1960s. Progressive English, as they define it:

> focuses upon personal aspects of experience, stressing the relevance and validity of each child's culture, language and self-expression . . . Working-class family and neighbourhood culture is explored via the pupils' own creative writing and through 'themes' and projects
> (p. 60–1)

Working class culture — and, by implication at least, the popular media — are seen here as a 'vital, meaningful and valid alternative' to the élitism of the great literary tradition.

By contrast, the radical version of English takes a critical rather than a celebratory stance, offering 'an analysis of the political and economic conditions that produce inequality.' According to the above authors, radical English 'takes seriously both the lives and culture, and the alienation and lack of opportunity, of working class pupils'.

These different versions of English clearly embody different political and pedagogic strategies. While progressive English is 'alternative', radical English is directly 'oppositional'. And while progressive English adopts a broadly 'child-centred' approach, radical English 'involves the construction of a working-class curriculum, often taught in a traditional authoritarian manner'. These two approaches might broadly be aligned with what the Cox Report terms 'personal growth' and 'cultural analysis' — although Cox is predictably somewhat more evasive about questions of class and politics.

Of course, such distinctions are bound to oversimplify. They offer 'ideal-typical' definitions which are unlikely to correspond to the realities of classroom practice — although they may well play a significant part in how teachers *account* for what they do, both to themselves and to their colleagues.[12] Even at this level, however, it is clear that these approaches would define the purposes of teaching about popular culture in quite different ways.

At least potentially, the progressive version of English would seem to lead to a celebratory approach, in which the media would be welcomed alongside other aspects of 'the whole world outside the classroom'. The canon of approved literary texts would be dismantled, and elitist criteria of artistic value abandoned. Students would be free to explore the diversity of their own cultural investments and concerns. In practice, however, the degree of freedom and cultural relativism adopted here has been rather more circumscribed. In so far as progressive English acknowledges popular culture, we would argue that it often does so in a sentimental and patronising way. It looks for signs of an 'authentic' culture that offers continuity and values, and attempts to recast that culture in the image of the dominant culture. The selection of approved elements of working-class culture is accordingly a limited one[13] — and the 'mass-produced' culture imposed by the media continues to be approached in a spirit of condemnation which seeks to demonstrate its inadequacies and deceptions, and thereby undermine its influence.

At least when it comes to the media, then, there is a considerable overlap here with the more 'oppositional' approach of radical English teaching. Here, the media are identified not as part of the culture of students but on the contrary as a means whereby the ruling class secures its power. Analysing the media in order to identify the covert ideologies that they contain is thus seen as an essential element of this broader process of political education. As Ball and others note,[14] the focus of attention here has shifted since the 1970s, as the preoccupation with class as the main dimension of inequality in society has faded, and more attention has been paid to oppression on the grounds of 'race' and gender. Teaching about the media has thus become a central element in anti-racist and anti-sexist teaching: analysing representations of oppressed groups, and detecting evidence of 'stereotyping' and 'bias', have become routine activities for English teachers.[15]

The dominant paradigm for media teaching in the 1970s and 1980s — both within English and increasingly in separate, specialist courses — was largely based on this 'oppositional' approach to popular culture. The media were seen as a central element of young people's lives, but also as the primary means whereby the 'dominant ideology' was imposed upon them.[16] Far from celebrating their experience of popular culture, this approach places a central emphasis on 'objective analysis'. Len Masterman, for example, proposes that students and teachers should put their 'personal feelings and tastes' to one side. Rather than seeking to arrive at value judgments, they should aim to analyse the media systematically using broadly semiotic methods: only in this way will it be possible to identify how media texts are constructed and selected, and hence reveal their 'suppressed ideological function'. 'Such an education', Masterman argues, 'will also necessarily be concerned with alternative realities — those constructions implicitly rejected, suppressed or filtered out by the images that appear.' Teaching about the media thus becomes a process of 'demystification', of revealing underlying truths which are normally hidden from view.[17]

Despite its very different kind of rhetoric, this approach clearly has much in common with the Leavisite version of English teaching.[18] Both regard the media as imposing a seamless and homogeneous set of dominant values: 'alternative realities', to use Masterman's phrase, can only be found *outside* the media themselves. Both implicitly define young people as 'passive consumers' both of the media and of the values that they are seen to contain: seduced and mesmerised by their overwhelming power, they are seen as effectively helpless to resist. Both perspectives see this power as deriving primarily from the *emotional* appeal of the media: the only hope of resistance or change is seen to lie in the application of rationality, and of 'objective' analysis. And finally, both define the teacher as a kind of political or cultural saviour whose attempts to lift the veils of illusion from students' eyes will automatically meet with their assent.

In many accounts of media education, however, there are often contradictions between the kind of 'transmission teaching' implied by this radical approach and the call for more progressive teaching styles. The emphasis on analysis often sits uneasily alongside arguments both for an 'equal dialogue' between teacher and student and for a process of open investigation.[19] In practice, this often results in considerable tensions, and even a degree of hypocrisy: as we have argued elsewhere, much of what students are expected to 'discover' in such teaching is predetermined, and much of what passes for 'analysis' is simply a sophisticated exercise in guessing what's in the teacher's mind.[20] Meanwhile, the possibility that students might *resist* what they perceive as an attack on their pleasures and preferences, as yet another attempt by teachers to impose their values and beliefs, seems to have been ignored.

This notion of media education as a form of 'demystification' is one which we would want to contest on a number of grounds. It offers a view both of popular culture and of young people's relationships with that culture, that underestimates the complexity and diversity of both. In particular, it neglects the pleasurable or emotional dimensions of that relationship: pleasure, it would appear, is highly dangerous, and can only be dispelled by a good dose of objective, rational analysis. This leads in turn to a set of prescriptions for teaching that we would argue do not actually *work* in practice. Our own research in *Watching Media Learning*, as well as recent work on anti-racist and anti-sexist teaching,[21] suggests that this kind of propagandist approach significantly neglects the power relationships of classrooms. Despite the rhetorical optimism of its advocates, the notion of media teaching as a form of radical political 'empowerment' seriously overestimates the power of teachers.

In offering these criticisms, however, we should emphasise that we are *not* advocating a merely celebratory approach to teaching about popular culture, of the kind implied by the 'progressive' approach to English teaching. This is not simply an either/or choice. As we have implied, the 'progressive' approach runs the risk of simply leaving students where they are. And where it has been adopted, such an approach has often seemed to confirm students' (and indeed other teachers') perceptions of media education as a 'soft option': while students may find it enjoyable, it is rarely seen to involve much 'real work', let alone much actual learning.[22] As we shall indicate in the final section of this chapter, while teachers may perceive themselves to be 'validating' students' cultures, it is not at all clear that students themselves perceive this to be happening, or that they even perceive it to be necessary in the first place. By contrast, what we hope to provide is an approach which has rather more modest and realistic aims but which might enable us to move beyond the limitations of both 'progressive' and 'radical' approaches to teaching on popular culture.

English and Media Studies: Defining Subjects

The propagandist approach that we have identified here probably remains the dominant approach to media teaching, although there are signs that a more constructive and less defensive approach has begun to emerge in recent years. New Media Studies curricula at GCSE level and A level, as well as developments in primary and lower secondary schools (largely, though not exclusively, within the context of English), embody a rather different perspective, which in many respects draws upon the more 'progressive' approach that we have outlined above. Questions of learning and progression, formerly much neglected, have now begun to emerge as central concerns of media teachers. The British Film Institute's influential Curriculum Statements[23] and the work of the English and Media Centre in London[24] embody a rationale for media education that moves beyond the rhetoric of earlier approaches and offers much more realistic teaching strategies. Meanwhile, the book *Watching Media Learning* has initiated a growing interest in classroom research, and encouraged a more fundamental questioning of the relationships between theory and practice.[25]

Nevertheless, the relationship between English and Media Studies remains a highly paradoxical one. On the one hand, many specialist Media Studies teachers tend to adopt a principled rejection of English as a repository of 'liberal humanism' — one of the Left's favourite 1970s swear-words.[26] Yet the predominant response to media education among English teachers has been to welcome it on board, and to incorporate it along with other elements of the subject.

Of course, it would be simplistic to suggest that there is a single definition of English — or indeed of Media Studies, for that matter. The Cox version of the National Curriculum, for example, provides a highly *inclusive* definition of English, in which seemingly incompatible perspectives are combined in an uneasy harmony. Nevertheless, the 'radical' approach to teaching about popular culture that we have identified above — and which roughly coincides with what Cox terms 'cultural analysis' — remains very much at odds with other aspects of English teaching, particularly the 'cultural heritage' approach. Despite the fact that most Media Studies teachers are primarily (and by training) English teachers, the approaches that they adopt in the two areas are often significantly different. The way in which an English teacher approaches a poem or a class reader is likely to be very different from the way in which a Media Studies teacher approaches an advertisement or a television programme — even where, as is often the case, the English teacher and the Media Studies teacher are in fact one and the same person. If we compare English and Media Studies courses, some consistent differences emerge, not merely in terms of their respective 'objects of study' but also in terms of their underlying theoretical framework. Ultimately, the two subjects do appear to embody very different theories of 'reading' and 'writing' and of the relationships between readers and texts. These theories in turn give rise to some quite fundamental contrasts in pedagogic practice.

These differences are most apparent in the upper years of the secondary school, where Media Studies is increasingly available as a separate subject at both GCSE and A level. In an article published in 1990, David Buckingham outlined four key differences which he detected in GCSE syllabuses, and which are summarised below.[27] (While the situation has changed somewhat since that time, we would argue that these points remain significant.)

1. The first, and most obvious, of these differences relates to the respective objects of study. English is of course predominantly concerned with written texts, and more particularly with books. Media Studies, by contrast, often seems to be concerned with everything *except* books — although some Media Studies syllabuses do in fact make reference to popular fiction. Yet the distinction is not simply between books and other media — or indeed between modern 'mass' media and more traditional forms. On the contrary, it is essentially a distinction between approved forms of 'high culture' and forms of 'popular culture' that are seen as intrinsically less valuable and worthwhile — a distinction that is obviously bound up with broader relationships of power within society.

Thus, in practice, English is not in fact concerned with all books but instead almost exclusively with those that it chooses to define as 'literature'. Of course, the received canon of texts which are seen to merit the term 'literature' has progressively widened in recent years, and is no longer so exclusively confined to the works of (preferably dead) white men. Nevertheless, the use of genuinely popular literature remains comparatively rare in English teaching. While there are signs that more 'literary' genres such as romance or 'classic' crime fiction *are* being recuperated by English teachers, the chances of a Jackie Collins novel being chosen as a class reader, or of Stephen King finding his way onto anybody's list of set books, remains highly remote.

As literary theorists have acknowledged, the way in which the object of study is defined in English is deeply ideological in nature. It is part of a process whereby certain people's tastes are validated while others' are merely dismissed. Yet the very criteria by which the category of 'literature' is constructed, the processes by which it is maintained and the interests that it serves are rarely open to inspection or critical study.

Perhaps more fundamentally, teachers are likely to approach these different objects of study with quite different assumptions about how they are, and how they should be, read. 'Literature' is seen to have broadly humanising effects on the reader: it encourages the development of sensitivity to language, culture and human relationships. The media, as we have indicated, are often seen to have predominantly negative effects: they manipulate or deceive readers into accepting false values in ways that readers themselves may be powerless to resist. If literature teaching is seen to be about developing students' receptiveness to something which is seen as fundamentally good, a great deal of media teaching is about encouraging them to resist or 'see through' something which is seen as fundamentally bad.

2. The broad frameworks which define and organise the two subjects at this level are also strikingly different. English is defined in terms of a set of practices — reading, writing, speaking and listening. These are further

subdivided, for example, into 'imaginative', 'discursive' and 'instrumental' types of writing. Media Studies, by contrast, is defined in terms of a set of concepts — media language (or 'forms and conventions'), representation, institution and audience.

On the surface at least, Media Studies appears to be much more overtly 'theoretical'. It is predominantly concerned with conceptual learning rather than with the mastery of skills or processes, or with the articulation of experience. This kind of learning is seen to be manifested in the use of a specific 'technical' terminology — both in the case of the 'key concepts' themselves, and in the use of terms drawn from sociology and literary theory. While English syllabuses do use 'technical' terms, students are much less likely to be required to use these themselves.

Of course, this is not to suggest that English is somehow atheoretical, or even anti-theoretical, although, historically, it has tended to present itself in this way. The criteria which are used for assessing students' work, for example, are notoriously vague and intuitive. Just as students are expected to respond 'personally' and sensitively to literature, so teachers are expected to respond personally and sensitively to students' writing, and to distinguish the 'vivid' from the merely 'effective'. There clearly is a theory underlying these judgments, but it remains almost wholly invisible.

By contrast, the problem for Media Studies is the extent to which the ability to use an academic discourse — for example, to deploy terms such as 'representation' and 'genre' — can itself be taken as evidence of conceptual understanding. There is a danger that the 'key concepts' may be reduced to a set of definitions to be learnt and regurgitated — and indeed that they may come to be seen as a form of academic character armour that will protect the student from influence. This is an issue to which we shall return in subsequent chapters.

3. While it might be possible to redefine Media Studies in terms of practices, it would appear to be much harder to redefine English in terms of concepts. While Media Studies obviously involves all the four practices — reading, writing, speaking and listening — involved in English, there are a number of Media Studies concepts which have no obvious equivalent in English teaching. For example, 'institution' (or 'industry') is one of the key concepts in Media Studies syllabuses. Under this rubric, students are required to consider aspects such as the ownership and control of media organisations, the economics of media production and distribution, the role of advertising and the relationships between the media and the State. Yet this is an area that English largely neglects. Publishing is obviously a major industry, in which the profit motive plays a vital role. Publishers act as 'gatekeepers' who determine what we are able to read and — through advertising, marketing and promotion — significantly influence the ways in which we read it. Book publishing is increasingly becoming a multinational, monopolistic enterprise, and one which is intimately connected with other media industries. In

neglecting these factors, English implicitly sanctions the view of publishing as a genteel cultural enterprise, and as a result adopts an idealised, asocial view of cultural production.[28]

Similar points could be made about the concept of 'audience', which we have considered in some detail in previous chapters. Despite the current emphasis on the 'sense of audience' in English, and despite the growing influence of 'reader response' approaches,[29] both the reader and the writer are typically perceived as isolated individuals. Reading and writing are abstracted from the social contexts in which they are performed and placed in a supposedly 'pure' personal space. By contrast, Media Studies goes beyond the individual student's own behaviour and responses to consider the different ways in which specific social audiences use and make sense of texts. If English is concerned with the individual reader's personal response to the individual writer's personal vision, Media Studies is concerned with the *social production of meaning*, both on the part of audiences and on the part of media institutions.[30] Yet at the same time, the emphasis on the 'social' in Media Studies can often serve actively to exclude the 'personal'. If English appears to suffer from a celebration of untrammelled individual subjectivity, Media Studies (as we have seen) often suffers from the attempt to suppress it.

4. Finally, there are further differences in terms of how the two subjects conceive of the practices that they entail — and in particular as regards their notions of 'reading' and 'writing'. Despite the recent emphasis on 'knowledge about language', English regards language primarily as a means of expression and communication. Language *study* is thus located firmly in the context of language *use*. Perhaps ironically, it is Media Studies that seems more preoccupied with the formal analysis of language, as we have seen in the case of the 'demystification' approach. Semiotic approaches to studying 'media language' involve a comparatively technical deconstruction of texts which can seem as dry and pointless as traditional approaches to English grammar teaching.[31] This emphasis on 'critical analysis' as a means of detecting underlying ideological meanings is effectively absent from English syllabuses, at least at GCSE level.

At the same time, the two subjects give a rather different weighting to reading and writing — or, in the case of Media Studies, to 'theory' and 'practice'. In English, the boundaries between the two are fairly fluid: while a certain proportion of students' writing is expected to be 'in response to literature read on the course', the nature of that response may in fact involve 'creative' as well as 'critical' writing. By contrast, in Media Studies the emphasis is on critical and analytical reading: practical production is often in the form of 'exercises' which are designed to illustrate pre-determined theoretical arguments. These practical productions are also partly assessed in terms of the written documentation that accompanies them, which is seen as a further source of evidence of the student's critical and analytical capabilities.

The differences between the two subjects, at least at this level, are thus particularly striking. English places a central emphasis on writing as self-expression, whereas Media Studies is concerned to promote the much more self-conscious 'construction' of meaning. English values reading as personal response, while Media Studies values analytic deconstruction. In English, the student is implicitly seen as a free agent whose relationship to language is purely 'personal'. In Media Studies, the student is seen as a potential victim of language who must learn to *resist* through rational analysis.

In seeking to identify differences rather than discover common ground, this account inevitably tends to polarise the two subjects. Classroom practice is of course much more ambiguous and contradictory than these broad definitions would lead us to suppose. Furthermore, as we shall indicate in the final section of this chapter, our own perceptions of our aims and priorities may well not coincide with those of our students.

The advent of the National Curriculum also complicates the argument. On the one hand, there is a welcome (if inevitably somewhat partial) commitment to media education as an essential part of English teaching — even if, at the time of writing, its survival hangs in the balance. Despite some revealing ambiguities and contradictions — for example in the various definitions of the term 'text'[32] — the original National Curriculum documents contain many examples of teaching activities that involve film, television, radio, the press and other media. What is notable, however, is that the *compulsory* elements of media education, embodied in the Statutory Orders for English, appear to refer only to non-fictional media — that is, to news, documentary and other information texts. Ironically perhaps, the aim of 'distinguishing between fact and opinion' in non-fictional media would seem to be one which unites those of quite different political persuasions — although of course where the Right complain about the left-wing bias of the BBC, the Left have traditionally made the opposite charge. By contrast, teaching about the kinds of popular texts that children actually read and enjoy would appear to be much more controversial; and the possibility of extending Media Studies concepts such as 'representation' and 'institution' to the study of literary texts seems to be much more problematic to entertain.[33]

Yet the National Curriculum, and the narrow debates that currently surround it, is only one of the current dilemmas for media teachers in Britain. Within the field as a whole, there are both positive and negative signs. On the one hand, Media Studies is enjoying a rapid increase in popularity at GCSE and A level, as well as in Higher Education, to the point where training cannot keep pace with demand. Yet GCSE itself is now under considerable pressure as it gets swept up in a broader 'rationalisation' of the curriculum. Meanwhile, the growing emphasis on 'vocational relevance' in Further Education, while not without its positive potential for media teachers, is similarly contributing to a redefinition of its aims and methods.[34]

The constantly changing terms of these debates require more immediate and strategic interventions than we can offer in this book. Our aim here is to suggest an approach to teaching about popular culture that is grounded in current practice, and yet which is also sufficiently rigorous to sustain the argument beyond the limitations of contemporary policies. Our approach is one that seeks to build upon what we have identified here as the strengths of both English and Media Studies. As we have argued, Media Studies offers a theoretical approach to cultural production which is in most respects more rigorous and powerful than that provided by English. At the same time, English places a central emphasis on subjectivity and agency — albeit one which is often defined merely in terms of *individual* 'creativity'. The challenge, we would argue, is to find ways of integrating these two elements in the context of a broader concern with what we have called the *social* production of meaning.

Going Back to School: Some Views from the Other Side

In a sense, the arguments we have considered in this chapter have all been part of a debate between teachers — or indeed between academics. Yet in the day-to-day business of teaching, the kinds of assumptions that we have considered will rarely be made explicit. As we have indicated, Media Studies poses a challenge to many of the dominant approaches to English. And yet, as Media Studies itself becomes institutionalised — in the form of syllabuses, examinations and teaching materials — it too develops a set of common-sense practices that come to be taken for granted. In practice, the differences and tensions between the two subjects are rarely seen to be problematic, and the underlying assumptions on which they are based tend to remain invisible.

Furthermore, students themselves may have significantly different interpretations of our aims and motivations, that will in turn play a part in how they make sense of what happens during lessons. At various stages across the four-year period covered in this book, we have interviewed both individuals and groups of students in an attempt to probe some of these interpretations. Perhaps inevitably, these interviews were comparatively 'artificial' occasions: students are rarely asked to give their opinions of school subjects, much less speculate about the motivations of their teachers. Indeed, their comments demonstrated very clearly their lack of control, and lack of participation, in deciding what and how they were to be taught — even within a comparatively 'progressive' subject and at a comparatively 'progressive' school. Their responses to our questions often tended to be somewhat 'formal', suggesting an attempt to articulate what they thought we would have wanted to hear — although this was not always the case. Nevertheless, our most abiding impression from these interviews is that our agenda as teachers, and the broader debates about culture that it entails, are simply irrelevant to the vast majority of these working-class students. In many respects, what these students said reinforces our sense of the limitations of generalised polemic.

Throughout the interviews, the rationale that the students offered both for English and, to a lesser extent, for Media Studies was essentially a *utilitarian* one. English was primarily about developing skills, for example in spelling and punctuation, which were necessary both for other school subjects and for future employment — although, as Zoe noted in a moment of realism, you probably wouldn't need it to become a road-sweeper. When asked what they enjoyed about English, a number mentioned 'oral work', although a distinction was often made here between 'discussion' and 'work' — the latter essentially meaning writing:

> Sophie: Yeah, I like discussing the work as well; I like discussing about what we're doing. Because sometimes if you just get down to work, you don't exactly understand. But if you and the teacher can discuss the work in all the group together, it's taught better.

Likewise, Sophie's rationale for reading focused not on the pleasure that this might offer, or indeed on the importance of developing sensitive personal responses, but instead on its value as a means of building vocabulary:

> Sophie: I think the reading was quite good as well, because, like, we read a lot, quite frequently in this school, and it brings out your vocabulary more, learning more words and things like that.

Very few of these students had much sense of what 'literature' might be, and perhaps as a result, any sense of the 'civilising mission' of English teaching was simply lost on them:

> DB: So why do you think the school does literature?
> Carol: Makes you more aware of things going on.
> Sophie: Increasing your vocabulary.
> Nicola: You need it for jobs when you leave school. If you've got a job you need it.
> Natasha: You've learnt to read, you might as well make use of it.

While Carol's comment here perhaps comes closest to a more 'liberal' and less utilitarian aim for English, it also relates to notions both of social education and of 'citizenship', which characterised their account of Media Studies.

However, some students did seem to perceive a broader social purpose in English, which was detected in the range of books which were selected for study. Books were seen to offer insights into other cultures or historical periods, although this was occasionally somewhat vague:

Darrell: We need to read the books so we can understand other things.
Costas: Some books tell us what happened before, do you get me? Like *The Basketball Game,* how it was, the blacks and whites in Africa. Was it Africa? America, something like that.

By and large, however, English teachers were accused of choosing books that were out of date and that had 'nothing to do with today' or with 'realistic things'. Despite the fairly contemporary selection of class readers that had been covered — *Underground to Canada, Journey to Jo'burg, The Basketball Game* and *The Friends* — these books were broadly condemned as having 'nothing to do with us'. Indeed, where teachers' attempts to select 'relevant' material were acknowledged, they were also explicitly rejected:

Karen: Anyway, most of the books we read have got to do with practically the same subject. Like family life, school life. [. . .] If it's not got to do with school life, it's got to do with home life. [. . .]
DB: Why do you think you always get that?
Michael: They can't pick any good books.
Zerrin: They want to teach us about how family life can be, how hard it can be, and how you can sort your life out.
Karen: It doesn't sort nobody's life out, 'cause it's all different to somebody else's.
DB: What, so you mean the families you read about in these books are not like your family?
Karen: They're make believe, they're exaggerated.
Michael: There's nothing realistic about it.
Karen: They exaggerate in them books. 'Oh, he hit me like this, he hit me like that.' [. . .] Half of the books we read in class set your mind back. They make you think that you should go out and do this and do that, and it's a whole load of rubbish. Like the family-life books. They go back and they say how you should solve the problems, 'Don't do this and do that,' but you can't do that in real life, you'll just make things worse.

It became quite apparent here, and in some later 'autobiographical' work carried out during this group's English lessons, that the students regarded this kind of 'personal problem' story as a genre in itself, with its own clichés and conventions. Despite the claim that these stories serve a therapeutic function, or at least offer 'useful advice' to troubled adolescents, it became clear that the students did not necessarily perceive them as relevant to their own lives; nor did they necessarily invest any of their deepest fears and concerns in this kind of writing. Perhaps, as in Karen's case, they resented the intrusiveness, as well as the patronising tone, of these adult attempts to connect with 'teenage problems'.

Nevertheless, what emerged very clearly both from these interviews and from the English lessons themselves was that the students had very little conception either of 'high culture' or of the debates about cultural value on which the opposition between 'high culture' and 'popular culture' is based. Despite the fact that they were following a joint English Language and Literature course, very few were able to explain what 'literature' might be beyond a vague sense that it might involve 'history', or be 'about the past'. Yet while literature might be 'for older people' or for 'posh' people, it certainly was not for them. As Jennifer said: 'We prefer things that include us.'

Thus, Shakespeare was identified by a number of students — as indeed he was in the original National Curriculum — as a solitary example of 'literature' largely on the grounds that he was 'famous' and 'old'. Studying Shakespeare might possibly serve as a means of learning about 'life in olden times', but there was little sense of any broader cultural or moral purpose here. Certainly, students' experience of reading the plays themselves had been at best ambivalent. While some expressed enthusiasm for *Macbeth,* largely on the grounds of the bloodthirsty story line, Shakespeare was almost universally condemned as boring and irrelevant, despite attempts to enliven the plays by using video- and audio-tape versions:

Debbie: *Macbeth,* it is so *dry*! We've read the book about two times now, and now we're watching the video. That is so boring. The scenes, it's so fake, you can just tell it's a set scene. It's *so* boring.
Claire: We've got a book [*Hamlet*] and we have to sit there and follow it, and we're listening to it on tape, and it is dead boring.
Debbie: Oh, that must be so dry!
Claire: It is dry, it's drier than dry. It's even drier than that.
DB: So why do you think you have to do Shakespeare?
Claire: Because I think we have to learn how they used to talk in the olden days, and the way things were . . . it hasn't really got nothing to do with us. It's past our time, innit.
Debbie: But if we've got to learn about Shakespeare, we should be doing that in History, don't you think? I mean, it *is* to do with English, the way he writ and everything, but it's not what we wanna learn. It's not the sort of thing . . . We're *fifteen,* you know. We don't wanna learn about Shakespeare!
Claire: We've got other things on our minds . . . it's suicidal. I feel like killing myself.

At the same time, it was clear that their own preferred reading out of school was of a very different order. As we indicated in Chapter 2, very few of the boys appeared to read books at all, beyond the occasional 'graphic novel'. Some of the girls were more enthusiastic about reading, although little of what they read could have been defined as 'literature'. Yet despite their enthusiasm for the likes of Jackie Collins, it was clear that they did not see this as appropriate reading for school — although, significantly, the reasons for this were not primarily to do with concerns about cultural value but rather with the issue of sexuality. The girls argued that their teachers would disapprove of the explicit sexual content of these novels, although they pointed to a degree of hypocrisy here:

> DB: So you think teachers would think that those books, like Joan Collins books or whatever, are too adult for you?
>
> Natasha: Yeah. But then when there's something else, they start to call you a 'young adult', and all this business.

The girls went on to point out the contradiction between having sex education classes and the teachers' rejection of some reading matter as too 'adult'. As Natasha implicitly acknowledges, the terms 'adult' and 'child' are key bargaining counters in adult-child relationships both in school and in the home.[35] Similarly, many of the girls in particular tended to reject the books that they had studied in English as 'children's books':

> Kerry: I'd rather read something to do with our age group, things that happen to us, at our age, not as fiction stories . . . it doesn't do things to do with what really happens, in the books we read. I mean, nothing that happens in the books we've read happens to everyday 14- or 15-year-olds.

What is notable here, however, is that their rejection of Jackie Collins and other popular fiction as possible reading matter for school is not based on any sense of its being too 'trashy'. Only one girl, Emily, suggested that what she called 'quality' might be an issue here, and that romances of the *Sweet Valley High* variety might be rejected for this reason — although it is significant to note that Emily was one of the very few middle-class students involved here:

> Emily: There's about 60 of them, and they're all just turned out every week, and it can't be like well-written. Some books take years to write . . . A book can't be turned out in a week and be excellent, can it?

Of course, all these responses were heavily determined by the context. The perceived formality of the interview might also account for the fact that students failed to acknowledge some of the less immediately 'educational' reasons for choosing Media Studies. In a less formal context, students will often admit that they choose Media Studies in the hope that it is basically a matter of sitting around watching videos, and occasionally getting to bunk off for the afternoon with a video camera. Students who admitted to such expectations in these interviews also confessed that they had been somewhat disappointed. Nevertheless, it was the practical elements of the subject that seemed to be most attractive, both for boys and girls. Georgina, for example, acknowledged that there might be an element of glamour here — 'most kids are fascinated by doing something on TV, in front of a camera, like being a pop star' — although she was keen to assert that her own reasons for taking the subject were much less superficial than this. In general, it was felt that there was more 'freedom' and choice in Media Studies than there was in English — and as Jennifer acknowledged, this also involved the freedom to 'muck around'.

Nevertheless, the predominant rationale for choosing Media Studies also seemed to be a utilitarian one, for example as offered here by Michael:

> Michael: Well, I want to be a lawyer when I get older, and I heard about all the stuff that it involves, so I was saying it might actually help me when I get older, so I chose it.
>
> DB: In what way do you think it's gonna help you?
>
> Michael: Well it's got a lot to do with people, and the way their life, about their life stories and stuff like that, magazines and articles they put in newspapers and stuff like that, the false bits they put in and things like that. So I just thought it'd be good to take it, so I took it.

Indeed, Michael was not the only prospective lawyer here, and there were other instances of students selecting Media Studies as a hopeful first step on the way to a career in journalism, or to running their own advertising agency — exactly the kind of vocational aims which media teachers have traditionally rejected. The significance of career choice had obviously been emphasised by staff during the process of option-choice, although throughout these accounts there is a sense in which students are balancing what they enjoy against what they feel they 'need' for a job, as well as balancing the potential requirements of an 'ideal' job (like Michael's) against more realistic estimates of their future prospects.

However, some groups offered an additional rationale for Media Studies, which defined it primarily as a form of social or political education. At times this was relatively vague: Michael, for example, felt that Media Studies might 'get people more aware of stuff that might even happen to them', while Chris suggested that it would let you know about 'what's going on in the world'. However, even here, it would seem that Media Studies was defined primarily in terms of factual information: in Michael's words, it would be about 'how they select information' — a formulation which significantly reflects the emphasis (noted above) on non-fictional media in the current National Curriculum. This emerged more fully in another discussion:

> Michael: [You can learn about] the kinds of tricks that photographers use. If you look at newspapers, most of the photographs aren't

the actual photograph. Like there's this photo of Michael Jackson's mum, yeah, and they done something to the eyes. I don't know what they've done, but the eyes on the photograph weren't the actual photograph's eyes, if you know what I mean.

Karen: It would be nice to look into *The Sun*, to see what it is really like, what they write about, where they get the information from, and they add a little bit extra, and they say, like, she did this . . . I've got no choice, my mum buys it, right. You know the reason why they buy it, 'cause it's got more gossip in it. And half the gossip in that is lies.

Sarah: You don't believe it, but you read it anyway.

This group went on to discuss fabricated news stories in the infamous *Sunday Sport*, as well as the false predictions about the soap operas as instances of the general shortcomings of the popular press — although this did not imply any interest in the so-called 'quality' newspapers, which they generally rejected as 'pathetic' and 'too big' (!).

Likewise, Cheryl offered a rationale for Media Studies which came close to 'demystification':

Cheryl: You find out things about the media that you would never have thought of before . . . so I don't see it for the face value, I see it for its true thing.

Here, the discourse of 'citizenship' shades across into a 'common-sense' conspiratorial view of the media — of the 'never believe what you read in the papers' variety — which is quite close to the position of some advocates of media education. However, this display of cynicism also serves a social function: it defines the speakers as 'adult' and 'sophisticated', and implicitly presents them as more intelligent than the 'other people' who read this stuff and actually believe it (Karen's mother perhaps?). Nevertheless, Sarah's comment here points to some of the contradictions that we noted in Chapter 2, and in particular the sense in which you don't have to believe it in order to enjoy it.

On one level, of course, what these students said merely reflects the discourses that are available to them, and the terms in which they define the purposes of education — discourses to which different social groups clearly have different degrees of access.[36] Yet it remains significant that, with a few exceptions, the issue of cultural value and the high culture-popular culture debate which we have identified as central to the relationship between English and Media Studies was actually quite meaningless — or at least insignificant — for these students. On the contrary, their concerns were much more utilitarian — although that does not necessarily mean they were always realistic. Whether or not this is a good thing is certainly debatable, but it also implies that some of the claims both for the 'radicalism' of Media Studies and for its ability to challenge these distinctions may be overstated. While there is undoubtedly a certain *frisson* which may be derived from the transgressive act of showing a game show in an undergraduate seminar, this act has a rather different and less 'radical' significance in the context of a working-class comprehensive school. Watching *Robocop* might be more interesting and enjoyable for many students than reading *Paradise Lost,* but it may only be the teacher's cultural values that are being challenged by doing so.

Nevertheless, these more reflective comments about the aims and values of school subjects may ultimately explain very little about how students engage with them — or indeed about teachers' own practices. In the following chapters, we will address questions of teaching and learning more directly by investigating our students' written and practical work in both English and Media Studies. Chapter 8 raises some broad questions about evaluation, and the relationship between 'school knowledge' and 'common-sense knowledge', in discussing two students' photographic productions. Chapter 9 examines one student's written work in both subjects in order to address the nature of 'critical' understanding. Finally, Chapter 10 considers the broader political aims of teaching about popular culture, through an analysis of practical media work on the theme of representation. As we shall indicate, investigating the ways in which students learn about popular culture leads us to question not merely our methods as teachers but also many of our fundamental aims.

Notes

1. See Mulhern (1979), Eagleton (1983) and Doyle (1989).
2. Masterman (1980). See also Masterman (1985) and Alvarado, Gutch and Wollen (1987).
3. For example, by Swingewood (1977). These similarities are particularly apparent in comparing the work of Q. D. Leavis (1932) and Adorno and Horkheimer (1979).
4. There are, of course, some interesting parallels here with the arguments about 'authenticity' in popular music, referred to in Chapter 4.
5. See Masterman (1985) and Alvarado, Gutch and Wollen (1987).
6. See Thompson's editorial contribution in Thompson (1964).
7. See, for example, Hoggart (1957) and Williams (1958, 1961).
8. The most substantial example of this move is found in the work of Stuart Hall and Paddy Whannel (1964).
9. Masterman (1980).
10. In addition to the above sources (in Notes 1 and 2), see Mathieson (1975), Batsleer *et al* (1985), Brooker and Humm (1989) and Goodson and Medway (1990).
11. Ball, Kenny and Gardiner (1990).
12. Sharp and Green (1975) and Edwards and Mercer (1987), among others, point to significant contradictions between teachers' *accounts* of their practice and the practice itself.

13. This could be exemplified by the changing fashions in class readers in British schools — for example by the move from a certain sentimentalised notion of Northern working-class experience — in the use of books like *Kes* — to the more recent (and, many would argue, equally sentimentalised) emphasis on black urban experience — for example, in the study of books by writers such as Rosa Guy.
14. See, particularly, Brooker and Humm (1989).
15. Good examples of this work are described in *The English Centre* booklets on gender (1984) and race (date unknown).
16. This Althusserian notion of ideology was particularly prevalent in the vanguard journal *Screen Education*: see Buckingham (1990b).
17. Masterman (1980); see also Bethell (1984).
18. Some of these similarities are noted by Moss (1989); although she fails to distinguish between different 'versions' of Media Studies.
19. This contradiction is most apparent in Masterman (1980). See Alvarado (1981) and Buckingham (1986) for highly contrasting critiques.
20. Buckingham (1990b, Ch. 2).
21. Notably, Williamson (1981/2), Cohen (1988), Ellsworth (1989) and Britzman (1990).
22. This has been particularly apparent in the debates about the role of practical production in media education: see Ferguson (1981) and Dewdney and Lister (1988).
23. Bazalgette (1989) and Bowker (1991).
24. See, particularly, Grahame (1991).
25. This is apparent, for example, in Alvarado and Boyd-Barrett (1992).
26. See Spicer (1987) and Masterman (1985).
27. Buckingham (1990b).
28. For an indication of possible approaches in this area, see Sefton-Green (1992).
29. See Corcoran and Evans (1987); Gilbert's (1987) concluding piece in that volume offers a useful critique of the overall approach.
30. For a fuller account, see Buckingham (1991).
31. This criticism could be levelled at some of Andrew Bethell's work, for example at parts of his *EyeOpeners* booklets (Bethell, 1981) and his *Media Tapes* (Bethell, 1985).
32. See Buckingham (1990a).
33. For a more extensive critique, see Buckingham (1990a).
34. See Buckingham (1994, forthcoming).
35. See Buckingham (1993c, Ch. 5).
36. See Richards (1990).

Chapter 8

In Other Words: Evaluation, Writing and Reflection

The process of evaluation often raises fundamental questions about the aims and methods of education. In order for teachers or students to evaluate their work with any degree of confidence and consistency, they need to have explicit criteria for what counts as evidence of learning. Yet such criteria are often unstated or vaguely defined, and in many instances prove to be contradictory.

In practice, however, teachers' assessment of students' work is generally seen as a routine exercise, whose basic principles are rarely questioned. This is particularly the case with more established areas of the curriculum, where teachers will often claim to know intuitively that a particular piece of work merits a particular mark — although, of course, this is not to say that their intuitions will not conflict with those of others.

Nevertheless, this may be more problematic with 'newer' subjects such as Media Studies, where such intuitions have had much less time to become settled. Despite the apparent confidence embodied in attainment targets for media education,[1] we still have very little clear idea of what we might expect children of different ages to know about the media. There is no widely accepted model of progression, nor any definitive account of the nature of learning, on which such an account might be based. In our experience, moderation meetings for GCSE- and A-level Media Studies have often been the occasion for quite intense and still unresolved debates about the criteria which are being used in assessment.

Yet assessment is only part of evaluation — and indeed, it may sometimes actively *prevent* it. For example, in showing some of the students' work that we have discussed in this book to groups of teachers, we have been struck by the readiness with which they have assumed the role of examiner. Of course, the act of grading students' work is a crucial source of power for teachers. Yet once they begin to make confident assertions about 'the candidate's' strengths and weaknesses, we can be fairly certain that they have ceased to look at what is actually in front of them. Particularly in the case of media education, there is very little tradition of looking carefully at students' work in its own right, as we are attempting to do here — which is very different from the situation in relation to children's creative work in English or in Art, for example.

The uncertainty that sometimes seems to characterise the assessment process in media teaching also extends to the ways in which teachers respond to students' work and to students' own self-evaluation. Thus, while all Media Studies courses place a central emphasis on self-evaluation — particularly in the form of the written 'log' or critical essay which is required to accompany practical projects — there is often very little guidance as to the form that this should take. While examiners often emphasise that they are not looking for a 'blow-by-blow' account of what happened, teachers often complain that they are much less clear about what they *are* actually looking for.

In this chapter, we focus on this question of evaluation by considering the work of two students as they progress through their GCSE Media Studies course (during years 10 and 11). In particular, we consider the relationship between practical work and written reflection, and these students' own perspectives on this issue. As we argue, this raises fundamental theoretical questions about the kind of learning that we are seeking to bring about, and about how we might begin to identify it. In order to open up these questions, and before proceeding to the empirical data, we need to provide a more abstract account of the issues at stake.

Rethinking Media Learning

As we have noted, media education in Britain has increasingly come to be defined in terms of 'key concepts' — in contrast, for example, to the dominant definition of English in terms of *practices* or *skills*. While there are several advantages to this emphasis on conceptual learning, it also begs some difficult epistemological questions. In particular, there is the question of what one takes as *evidence* of conceptual understanding: what is the relationship between understanding itself and the language in which that understanding is embodied?

Media Studies has typically emphasised the importance of students' acquiring a specialist academic discourse. For example, one recent GCSE examination paper in Media Studies required students to provide a definition of the term 'representation' — although apparently, only one candidate was awarded the full three marks.[2] This is, certainly, one kind of evidence of conceptual understanding — although it is one which most teachers would probably regard as pretty inadequate. While it certainly serves as a useful measure of students' ability to regurgitate what teachers have fed them, the ability to use an academic discourse in itself clearly tells us very little about 'understanding'.

In the final chapter of *Watching Media Learning*, we sketched out some of the possibilities and limitations for media education of the work of the Soviet psychologist Lev Vygotsky.[3] In revisiting and questioning some of these ideas in the light of our current research, we want to argue that this relationship between discourse and understanding is a central dilemma in teaching about popular culture.

Over the past decade, Vygotsky's work has become increasingly fashionable in educational circles — a fact which should itself give rise to some suspicion. Teachers have good reason to be wary of the ways in which psychology has functioned as a 'regime of truth', which is used to regulate practice. In Vygotsky's case, however, several different 'versions' of the theory have emerged during the course of its being imported from post-revolutionary Russia and popularised in the West.[4] Some writers have sought to disavow Vygotsky's relationship to Marxism and stress the links between him and other contemporary psychologists; while others have seen the historical materialism of Marx, Engels and Lenin as the primary source and inspiration of his work. Educationally speaking, the theory has been used to justify some widely divergent ideas about pedagogy. Some have attempted to accommodate Vygotsky to a 'child-centred', progressivist approach, conveniently ignoring his emphasis on the necessity of formal instruction — and, indeed, on the benefits of teaching grammar.

The value of Vygotsky's work, from our perspective, derives from the fact that it offers a *social* theory both of consciousness and of learning. The development of the 'higher mental functions', according to Vygotsky, depends upon the linguistic (or, more broadly, semiotic) tools and signs that mediate social and psychological processes. Learning is, in this sense, a matter of the acquisition of symbolic codes, codes which are inevitably social and historical. Our 'version' of Vygotsky is thus one that emphasises his relationship to historical materialism — although there is a sense in which we would want to go further than Vygotsky in considering the social functions of language. Educationally, Vygotsky appears to offer a way of moving beyond the sterile dichotomy between 'progressive' and 'radical' approaches to pedagogy that has been particularly apparent in media education.[5] Learning, from this perspective, is not simply about discovery and spontaneous growth; nor, on the other hand, is it about the passive reception of radical ideas transmitted by the teacher. The *dialogue* between teacher and student, and between students themselves, is central to this process — although, of course, this is not to suggest that dialogue in itself guarantees that learning will occur.[6]

In *Watching Media Learning*, we focused particularly on Vygotsky's distinction between 'spontaneous' and 'scientific' concepts.[7] Briefly, spontaneous concepts are those developed through the child's own mental efforts, while scientific concepts are those that are decisively influenced by adults, and that arise from the process of teaching. Scientific concepts — which include social-scientific concepts — are distinct from spontaneous concepts in two major respects. Firstly, they are characterised by a degree of distance from immediate experience: they involve an ability to generalise in systematic ways. Secondly, they involve self-reflection, or what psychologists term 'metacognition' — that is, attention not merely to the object to which the concept refers but also to the thought process itself.

To a certain extent, we might consider children's existing understanding of the media as a body of spontaneous concepts. While these concepts become more systematic and generalised as they mature, media education might be seen to provide a body of scientific concepts which will enable them to think — and to use language (including 'media language') — in a much more conscious and deliberate way. The aim of media education, then, is not merely to enable children to 'read' — or make sense of — media texts, or to enable them to 'write' their own. It must also enable them to reflect systematically on the processes of reading and writing themselves, and to understand and analyse their own experience as readers and writers.

Reflection and self-evaluation would therefore appear to be crucial aspects of learning in media education. It is through reflection that students will be able first to make their implicit 'spontaneous' knowledge about the media explicit, and then — with the aid of the teacher and of their peers — to reformulate it in terms of broader 'scientific' concepts. Vygotsky argues against the 'direct teaching' of concepts — which he suggests will result in 'nothing but empty verbalism, a parrotlike repetition of words by the child'. However, he does argue that children need to be introduced to the terminology of scientific concepts — in effect, to the academic discourse of the subject — and that only gradually will they take this on and come to use it as their own. Instruction, he argues, should precede development, rather than waiting until children are 'ready'.

From this perspective, then, 'media learning' could be regarded as a three-stage process: it involves students making their existing knowledge explicit; it enables them to render that knowledge systematic, and to generalise from it; and it also encourages them to question the basis of that knowledge, and thereby to extend and move beyond it. At each stage, this is seen as a collaborative process: through the encounter both with their peers and with the academic knowledge of the teacher, students gradually acquire greater control over their own thought processes. The act of moving between one language mode and another — for example, by 'translating' the insights gained through practical media production into the form of talk or writing — would seem to be a particularly important stage in this process.

An illustration from our own teaching might help to explain this. This is an activity that we have used both with school students and with trainee teachers, often at a fairly early stage in their course. The students are asked, in groups, to take a number of photographs from a list which includes a range of generic possibilities. Depending on the context and the group, this might include more specific requirements — for example, that of an illustration for an article on 'The Young Designer of the Year' for *The Sunday Times*, or that of an advertisement for the housing charity Shelter — or else broader generic possibilities — for example, a frame from a photostory, or a record cover for an indie band. With A-level groups, for example, we have used this approach to introduce a unit of work on film stills and film trailers: here, the students were asked to produce stills and publicity shots for films in specific genres such as horror, documentary and the musical. Once the photographs have been processed, they are initially returned to a different group, so that they can try to identify which image is which; readings are then compared among the groups. In the original groups, students then put captions to their photographs, and label the particular conventions in the image that indicate which genre it comes from. In some instances, we have developed this work further, asking students to write more extended pieces that relate to the images (such as sleeve notes from the record album, or copy for the advertisement).

This activity clearly assumes an existing knowledge of generic conventions on the part of students — and of course, it is important to devise the possibilities with that assumption in mind. Yet in taking and subsequently captioning the photographs, students are required to manipulate those conventions, which they often do through parody. And in subsequently reflecting on their work, they are being required to make their knowledge explicit, and to question it. In a sense, this exercise forces students to acknowledge consciously what they already know 'unconsciously'; yet it also forces them to question both *how* they know what they know and *where* that knowledge comes from. The fact that this is a collaborative activity — both in devising the images and in subsequent gauging of others' readings of them — is of course crucial to its success. Finally, it is an activity that involves an interaction between a number of different 'language modes' — and here we would include the visual language of photography, as well as talk and writing.

Interestingly, this kind of approach has much in common with some of the work developed in the 'Knowledge about Language' initiative.[8] Although it is centrally concerned with teaching about the structures and functions of language, 'Knowledge About Language' avoids the sterility of conventional grammar teaching and, indeed, of some of the approaches to 'genre' which have been developed in English teaching in Australia.[9] This approach is based on a dialectical relationship between language *study* and language *use* — or, in Media Studies terms, between critical analysis and practical production. This may well involve students' acquiring a specialist terminology: for example, in the case of our photography activity, it can be a useful way of 'systematising' what students may already know about camera angles and positions or about the semiotics of dress or posture — in other words, their 'spontaneous' concepts. And it is also likely to involve considered intervention by teachers, for example, to encourage students to compare different instances of the same genre, or to ask why particular images are seen to 'fail', and thereby to move them on to broader insights about the social and historical diversity of language.

At the same time, there are several problems associated with this approach, as well as with the theory on which it is based. Vygotsky's distinction between spontaneous and scientific concepts is perhaps more problematic than might at first appear. For example, we might well ask whether this is not simply a difference in degree rather than a difference in kind. Is it necessarily true to say that spontaneous concepts are always less systematic than scientific concepts, or that they develop in different ways? More significantly, we might ask whether the difference is merely to do with the social *contexts* from which they derive, and the conventions of the language in which they are couched, rather than with something inherent in the concepts themselves. Interestingly, the words 'spontaneous' and 'scientific' could equally well be translated as 'everyday' and 'academic' (or 'scholarly') respectively,[10] which may be a more accurate reflection of these different origins. Yet the language of scientific concepts, and the processes by which they are validated as scientific in the first place, are clearly subject to particular social conventions and power relationships.

There are two other perspectives which might strengthen this challenge to Vygotsky's apparent optimism about the role of scientific concepts. The work of sociologists such as Basil Bernstein and Pierre Bourdieu[11] has emphasised the ways in which individuals' access to particular forms of language ('codes' or 'discourses') is determined by inequalities of power. From this point of view, the acquisition of academic discourse would be seen not merely in terms of its cognitive benefits but also as a matter of accumulating 'cultural capital', and thus as part of a broader process of social reproduction.

Similarly, from the perspective of recent work in discourse analysis, we could argue that Vygotsky's theory effectively neglects to consider both the social functions of discourse and its role in the social relationships of the classroom. From this perspective, acquiring or using a particular discourse is seen to have pre-eminently *social* functions: it serves to define the 'self' in relation to others, and it is crucially determined by the social and interpersonal context in which it occurs.[12] As we argued in Chapter 2, this is true of the ways in which students assume 'critical' positions when discussing the media and when staking out their own tastes — although it applies just as much to staff-room discussions about the aesthetic qualities of the latest Dennis Potter play as it does to classroom debates about the relative merits of Madonna and Kylie Minogue.[13] The decision to adopt a 'critical' discourse about 'the media' — rather than simply describing the good bits in the video you saw last night, for example — needs to be regarded as a social act with social functions and purposes, and not merely as evidence of cognitive understanding.

From this point of view, learning to talk about 'representation' and 'genre' could be seen to function as a way of distinguishing oneself from the 'mass audience' — who are presumed to be lacking in the required critical faculties; and in this respect, it could serve as a powerful means of class socialisation.[14] There is an ironic contrast here with the Leninist principles on which Vygotsky's original distinction between scientific and spontaneous concepts is based.[15] From this vanguardist perspective, the correct form of class consciousness would be embodied in the 'scientific' analysis of the Party; and the only remaining problem would be to find ways of transmitting this to the unenlightened masses.

As James Wertsch has argued, Vygotsky's theory can usefully be extended here by considering the notion of 'speech genres', developed by his contemporary Mikhail Bakhtin.[16] This focus on different types of speech, and the ways in which they are privileged and used in different social contexts, begins to move us beyond both Vygotsky's apparent privileging of the academic, 'scientific' mode and the vanguardist politics on which it appears to be based — although it also leads us to question the cognitivist assumptions which it entails.

This leads on to broader problems with Vygotsky's theory, and in particular with his emphasis on the 'higher mental functions' — in effect, on the intellect. Vygotsky's attempt to develop a social theory of mind led him and his colleague Luria to undertake extensive cross-cultural research, comparing the language and mental functioning of people in different regions of the Soviet Union.[17] Yet their conclusion that 'primitive' peoples were lacking in the 'higher mental functions' clearly points to the cultural bias of their own research. The fact that these people scored badly on conventional intelligence tests may simply reflect their lack of familiarity both with those tests and with the kinds of discourse required by the social situation of testing rather than any lack of intelligence. As numerous writers have argued, any investigation of such issues needs to begin by making crucial distinctions between cognitive development (or indeed literacy) and schooling.[18]

Finally, Vygotsky's theory also perpetuates the separation between 'cognitive' and 'affective' processes, and the comparative neglect of the latter, which is characteristic of cognitive psychology. Ultimately, his theory may lead to a limited, rationalistic account of the learning process, which neglects the fundamental significance of students' emotional investments in the media. As we have noted, the limitations of this approach have been particularly apparent in studies of anti-racist and anti-sexist teaching, where the attempt to displace students' pleasure merely through 'rational', critical analysis has often proven ineffective or counter-productive.

This discussion raises several troubling questions for media education, which we shall be pursuing in more concrete terms in the remaining chapters of the book. In particular, it should lead us to question the notion of academic discourse as a purely 'scientific' tool for understanding, which is necessarily preferable to the 'spontaneous' everyday discourses through which children already make sense of their experience of the media. All forms of discourse — including academic discourse — should be questioned in terms of their social functions and effects, rather than merely in terms of their role in cognitive processes. Similarly, the privileging of intellectual, analytical discourses may lead us to neglect much of the significance of what is taking place in students' learning about popular culture. Attempting to set aside emotional responses in favour of an 'objective' critical framework may result in a superficial approach, in which students simply learn to play the teacher's game without necessarily reflecting upon their own position. Nevertheless, as we shall argue, it is a mistake to view these issues in terms of simple either/or choices: we have to resist the separation between the social, the cognitive and the affective rather than seeking merely to 'redress the balance' between them.

Evaluation and its Discontents

The question of evaluation — and in particular the evaluation of students' practical work — brings many of these broader theoretical issues into sharp focus. Media teachers have often displayed a considerable, and to some extent justified, anxiety about the value of practical work. Advocates of practical work have often been criticised for a reliance on woolly-minded notions of 'creativity', or for a purely instrumental 'technicism' — in other words, for a neglect of theory. On the other hand, however, the privileging of theory has sometimes led to an approach in which practical work is reduced to a form of analytical 'deconstruction', which serves merely to illustrate the teacher's predetermined theoretical agenda.[19]

In principle, the aim of the written self-evaluation which accompanies practical work is to enable students to integrate their practical activities with theoretical insights. It is during the writing that students should be reflecting on why particular choices were made, and how they might have been made differently. In the process, they should be making their conceptual understandings explicit and reflecting systematically upon them.

However, as Jenny Grahame[20] has indicated, there are several problems with this approach. Obviously, the emphasis on a written log discriminates against those students who have difficulties with writing — yet these may be precisely the students who have contributed most effectively to the success of the practical work itself. Even for the more academically 'able' students in Grahame's study, the written evaluation seemed to be inhibiting and unrewarding. Many of the insights and understandings — in particular, those relating to the social, interpersonal aspects of the process — which Grahame observed in the course of her students' practical work were simply lost when it came to writing.

As Grahame argues, the insistence on written evaluation may derive from a kind of insecurity about what students might be learning from their practical work:

> However open-ended the project, we seem to need strategies which bring academic knowledge back to us in a safe and acceptable form. But by insisting that students must locate their individual accounts within a pre-determined 'objective' framework, we may be putting several important learning outcomes at risk. It may be that only by allowing students to write freely and subjectively about their own personal perceptions of the production process can we begin to reconcile *our* notions of appropriate learning with what *they* perceive as important to them.
>
> (p. 121)

This question of the written evaluation of practical media work thus goes to the heart of the broader theoretical concerns that we have discussed. In developing these arguments, we want to consider some work produced by two students as part of their GCSE Media Studies course, and their subsequent reflections upon that work.

Making Identities

The first two pieces of work that we shall consider were produced at a very early stage in the course, and represent a combination of two rather different practical assignments. For the first of these, the students were asked to take three photographs of themselves: one as they 'really' are, one as they would like to be and one as they think others see them. They were then asked to combine these images into a 'media identity poster', juxtaposing images of themselves with images of their favourite media stars or personalities. Finally, they were asked to write an account of their work using a series of directed questions.

This activity served as a way of introducing two of the main key concepts in the Media Studies syllabus. The first part of the exercise related most closely to 'forms and conventions': it required students to take a single subject (namely themselves) and to present and photograph this in a variety of ways in order to convey a series of different meanings. Thus, students might vary the background, pose, dress, camera angle, type of shot, and so on, in order to achieve different effects. The second part of the exercise built on this first phase by requiring the students to crop their photographs and juxtapose them with other images, — although it also drew in a second key concept, namely that of 'audience'. In parallel with this work, the students had been undertaking some research on their own media use, using a 'media diary'; this subsequently led into an ethnographic observation of other members of their family, as well as to a more wide-ranging survey of media use. The 'media-identity poster' provided a more exploratory approach to the same issues, although it was one which was significantly more 'affective'.

In retrospect, this series of activities seems to represent an uneasy compromise between two contrasting views of media teaching. The first activity (the three photographs) seemed to derive from an almost 'grammatical' approach to media language,[21] which emphasised systematic variation as a means of 'practical analysis'. By contrast, the poster activity offered a much more open-ended opportunity for students to explore their personal, emotional investments in the media — an approach which is, if anything, much closer to notions of 'expression' in English teaching than to the more distanced forms of analysis generally favoured in Media Studies.

In general, the exercise was undertaken with considerable enthusiasm, although there were some interesting variations and resistances. Many of the students, both girls and boys, found having their photograph taken an embarrassing and even painful activity. Two simply refused to co-operate. In some cases, they managed to negotiate the difficulty by only appearing in long-shot, with the result that the images of themselves contained in the finished posters were often very small and hard to detect. As we have noted in Chapter 5, there may be various reasons for this, although obviously for young people of this age, physical attractiveness is a major issue. Anything that involves the physical display of the self — and, it is worth noting, a lot of activities in Media Studies do — is likely to meet with this kind of embarrassment and resistance.

When it came to the finished posters, there were some significant differences between the boys and the girls, differences which are partly illustrated by the two examples that we will be considering in more detail below. Michael's poster (see Figure 8.1) was typical of most of the boys' insofar as it focuses on a single theme, in this case wrestling. Similarly, Stephen's focused on cars, and appeared to be making a statement about the contrast between his own disability and the mobility which they might afford; while Darren's (rather incongruously, or not) had several large pictures of fish, reflecting his interest in angling. These were not the only boys who departed from the brief. By contrast, Clare's poster (Figure 8.2) was extremely crowded, and contained a very wide range of images, including those of film stars, cartoon characters, musicians and even a horoscope. All the girls' posters took this form, although with different emphases: in some cases, there appeared to be a preponderance of 'hunky' male stars.

As we have argued, part of the aim in starting with photography is that it connects with a popular cultural practice in which ordinary people are 'producers' rather than merely 'consumers'. By contrast with the 'identity posters' discussed in Chapter 5, this approach relates much more closely to a particular popular cultural practice — namely, that of creating the notice-board or collage of pin-ups on the bedroom wall. Of course, engaging in these practices in the context of school inevitably transforms them — just as

Figure 8.1 Media Identity Poster, Michael

autobiographical writing in English could be seen to transform the out-of-school practice of diary writing. Yet the activity did also seem to capitalise on these practices in a productive way, and thereby give the students themselves a degree of status. When the finished posters were mounted on the classroom wall, they were a constant focus of discussion and admiration for the other classes who used the room. Indeed, many of the posters were cannibalised, with certain images being delicately peeled off and removed.

Although a number of students departed from the initial brief, our initial impression was that this had been a successful exercise. Despite the anxieties mentioned above, most appeared to enjoy it, and all of them came up with some kind of finished product. At this early stage in the course, motivation and enthusiasm were obviously qualities that we wanted to encourage. However, we were rather nonplussed when Michael, whose poster is reproduced here, asked us what grade we would give him. We both said we thought Michael's poster was 'good', although we were very uncertain about how best to answer his question. If we compare Michael's poster with Clare's, and if we also consider the pieces of writing that they produced to accompany them, this difficulty is compounded further.

Figure 8.2 Media Identity Poster, Clare

If we take the syllabus that we were using literally, we might locate the aims of this activity in terms of the two key concepts noted above — 'forms and conventions' and 'audience' — and of two of the pairs of skills identified in the assessment objectives — 'select and combine' and 'comment and analyse'. While this does suggest where the ticks in the boxes might be placed, it doesn't actually get us very far. For example, we might choose to give Michael higher marks than Clare for 'selecting and combining': we might say that the overall design of Michael's poster is more unified, and that he seems to have taken greater care in choosing how to juxtapose the images for example by placing himself behind the wrestlers. While Clare's poster has a definite 'energy' to it, the overall design is much more arbitrary, and there is little relationship between the images of herself and those of the media stars.

However, if we consider the accompanying written work Clare provides a more detailed rationale for her selection of images, and describes why she chose to combine them in the way she did. In describing the photographs of herself, she admits that the final images did not really 'represent' the three choices given in the brief, and yet there are a number of points where she notes the difference between 'reality' and 'appearances'. Of course, we might well question the extent to which her written account in fact reflects the thinking that went into her poster: at least some of it seems to be a form of *post hoc* self-presentation, which is an undeniable risk with this kind of approach. Nevertheless, in general, her written work does display a much more sustained attempt to 'comment and analyse'. By contrast, Michael describes why he chose to juxtapose the images, and he also notes that he included some in order 'to give it more class', but he does not define what he means by this. His evaluation of the finished product is also limited, and he fails to speculate about the effects of his choices. For example, one of the most striking things about Michael's poster is that he is the only black person included, and yet this is not an issue that he discusses in his writing.

Likewise, Clare's written work does show some acknowledgement of the issue of 'forms and conventions' raised in the first part of the activity (the three photographs), although this aspect is effectively missing both from Michael's poster and from his written account. On the other hand, Michael undoubtedly does show some implicit awareness of the 'forms and conventions' inherent in the images that he has chosen, and this is reflected in the poses that he adopts in his self-portraits. Again, the whole issue of 'self as audience' is much more explicit in Clare's written account: for example, she describes her 'varied tastes', and explains what it is that she likes about the stars that she has chosen. Michael also does this — he tells us that he likes strong and muscular people — but he makes no attempt to explain why, nor does he say anything more about the particular form of wrestling that he is interested in.

Thus, in terms of the assessment criteria, Clare's work almost certainly scores higher marks, even if neither emerges as outstanding. Yet while we would acknowledge the weakness of Michael's written work — even at this stage, he was capable of more sustained and thoughtful writing — our abiding impression is that his poster is a 'better' piece of work. This is partly a matter of what we would have to call the 'aesthetic' quality of the design — although, as we have seen, this is partly addressed by the assessment criteria themselves. Perhaps one reason for this view derives from the fact that Michael's collage has a single unifying theme while Clare's is intentionally more diverse, reflecting a greater range of facets of her identity, or her involvement with the media. Here too, Clare has stuck more closely to the brief, her work appears less 'coherent' as a result. Clare's poster looks much more like a bedroom wall and much less like a work of art than does Michael's.

There is a further quality in Michael's work which is even harder to define: it amounts to a kind of irony, a knowing distance from the material that he is dealing with, and it is particularly apparent in the way that he has juxtaposed his own image behind that of the wrestler. To some extent, of course, this reflects the irony which is characteristic of the wrestling culture itself, and which is also apparent in the 'heavy metal' imagery which it often employs. There is a kind of gross excess which is apparent in the images here, and indeed in the television performances of the wrestlers, which often seems to veer towards comedy. In his account of the pleasures of television wrestling, John Fiske[22] emphasises these elements of parody and excess. Wrestling provides a grotesque carnival, in which the pleasure is derived from the disruption of the rules and conventions of sporting behaviour. It is these aspects which, Fiske argues, typify 'working-class participation in cultural forms rather than middle-class appreciation'.

Of course, this is an academic interpretation, and it may say more about *us* than it does either about wrestling or about Michael. Certainly, there is little sense of irony in Michael's writing: for example, he describes the juxtaposition of himself and the wrestler simply as an attempt to 'look like I'm possing off [*sic*] with a wrestling star'. At the same time, however, it was clear from talking to Michael and other boys in the class that much of the pleasure of this material was based on a combination of fascination and repulsion, of admiration and disgust. Yet this kind of emotional ambiguity — indeed the broader subjective dimensions of the project as a whole — are bound to be much harder to articulate. Furthermore, the very articulation itself is bound to change the experience, and in ways which one might not necessarily wish for. John Fiske might enjoy watching wrestling as much as Michael, and for similar reasons; but one can see why Michael might not want to talk about it in the same way.

Obviously, we should beware of 'reading in' qualities like irony — or, indeed, conceptual understanding. This is certainly a danger which academic accounts of working-class culture, and particularly of working-class youth culture, have not always managed to avoid. The desire to validate subcultural forms often lapses into a kind of romantic celebration, which discovers elements of 'resistance' which the users of those forms would not themselves recognise. Michael's poster may be a fascinating sociological document for those of us who are interested in deconstructing the social production of masculine subjectivity, but in the end this is beside the point. The key question is surely: what does it mean *for him*?

The problem is that the means that we have at our disposal to answer this question are very limited. When it comes to assessment, we need to have 'understanding' *demonstrated* to us, primarily through the use of an academic discourse, rather than attempting to infer it. Ultimately, our assessment of the work privileges the written form, and because Clare is (at least in this instance) more capable of producing a discursive account of what she has done, she comes out better. In a subject that is expressly concerned with forms of communication other than the verbal, and that often claims to validate students' existing knowledge, this is at least paradoxical. Would we be making the same judgments if this work had been produced in an art lesson?

Conversations With Yourself

We want to move on now to consider some of the 'logs' written by Michael and Clare later in the course, as well as some of their retrospective comments about the nature and the purpose of such writing. To what extent did these students learn to use writing as a means of connecting 'theory' and 'practice'? How did they perceive the specific cognitive demands of writing — as opposed to those involved in talk, for example? What value did they attach to this kind of reflective writing? And how can we ourselves evaluate it?

At the end of the course, in one of a series of individual interviews, Michael went over his coursework folder and talked through what he thought he had learnt over the previous couple of years. Inevitably, such a situation, and such focused attention, will affect the kind of ideas discussed. Indeed, asking students to be explicit about what they have learnt will often produce limited or artificial responses. For this reason, we need to treat the comments that students make about their studies with a certain amount of scepticism.

Michael had never written easily and had needed a good dose of nagging to get his coursework completed. As he said himself, writing was always an unnatural activity:

> That's how I was. I wasn't really interested in doing the written work until late in the fourth year, early in the fifth year, when I actually sat down and did a few pieces of work and ended up enjoying it. At the beginning of the course, I didn't really like written work. I was like a lot more on towards the practical side, but as the course has gone along I've learnt that actually writing it down gets all the ideas out of your head, and it gets really enjoyable after a while, yeah.

Pleasure was much more important to these students' idea of Media Studies than one might imagine. Media Studies, they said repeatedly, was different from most other subjects because it was meant to be *enjoyable*. For many students, the emphasis in the course on collaborative and practical activities meant that writing became even more of a boring activity than usual. Yet Michael stressed the pleasurable nature of the writing process, and rather enthusiastically gave it a physical, almost emetic quality:

> A lot of people would disagree, but I think it, it expresses yourself. It gives you a big relief, in like, when you actually get a few [ideas] down on paper, I mean you, um, you add more than if you, like, keep it inside you, and it's . . . it's a great part of learning in Media Studies. It is.

If we compare this account to the brief factual account of the identity poster discussed above — where the writing is implicitly perceived as a meaningless chore — a remarkable intellectual shift seems to have taken place.

Other students in these interviews had been critical of the self-evident nature of log-keeping. It was predominantly seen as merely a matter of restating the obvious, or as yet another abstract examination requirement. But whereas the self-discipline that was required to account for practical work in a written form may have seemed pointless to some, Michael claimed that it offered a significant opportunity for reflection. As part of a project undertaken in collaboration with BBC Schools Television (and filmed for their *Scene* series), the class had effectively been commissioned by the advertising agency for Levi's jeans to produce a new Levi's advert targeted at their age group. Here, Michael was talking about his role in interviewing an executive from the agency. The class had questioned him about the lack of black people in Levi's adverts, and received a somewhat equivocal and inconsistent response:

> . . . The actual interview with, um, Mr Gash, um . . . When you think back, I mean it was obvious that he was hiding, but you think back and you can actually see his point of view, hiding and stuff like that, because he doesn't want to let everything go, and I mean even though you're, like, saying 'Oh, um, he's silly' and everything else. But I mean if you put yourself in his shoes there you realise that, um, there's a lot of [sense] in what he's saying. I mean, a lot of what he said was a load of nonsense, but he did make some good points, and that's not really obvious. I mean, you've got to sit down and think about it.

Michael is clearly grappling for expression in this extract, which reflects how this interview acted as a way of making explicit his own development over the previous couple of months. Reassuringly, these remarks seem to support the idea that writing serves a 'metacognitive' function, making explicit those cognitive developments which are largely implicit in the production process itself. In other words, by writing things down in the log, the student 'translates' those understandings arrived at empirically into a more abstract, theoretical understanding of media production.

If we look very closely at what Michael claims to get out of his new-found confidence in writing, we see that it is actually a *space* for reflection:

> Afterwards . . . you didn't realise there was a lot more. 'Cause I mean, you go into your own thoughts and your own conversation with yourself and you learnt a lot more that way, and that's what written work is really like as well.

It could well be that Michael's projection of himself as mature and reflective in this way is the best articulation of the insights that he now possesses. What he has drawn attention to is certainly a valuable and significant stage of development in media learning. But what he does not do is to credit the *act* of writing as distinct from the *opportunity* of writing. It may be splitting hairs to differentiate between these two uses, but it is important to our sense of the value of the written account itself. Being able to see the nonsensical Mr Gash's point of view is an impressive intellectual achievement, and only the quiet of internal reflection brings this about. Indeed, it is this sense of a continuous dialogue, *the conversation with yourself*, that Michael contrasted with English when he talked about the difference between practical projects and oral assignments in the other subject.

Yet there is also a sense in which Michael may be telling us what he thinks we want to hear. If we look at the written account that he is talking about here, it is notable chiefly for its length. For all its depth and attention to detail, it is not intellectually that far removed from the piece accompanying the identity poster. For example, the following extracts, taken from Michael's log of the meeting between the class and Mr Gash, are considerably less incisive than we might have deduced from his comments on the meeting's significance. There is a great deal of scene-setting:

> His class brought us into a kind of mini boardroom where we'd be talking to Mr Gash. We were served tea, coffee and carbonated mineral water.

When we get to the discussion of the debate, Michael recounts the argument as follows:

> Back to our discussion, we then asked: 'Why aren't there any black people starring/co-starring in any Levi ads?' His reply was that 'It would be hard to break into a European market because they aren't used to seeing black people on Levi ads . . .'

Michael takes issue with the ideas put forward in the narrative that he is retelling, but his writing is constrained by its sense of the present. He does not generalise or link different ideas into an alternative position, and as a result he cannot actually sum up the 'silly' Mr Gash in the way that he does verbally in the interview. The stage of writing, of ordering all the ideas into a chronology and a structure, has undoubtedly enabled him to make some extremely valuable connections, even if they are not wholly apparent in the writing itself. The writing process has thus played its part, although it is not the end in itself that Media Studies examiners might like it to be.

Clare also respects the importance of writing in Media Studies, but unlike Michael she can reflect upon the stage that follows that of retelling or thinking through:

> There is a good point to it, 'cause after you've done a project, otherwise you've just enjoyed it, you haven't learnt anything and it's not until you sit down and write about what you've done you think 'Oh! I've learnt that,' and I've thought 'Why did I do that?' It makes you think about what you've just done, otherwise it would just be copying out, basically.

Clare can see the difference between genuine reflection and merely copying out or stating the obvious, and as in Michael's case, the discipline of going back over the same ground in a different medium helps to develop new understandings. She also contrasts writing to enjoyment — suggesting that, at least in this respect, Media Studies has much in common with the traditional academic curriculum. However, like Michael's work, her actual writing does not demonstrate the degree of reflection and understanding that she suggests it does.

Clare's logs are irritatingly eloquent pieces of writing. They have poise and wit, but they lack hard analysis. This may well say something about the absence of an audience for this writing. Rather than serving any more specific social purposes, it is perceived as a demonstration of 'pure understanding', produced primarily for the benefit of an examiner.

Compared with Michael, Clare shows a greater degree of control in the way that she retells and sums up past events:

> A few ideas were tossed around in each group, but it was eventually decided to concentrate on the footwear campaign.

She can also use the evidence from the simulation and relate it explicitly to a perception of learning objectives:

> To show the rebellion factor, we came up with the idea of a young boy trying to escape.

However, Clare did not really enjoy this kind of writing. Despite what she says about its worth above, she clearly found it much too disciplined and rigid, and had to do several rewrites. What Clare liked doing was showing off how she could use the word 'deconstruct', and using the writing as an object of interest in its own right. Her logs often started off as dramatic narratives and had to be pulled back round, through teacher intervention, to the disciplined accounts that she found so exasperating. Indeed, because she was so well-developed as a writer, it may be that, for her, log writing — in the sense of a blow-by-blow narrative — was intellectually redundant.

As she indicates, Clare did appear to find the process of reflection valuable. Even if the writing was in itself a little empty and functional, the *opportunity* to write acted as a way of allowing other developments to take place, albeit ones which were oblique to the written account. In effect, we are led to a kind of paradox: the act of writing does help to make the learning explicit, but the evidence for this fact may not always be apparent in the writing itself. Here again, the log might more usefully be seen as a penultimate stage in any unit of work rather than its summation.

So what are the specific cognitive demands of this kind of writing, and how might we evaluate its significance? If we take Michael's comments at face value, writing becomes a kind of quieter talking, a way of listening to yourself and going back over the same ground in order to pick out contradictions or significant moments. Michael clearly values the same process in the talk associated with practical work. In effect, the value of the writing derives from its status as a kind of *dialogue* — albeit one with an invisible other, or merely with 'oneself'. What both Michael's and Clare's work seems to suggest is that it is the *social* aspects of writing (or rather the reverse, its individuality, its solitary nature) that are important — not, as the Vygotskyan model might indicate, its cognitive implications.

So What Did You Learn From That?

We have argued here that teaching and learning about popular culture need to be seen as fundamentally *dialectical* and *dialogical* processes.[23] They involve a constant movement back and forth between action and reflection, between practice and theory, between language use and language study. It is in this process of interaction and translation *between* different experiences and modes of language — talk, simulation, practical work, writing — that the most significant learning occurs.[24] In a sense, our aim in teaching about popular culture is not primarily to provide students with new knowledge — although of course, this is bound to play an essential part in some areas. On the contrary, it is more to encourage students to make explicit, to reformulate and to question the knowledge which they already possess. In this respect, reflection and self-evaluation are crucial aspects of the learning process. In considering the reasons why one reads and writes in a given way, and in comparing one's readings and writings with other people's, it becomes possible to realise why things are the way they are, and how they might be different. Above all, however, this should be seen as an inherently *social* process, as something which takes place within, and is motivated by, a particular set of social relationships — not merely between the teacher and the individual student but also within, and beyond, the wider community of the classroom and the school.

This, at least, is the theory. Like most teachers, both of us have taught students who have readily borne witness to the effectiveness of our teaching — 'I'll never look at an advert in the same way again', they tend to say. Of course, there is an undeniable pleasure to be gained from perceiving oneself as the person who sees what other people cannot. We might just be cynical, but we do feel that there are important reasons why we should be cautious about such statements — and not just because they are such craven attempts to 'please teacher'. Media teachers often seem to operate with a 'road to Damascus' theory of learning, which perhaps reflects the persistence of a kind of evangelical politics. Yet we would argue that the kinds of learning that we are looking for are likely to take place over a much longer period, and are inevitably very difficult to define. Attempting to identify what one has learnt from a particular activity or experience is comparatively easy when it comes to basic motor skills — such as learning to operate a video camera — or to information retrieval. But conceptual learning of the kind that we have been discussing here is almost bound to be much more elusive.

This raises important questions about our desire to have learning *demonstrated* to us, and about the form in which we expect that demonstration to occur. In practice, as we have shown, the process of reflection can become merely a matter of answering the teacher's questions, or of fulfilling examination requirements. Students' self-evaluation can become an artificial process, in which they struggle within the confines of a narrow discourse that does not even begin to describe the complexity of what has taken place. We need to ensure that reflection is a 'natural' process, or at least a motivated one, in the sense that it arises inevitably from the situation, and has genuine purposes for students themselves. Showing their work to 'real audiences' — i.e. those beyond the teacher or the class — and evaluating the responses of those audiences might provide students with more genuine opportunities for reflection about their aims and purposes than is often the case. Yet we need to ensure that reflection — whether it occurs in writing or in any other medium — is not the end of the process, much less its summation. To attempt to reduce it to a matter of merely 'demonstrating understanding' is to neglect its potential and to miss its central significance.

Notes

1. For example, in the BFI's Curriculum Statements for Primary and Secondary Media Education (Bazalgette, 1989; Bowker, 1991).
2. This question was contained in the LEAG (London and East Anglian Group) Media Studies paper for 1988.
3. See Vygotsky (1962, 1978) and Buckingham (1990b).
4. For contemporary examples, see Wertsch (1985a and b), Kozulin (1990), Moll (1990), Burgess (1993) and Newman and Holzman (1993).
5. For a summary and critique of these debates, see Lusted (1986).
6. See Tudge (1990).
7. See Vygotsky (1962, Ch. 6).
8. For theoretical and practical accounts of this work, see Carter (1990).
9. For a brief introduction to the debates in this area, see Reid (1987).
10. See Gallimore and Tharp (1990).
11. For example, Bernstein (1971) and Bourdieu (1977, 1984).
12. For examples of this approach, see Potter and Wetherell (1987), and Billig *et al* (1988).
13. For an account of the ways in which teachers and students talk about popular television, see Fraser (1990).
14. See the account of middle-class children's talk about television in Buckingham (1993c); and see also Buckingham (1993b).
15. Thanks to Ken Jones for making this connection.
16. See Bakhtin (1981), Wertsch (1990) and Buckingham (1993c, and particularly Chs 2 and 12).
17. See Cole (1990).
18. For example, Cole (*ibid*) and Street (1984).
19. For a brief review, see Buckingham (1987b).
20. Grahame (1990).
21. The approach here comes close to that of Bethell's *EyeOpeners* booklets (Bethell, 1981).
22. See Fiske (1989).
23. This notion clearly takes us back to Bakhtin and Wertsch's observations (see Note 15 above).
24. See Lorac and Weiss (1981, Ch. 12) for some interesting observations on this kind of 'translation' both between written and practical work and between 'active' and 'passive' knowledge.

Chapter 9

Going Critical: The Development of Critical Discourse

The development of students' 'critical faculties' has often been seen as one of the central aims of teaching about literature and popular culture. But what does it mean to be 'critical', and by whom is it defined? What counts as evidence of a truly critical perspective? And how do students themselves become critical?

As we argued in the first part of this book, young people's everyday uses of popular culture may well involve some extremely precise critical judgments. For example, as we showed in Chapter 4, the distinctions between popular musical genres, and between different instances of those genres, may involve the application of some complex and diverse critical criteria. Likewise, the ways in which students use popular forms in their own writing or media production activities often reflect the critical sophistication with which they read those forms — even if their judgments are not always made explicit. In terms of Vygotsky's theory, such critical perspectives could be seen to represent a body of 'spontaneous' (or 'everyday') concepts. While these concepts may well relate to those embodied in academic discourse, they are rarely recognised as such.

In this chapter, we want to consider this relationship between these 'everyday' critical practices and the different forms of 'academic' critical practice represented by the school subjects of English and of Media Studies. Inevitably, these different kinds of critical practice are embedded within particular forms of discourse and social relationships. We want to ask, therefore, what it means for students to acquire an academic critical discourse, and what might be gained or lost in their doing so.

This involves paying close attention to the way in which students employ the different discursive markers of each subject, and thereby locate themselves within a particular academic tradition. An apposite illustration of this comes from the work of one of the students that we have already considered. In her essay on 'Finesse FM' (see Chapter 4), Nicky initially wrote that she had used her 'lingo' in order to establish a relationship with her intended audience; and she went on to list a series of phrases like 'nuff respect' or 'dissing' to illustrate her argument. We recommended that she use the word 'discourse' instead of 'lingo' and put 'lingo' in brackets after it, because we knew what would appeal to an examiner's evaluation of her success in (as the syllabus puts it) identifying 'appropriate ways of targeting audiences'. The word 'lingo' clearly belongs to a repertoire that we would associate with popular knowledge, whereas 'discourse' (needless to say, perhaps) belongs to an academic repertoire. The concepts implied by the two words are, if not the same, then very similar, although both the word and the concept will have different meanings for different audiences. This example begins to indicate something of the intricate nature of the interrelationships both between everyday discourse and academic discourse, and between discourse and critical understanding, that we intend to consider in this chapter.

In investigating these issues, we will be looking in detail at the way in which one student — a boy named Stephen — has developed his critical writing in English and Media Studies. In effect, we want to examine how Stephen socialises himself into the appropriate academic discourse for each subject, and thereby develops some degree of control over the implicit values and discursive structures. By looking closely at Stephen's writing, we will attempt to identify what the critical discourses of these two academic subjects might actually look like and how they might relate to the more everyday discourses that we have considered thus far. In the process, we want also to ask some awkward questions about the cultural and political consequences of 'becoming critical'.

The Essays

We have chosen one essay from English and one from Media Studies from each of years 10, 11 and 12, which makes six essays in all. Neither of us taught Stephen English in year 12, but other than that, we have worked with him continuously. Stephen was unusual in the school because he came from a middle-class background and because his parents are both English teachers. He is also severely disabled. His incredible enthusiasm for Media Studies certainly kept us going at awkward times over the years, and he had a highly individual interest in the subject, beyond just doing well at school — so much so that he is now studying Media Studies at university. Stephen certainly did have a more developed and sophisticated understanding than his peers of some of the cultural arguments that arose in the late 1980s concerning English — particularly those concerning the role of coursework — and he was clearly comfortable using a wide range of language repertoires both from home and from school. We are not claiming that his work is representative, more that it illustrates with clarity the movement between the differing discourses of these subject disciplines.

Year Ten

The first two essays were probably some of the earliest pieces of 'critical' writing that Stephen had ever been asked to produce, and as such they show his early attempts to reproduce the conventions of the objective, discursive essay. His first piece for English was a comparison between the opening chapter of a 'novel' that he had written himself (for a publishing simulation) and George Orwell's *Animal Farm*.[1] Stephen himself chose *Animal Farm* to contrast with his own 'novel', a piece of adolescent drama centring on a young man, Andrew, who runs away from home to the streets of Tottenham and gets involved in gang warfare while working in the local McDonalds. We did not study the whole of *Animal Farm* in class, but we used the opening chapter, along with those of *The Disappearance* by Rosa Guy and a Mills and Boon novel, as examples of how different genres established readers' expectations.

The essay for Media Studies concluded a half term's unit of work on soap operas, and was entitled 'Do you think young people are represented fairly in soap operas?' It followed a detailed comparative study of the narrative patterns in *EastEnders* and *Neighbours* and a piece of practical work in which students wrote the opening episode for their *own* soap aimed at a youthful audience.

For both pieces, the students were given a set of questions to help them to structure their writing. Although this may be interpreted as undue intervention on our part, it is important that we do not attach undue emphasis to this aspect of the finished writing. Like all the students' writing, the essays are responses to set tasks, and they embody general values inherent in the subject as well as any specific peculiarities of the teaching. Thus, in asking the students to *make comparisons* (in this case, between opening chapters), we were involving them immediately in a conventionalised task found in the subject English: the 'compare and contrast' essay. Similarly, asking students to comment on the accuracy of representations in soaps is to conform to equally conventional expectations as to what is involved in Media Studies courses: that is, taking a critical stance towards popular representations. In this respect, the subject matter and the processes involved in both tasks already embodies the traditional values and structures inherent in both subjects.

The most obvious difference between the two essays is in the attitude that Stephen takes towards the texts he analyses and the implicit position that he adopts as a critic. In his soap-opera essay, he describes Sharon or Michelle's behaviour in terms of its stereotypicality and then goes on to qualify what this might mean:

> In 'EastEnders' 'Sharon' behaves in a very unstereotypical way. When her step parents were around they always spoilt her with money and presents, but gave her little of there time. Now she [is] older and her step parents have split up and moved away she has become a very sensible, strong young woman. But 'Sharon' is not perfect, she has got into slight debt through credit cards but she's gradually getting things sorted. She runs a pub with her boyfriend 'Simon' and she's best friends with 'Michelle'. Her character is original and both her character and behaviour are unstereotypical of a young women.
>
> The trouble with classing different characters as stereotypical or unstereotypical is that often characters will do something stereotypical and therefore be classed as a stereotype but at other times they maybe doing something very unstereotypical and therefore not be a stereotype. Often it doesn't boil down to whether the character is a stereotype or not but more about if they are used in a stereotypical storyline.

What is impressive about this extract (within the context of Stephen's development) is both its distance from the text and its control of a highly generalised and abstract level of argument. The ability to discuss the meaning of stereotypes within differing narrative structures shows a familiarity with an objective and 'theoretical' mode of discussion. It is particularly notable that Stephen shifts from an analysis of whether Michelle and Sharon are stereotyped towards a much broader discussion of the concept of stereotypicality itself. On one level, this could be seen as a clear illustration of Vygotsky's theory of conceptual understanding: Stephen's everyday concepts are gradually becoming more systematic as they encounter academic concepts such as 'stereotyping' and 'representation'. However, the notion of the stereotype is not merely an academic one: it is also a significant part of more popular definitions of what a 'critical' perspective on the media might involve. While acknowledging the complexity of Stephen's understanding, we can also detect here the way in which he is attempting to socialise himself into the specialist discourse of the subject.

His English essay is more immature by comparison. It was written a couple of months earlier. There are, however, significant differences in terms of the 'personal voice' between the two essays. This is particularly borne out by a comparison of the way in which Stephen uses the personal pronoun in both pieces of writing. Both essays use an 'I' narrator, in itself an important stylistic development in Stephen's embryonic control over this 'genre scheme' and its requisite discourse structures.[2] However, in the soap-opera essay, the

'I' involved is not one that feels but one that 'thinks' (the most frequent verb) or 'finds out' or is reflected upon: 'when I had a go at making my own soap opera, I was convinced'. This persona is objective and evaluative, and is able to summarise what has been learnt:

> From doing this project *I have learnt* that young people in most cases are represented in very stereotypical way in soaps. *I have learnt* how easy it is to write a soap as the quality of the storyline doesn't really matter in terms of attracting viewers as long as there is a reason for them to watch the next episode i.e. an unanswered question. [Our emphasis]

However, in the English essay, there is another kind of 'I':

> The opening chapter of 'McDonalds War' really creates a sense of danger and adventure. Most of the chapter is describing 'Andrew's' thoughts on whether he should take the plunge and run away. I particularly like one sentence 'Andrew was toying with the idea of running away'. The opening chapter introduces you to the main character as well as pulling into the story in a curious sort of way.
>
> The style of 'Animal Farm's' opening chapter is very good and I like it a lot. It has a lot of detail in it without a danger of becoming boring. If your an Animal Lover as well as an adventurous sort of person yourself the style of the first chapter will certainly make you want to read on.

Here, the author is trying to position himself as having a sensitive and judgmental persona. There is a more 'genuine' 'I' here, one who can express feelings and opinions: 'I particularly like one sentence . . .' Stephen doesn't explain why he likes this sentence, but clearly thinks that it is appropriate that he should express a preference of this sort. Indeed, the statement of this kind of preference does articulate a degree of discrimination and sensitivity that is seen as a key marker of success in English. With classical balance, the succeeding paragraph also contains a statement of taste: 'The style of 'Animal Farm's' opening chapter is very good and I like it a lot.' And this absolute is repeated in the conclusion: 'Overall I think I prefer "The McDonalds War's" opening chapter because it sounds like more my kind of story'.

The differentiation between the two subjects is clearly being practised here by a fairly immature and inexperienced writer. Nevertheless, he is beginning to replicate the emphasis on a personal response within English, and on an objective analysis in Media Studies, discussed in Chapter 7. While the Media Studies essay would seem to empower the writer by allowing him to adopt a politically 'critical' stance towards popular culture, the English essay also encourages a similar process of empowerment through the development of 'taste'. In many respects, this process is similar to the development of a 'critical' approach to popular music, as described in Chapter 4. Thus, Stephen makes comments like 'It has a lot of detail in it without a danger of becoming boring' or 'Even though the book creates this kind of atmosphere it remains with a slight comic tone to it.' There is more at stake here than just the rehearsal of a position from which one can write 'sensitive' English essays: the process of making judgments also puts the writer in a position of authority over the text.

A second aspect of the discourse structure that we want to consider involves the strategic use of evidence and quotations. In an interview that we conducted with Stephen at the end of year 12, he offered a concise and almost cynical definition of his approach:

> In English, all you have to do is whatever question you get, you take quotes, you take parts of the book, parts of the play, parts of the poem, say how this relates to the question, whether it proves the question right or wrong or whatever, and back up your points, keep backing up your points with evidence, and when you pick out a quote, analyse the quote. It's sort of really systematic, and you just bring them all together in your final conclusion and you get a nice C or a B.

Thus, in the English essay, we see the use of a direct quotation to verify the author's first-hand experience of the texts involved: 'His mum is the only other character mentioned in the opening chapter. She is a night nurse and when she is not working she is described as "either moping around the house or catching up on lost sleep".' What does the quotation do within the framework of his argument, and why does he feel the need to use a quotation to make his point in the first place? The answer would seem to lie in the fact that Stephen is attempting to reproduce what he perceives are the hidden requirements of English. In particular, this kind of structure reveals the necessity for the style of 'close reading' recommended by I.A. Richards.[3]

In the Media Studies essay, there are no references of this kind, perhaps partly because there is no assumption that anyone could question his knowledge of the text: it is an assumed 'common culture'. There are no references to detailed moments, but instead merely the adduction of general story lines in support of large hypotheses:

> For example *Neighbours* seems to suggest that the minute a young person gets into trouble or has an argument with someone older than them there first reaction is to run away. 'Todd' has an argument with 'Helen' so he runs away and hides in a disused house. If this was the only occasion this would give a fair impression. 'Sharon' tried to run away when she had an argument with 'Harold' and 'Toby' tried to run away and hide when he had an argument with his dad. This portrays young people in very unfair way as it suggests that young people are not prepared to face up to there problems.

By contrast with the English essay, there is no direct quotation here *to support* the argument. Instead the evidence is already summarised — in effect, interpreted — before it is really used. On one level, it is almost as though it is assumed that no reader is likely to question its veracity. However, on another level, the evidence itself seems to have less inherent status: the texts themselves do not appear to *deserve* close reading. In the end, it does not matter that much if you have not watched *Neighbours*; you are still entitled to have your opinion about it. By contrast, in English, your opinions are only admissible if they are supported by detailed evidence of a sustained and intimate relationship with the text.

Thirdly, as we have already implied, each of the essays offers a different opportunity for the author to generate his own theory in relation to the material studied. In the Media Studies essay, Stephen speculated as follows:

> I think that here are many reasons why producers use this kind of representation. Their argument is that it is what the viewers want to see. But I believe that the producers and writers just take the easy way out. The trouble with soaps is they just touch the surface. It is also a cheap way out in terms of the amount of actors and sets they need.
>
> Another reason why writers and producers use this type of representation is that there idea of what is stereotypical may be different to other peoples. The fact that a lot of people find soaps give a stereotypical view of everything doesn't seem to effect the size of the audiences they attract.

In an interview, Stephen commented on the way business and politics could be integrated into Media Studies work, whereas English was 'more specialist' — an ironic and provocative word to use in the face of the liberal notion of English as a kind of general education in human values. In fact, there is very little general speculation in Stephen's English essay. It is far more oriented towards proving its case about the text in hand rather than opening out to offer broader arguments. Thus, his English essay can assert emotive statements — 'The opening chapter of 'McDonalds War' really creates a sense of danger and adventure' — and use evidence to support the assertion: 'Most of the chapter is describing "Andrew's" thoughts on whether he should take the plunge and run away.' This kind of argumentative position is quite different from the assertion, quoted above, about the motives of soap producers. In his English essay, the mode of argument is pseudo-technical, showing how 'technique' creates 'effect' — for example, how 'quick short sentences create a sense of action'. In the Media Studies essay, the aim is to develop a general argument that empowers a critical and distanced author, and thus persuades the reader through rational argument. In English, it is to demonstrate to the reader that the author is able to understand and feel;

and the reader is to be persuaded almost through a process of identification with the writer.

Year Eleven

As we followed Stephen's development over the following two years we wanted to see the ways in which the act of 'becoming critical' serves as a form of empowerment. One of the most obvious changes was that as he became more accomplished, the differences between the two subjects became more pronounced. As we have seen, Stephen was quite explicit about the differences between the two subjects by the end of year 12; yet he didn't comment on those differences in the interview held at the end of year 11 and he seemed quite happy to move between the differing styles used in English and Media Studies respectively without realising that he was moving in contradictory directions.

The work we want to look at next was produced for his GCSE folders in the two subjects. The Media Studies piece, entitled simply 'Genre', is a very direct account of the concept of genre in television and film, and it includes an extended analysis of the generic antecedents of the film *Robocop*. This essay was the conclusion of an extended unit of work on this theme. To begin with, the class had to sort a number of television programmes into generic categories of their own choosing and then reflect on those programmes that were difficult to categorise. We then watched *Robocop* as a class, and tried to analyse the various generic elements of the film, such as character, image, plot and ideology. These two exercises were brought together in a piece of writing in which the students were also asked to reflect on some of the implications of the idea of genre for producers and audiences. The essay itself was thus broken down into a series of short sections entitled — 'Westerns', 'News', 'Frankenstein', etc. — in which the various genres or programmes were discussed.

Stephen's English essay was a study of three poems entitled 'Oh Bring Back Higher Standards', 'Gold Fish' and 'The Lesson'. This essay followed on from a fairly extensive study of poems from an anthology called *Strictly Private*[4]. The students were asked to choose poems they liked from the anthology and present them to the class for a group discussion, we then discussed the poems in class and 'taught' an appropriate method of analysis for poetry. The students then had to focus on three poems and write a study of them, concentrating on their differences and similarities. This essay went through each of the poems in turn, before coming to a general conclusion. Like the work carried out year 10, these assignments are relatively typical of the range of work submitted for GCSE moderation.

To an even greater extent than the year-10 essays, these pieces illustrated the significant differences, outlined in Chapter 7, between English and Media

Studies. Thus the Media Studies essay aimed to demonstrate a broad theoretical understanding of the concept of genre, while the English essay aimed to demonstrate expertise in the technique of analysing poetry. Unlike the Soap essay discussed above, the 'Genre' essay explicitly rejected the use of a conventional essay format, with its segmented structure, and argued on a self-consciously abstract and generalised level. The poetry essay showed a 'mastery' of technical terminology (which is ironic when it is normally considered that Media Studies has the monopoly on specialised jargon), and demonstrated control of the 'system' of essay writing that Stephen referred to above.

Again, the positioning of the author/reader in relation to the text is the main focus of our analysis. Broadly speaking, the Media Studies essay emphasises critical distance, while the English essay privileges close critical reading. The Media Studies essay implies a mind taking an overview, while the English essay displays a sensibility subject to the effect of the material discussed. The Media Studies essay does not bother with detailed analysis or examples in its pursuit of generalised abstractions; whereas the English essay is totally bound up with the moment of close reading. The Media Studies essay emphasises analysis as its dominant mode, while the English essay favours judgmental discrimination. Both essays, as we shall argue, imply a different model of what it means to be critical.

The opening sentences of the Media Studies essay exemplified many of these points:

> Genre is a way of describing the form of a Television programme or film with its own set of conventions and is used by programme makers and film producers as a way of defining the type of programme or film they wish to make. Often when a television company wants to make a new programme they use genre as a way of categorising different tried and tested formats.

The very wide implications of the definition and the abstract nature of the argument are reminiscent of the soap essay we have already discussed. And the moves between understandings about finance, audience and textual conventions all indicate a grasp of the conceptual implications of the idea of genre. Stephen also shows that he can move from a discussion of the text itself to a wider critique of popular culture:

> *Brazil*
> The scenery in *Brazil* is set in the future and *Robocop* has used a similar look. Both films show an image of capitalism in a multinational corporation. They use the idea of one man taking on the system.

This is an exciting insight, and one generated by the broad requirements of the task. The application of concepts like 'capitalism' or 'the system' to an ideological reading of specific genres is extraordinarily encompassing.

By contrast, Stephen's poetry essay did not move beyond its own boundaries:

> 'The Lesson' uses a slightly slower rhythm. The poem opens with an introduction letting the reader know that the poem is answering the question 'Should capital punishment be used in schools?' From then on the poem mainly sticks to the same rhythm. This use of a regular pattern of rhythm in each verse makes it easier for the reader to examine each section of the story in detail. Each verse contains one main image or scene and the constant pattern helps to link them together.

There is a strong element here of self-justification and of *post hoc* rationalisation. Why, for example, should a regular rhythm make it 'easier' for a reader to 'examine' each section? And is that how such a putative reader would read anyway? There is a crucial difference between the two essays in terms of how they conceptualise the potential consumers of the texts they discuss. While the Media Studies essay is ultimately concerned with real audiences, the English essay fabricates a single, hypothetical reader. Thus, the 'Genre' essay talks about 'the relationship between the producer, the product and the targeted audience', and offers generalisations like 'Everyone likes a hero'. On the other hand, the English essay purports to trace the effects of the poems discussed either on an ideal reader, as in the quotation discussed above, or on the author himself — except that he cannot be entirely personal in his response, and as a result acts more as a sort of stand-in for the 'general reader'. Thus, Stephen wrote: 'The use of rhyme here ensures that *the reader* understands that the poet is being ironic and doesn't agree that corporal punishment is needed in education, by connecting "pain" and the "cane".' This kind of comment duly received its tick in the margin, but we have to ask on what basis Stephen is able to comment on the text/reader relationship. Surely it isn't 'the reader' who understands the irony of the poem but Stephen, and the discursive use of 'the reader' is a modest way of declaring one's own insights.

Of course, generalising about audiences, as in the genre essay, can also serve as a way of passing off one's own insights as those of people in general. However, this way of talking about media audiences does at least allow the possibility of supporting such assertions with empirical evidence — and (as we have noted) audience research is an important element of most Media Studies courses. By contrast, the suppositions that underlie Stephen's concept of the ideal reader can only derive from the discursive repertoires of the English critical essay. In effect, this ideal reader is a purely hypothetical creation; the possibility that real readers might read texts in very different ways is one that cannot be entertained, let alone investigated through empirical research.

When we asked Stephen at the end of his GCSE course what he thought he had learnt from the 'Genre' essay, he first said that he thought he had learnt why *Robocop* had been successful. Yet he went on to speculate on the wider principles at work in this particular example:

> Stephen: If you include enough things into something, because it's such a mixture of stuff, it becomes original.
>
> DB: But isn't that just stating the obvious?
>
> Stephen: Up to a point, you are stating the obvious. But then you're meant to try and look further into the programme, because that film wasn't made in one lesson, that film was made over months and months and months, yeah? Therefore, someone must have thought deeper than the obvious.

The Media Studies essay clearly encourages a process of abstraction and generalisation, of the kind implied in our discussion of Vygotsky's theories of conceptual development. Crucially, Stephen is himself conscious of this process. 'Being critical' in this context privileges the perceptions of the critic. As Stephen puts it, '. . . someone must have thought deeper than the obvious' — and if he can see deeper than the obvious, then he is in some ways different from other people.

Both essays actively construct this kind of privileged 'critical self', although in different ways. In English, the critical self emerges from the manipulation of the conventional discursive structures of the English essay, such as speculating about the responses of a hypothetical reader, or making technical observations using a specialised critical repertoire, like the effects of irony or rhyme. In Media Studies, the critical self is primarily manifested in the distance between the critic and popular culture, and in the capacity to construct an analytical framework. This is, as Stephen states, a matter of seeing 'deeper than the obvious', or as he commented earlier in the same interview:

> It's kind of easy to talk about basic things, like how the title will attract people, but when you have to really look, you start noticing little details that you would have just taken for granted. So to do it really well, it's a bit more tricky.

There is an implied critical self here who can look beyond what is taken for granted — which is in effect the rationale for the 'Genre' essay.

It is noteworthy that during year 12 Stephen referred back to the 'Genre' essay several times, and (although we did not count this) we would also guess that genre was the most frequently used media term in general class discussions. The intensive analytical format of the essay clearly offered Stephen particular pleasures, which — if his rather disparaging comments about the 'system' required for good English essays can be relied upon — were not available to him in English.

Of course, one of the risks of privileging analysis and a distanced approach to popular culture is that it can lead to a position of arrogance and superiority, and even a form of contempt for the mass audience.[5] For middle-class students, this can be a powerful marker of 'taste' and distinction, and thus a means of socialising oneself into class membership. However, there is very little of this in Stephen's writing. Indeed, he seems to emerge with an enhanced respect, both for the skill of media producers and for the pleasures of audiences. Part of the explanation for this must lie in the social context of the school, and Stephen's realisation that he and his peers were in fact quite different from the mindless mass audience so despised by media critics.

Year Twelve

By the time Stephen came to write the final pair of essays we want to consider, it is fair to say that his 'literary' development had reached a recognisably adult standard, and that the kinds of positions we have analysed had now been properly subsumed into the production of the required critical styles. As we have already indicated, Stephen was uncommonly aware of this process himself, but this did not result in a mechanistic or cynical approach to his work so much as a theoretical deconstruction of the value of traditional English studies.

The Media Studies essay we will be examining was written to accompany a storyboard which was submitted as a practical exercise for the first module, entitled 'Textual Analysis', in Stephen's Media Studies A-level course. The storyboard was for a trailer advertising an imagined forthcoming film. Like the English essay, it was written in the first term of his year-12 studies, but whereas the English assignment (entitled 'Comparing "The Express" by Stephen Spender and "Edward, Edward" an anonymous ballad, in their use of rhythm, language and drama') was written as part of ongoing studies, the Media piece was polished up for an examiner.

One of the main threads in this chapter has been to follow the relationships between the critical and the personal as they have been constructed through the discourse of critical writing. This Media Studies essay of Stephen's brought together these two elements in an interestingly different way. Stephen used an 'I' throughout the essay to show how he (the creator) manufactured the storyboard he was describing. However, the narrator in this essay is characterised not so much by personal feeling as by the interplay of theory and ideology.

We had given two pieces of reading to the class, and actively encouraged them to use these in the analyses of their own trailers. The first was a summary of Todorov's theory of narrative, and the second was a chapter from Bordwell and Thompson's *Film Art,* describing the classical Hollywood system of continuity editing.[6] Whereas one of Stephen's classmates got no further than noting that Todorov was a Russian who had invented a theory of narrative[7], Stephen distances himself from his own invention and uses the academic theory as a way of interpreting his own work. Thus, for example, he writes of the overall pattern of his trailer:

> Using Todorov's theory I decided to reveal the basic storyline just past the peak of Disequilibrium. That way the viewer is left with a cliff-hanger: Is Scott guilty? and if not, will he be able to prove his innocence?

Later on in the essay, he uses the film grammar of Bordwell and Thompson to analyse sequences in his storyboard. For example, he talks about the way he uses shot-reverse-shot patterns, or constructs establishing shots. Besides applying the theory so succinctly, he also summarises its implications. Thus, he writes at one stage:

> Continuity editing is seen as the grammar of film and montage editing is where you forget all these rules and just cut different shots to get the effect required and can be compared to the use of collage in art. In a trailer both methods of editing can be useful.

Being able to integrate the theory in this way was the main point of differentiation between the students in the class. However, we need to ask whether integrating ideas from somebody else's writing really made a difference to the quality of Stephen's critical thinking, or whether it merely marked a stage in the 'system' of media essays that Stephen was so clearly mastering at this point.

It might be useful here to return to Vygotsky's distinction between 'everyday' and 'academic' (or 'spontaneous' and 'scientific') concepts. The academic concepts here derive from an established body of critical writing that is in the process of being canonised in Media and Cultural Studies courses: *Film Art,* for example, is widely used as an undergraduate textbook. By contrast, the everyday concepts emerge through a process of reflection on more concrete experiences — such as Stephen's viewing of soap operas, discussed above. Academic concepts are passed down to the student from the teacher, while everyday concepts progressively become more systematic, and eventually come to merge with the former. The moves that were occurring within Stephen's discussion of the notion of 'stereotyping' (considered above) provide a useful illustration of this process: in effect, they reflected the ways in which academic theory interacts with students' more 'common-sense' theories about popular culture.

Inevitably, it is difficult to discern the difference in Stephen's writing between the use of academic concepts as part of the dressing of A-level critical writing and the elements of 'genuine' critical practice. Obviously, the learning process may often involve using techniques or language by way of practice before such techniques become more automatic and meaningful. As Vygotsky argued, the syntax of speech might precede the syntax of thought: students might be instructed in 'initial verbal definitions', which would only gradually acquire meaning for them.[8] Stephen's use of terms like 'montage', or phrases like 'the grammar of film', may therefore serve as much as a way of teaching himself how to enter another stage of critical understanding as they would as a way of providing an insight into the structure of film narrative.

In this respect, it is interesting to consider the particular effects of using academic concepts in conjunction with such a personal mode of writing. If we look back at the excerpts we have quoted from this essay we can see that Stephen is referring, in the same sentence, to 'my' storyboard or how 'I' constructed the narrative, as well as to Todorov, or Bordwell and Thompson. We would argue that the conventional propriety for quoting references or applying theory is to do so in the objective or passive mode, and distinctly not in such a personal way. Of course, Stephen is not being personal in the same way as he is in the English essays we have discussed. Nevertheless, he is positioning himself as an equal to the theorists he is using: indeed, we might even suggest that this represents a democratisation of power relations between the learner and the body of knowledge to be learnt.

At the same time, Stephen is moving between different stages in the learning of Media Studies theory. He has not just absorbed theory from a book and reproduced it — as one might suspect from a sentence like 'Continuity editing is seen as the grammar of film'. He has also used and applied theory both before and after his own creation. We would see this integration of independent creativity and theoretical reflection as one of the most important aims of media education. Stephen has tried and tested the theory in practical work, and thus he does not have any great respect for it: it just offers a useful way of explaining his own understanding back to him (and, of course, to us). This kind of reflection, thus, represents a significant progression from the notion of an internal dialogue, or a 'conversation with yourself', that Michael articulated in Chapter 8. The academic discourse offers a way of articulating common sense and popular knowledge which would otherwise remain unknown and indistinct. And one added benefit of using this discourse is that it offers the possibility of joining a particular interpretative community. Thus, to be able to refer to Todorov, or to Bordwell and Thompson, is not just a matter of joining a club of name droppers; it is also a matter of asserting oneself, and validating one's own understandings as intellectually pertinent.

Of course, we might equally interpret Stephen's use of this academic discourse in terms of his acquisition of an appropriate style for this level of critical writing. In fact, however, this is one of the most problematic issues at A level. The syllabus that we were using states that this level of quotation and reference is not required; and at several conferences and meetings, the then chief examiner also argued that he was looking for familiarity with the ideas rather than the names of specific authors. Nevertheless, students who could quote and refer to named theorists definitely did better in terms of exam success. We became quite cynical about encouraging students to use references in this way to help them to get marks — although, as we have noted, there were students for whom Todorov's Russian origins were at least as relevant as his theory of narrative. Quite why the syllabus preferred to be disingenuous about this matter remains unclear. There may be a naïve idea that students could somehow learn the ideas but not get bogged down in the theory, or that exposure to the theory would somehow taint their 'natural' use of the ideas. While there remain significant problems in regard to making academic writing 'accessible' to such students, we hope that our analysis of Stephen's writing has suggested something of the importance of this task.

The origins of this anxiety about an 'excess' of theory do however lie in part with the critical tradition of English, which has unavoidably informed the development of Media Studies. To examine this further we need to look at the English essay Stephen produced in year 12. What is striking about this essay is how similar it is to the other English essays we have discussed and how it is almost impossible to trace the qualitative growth that we have analysed in the three Media Studies essays.

Inevitably, the essay is much more 'naturalised' in its command of the appropriate critical discourse, and it uses a more extensive range of 'technical' terms:

> In 'The Express' the rhythm of the poem gradually gets faster simulating speed and this is achieved by the long vowels and strong consonants used in the opening lines.

This, however, is a development in degree rather than in kind. There is no equivalent argument to be had here about the role of academic concepts in Stephen's development: indeed, the theory behind the reading of these poems remains completely implicit and hidden.[9] Unlike Stephen's struggle to find a way of explaining himself both in the 'Genre' essay and his account of the storyboard, the English essay serenely ignores such methodological concerns, and launches into its argument without any self-justification at all. The essay concludes rather flatly. We might almost infer that the absence of ideas in the structure of the essay has resulted in a sense of pointlessness:

> From comparing the two poems I don't think they have any real point of contact as far as meaning. They are interesting to compare

technically as each poem uses particular techniques to write about different topics in two very different styles.

Clearly, Stephen did not particularly like these two poems, and did not get a lot out of the comparison. More than that, however, it seems as if having perceived the hidden agenda behind this kind of essay it no longer has any point.

If we return to the observation we quoted earlier, about the use of a system to write English essays, it seems as if being aware of the system acts as a way of undermining the point of the game. Later in the discussion from which that comment was taken, Stephen acknowledged that Media Studies essays also involve a system — or what we would call a critical discourse. However, he also discussed in an animated fashion, quite how pointless he found English as a subject compared to Media Studies:

> If you're, like, doing Media Studies, yeah, you're probably moving up, you have some understanding of the media already, and certainly an interest, a natural interest in certain elements of the media . . . and that's a start. If you're not that interested in reading, then English is hard to get into, and there's not, like, much scope for your own interest . . . with English, you read a book and it's a book you may enjoy, you may think it's a really good book, but then you've got to start doing essays on it, you've got to break it down, and you start seeing it not as a piece of art but as something very technical.

Students often complain about having to analyse a text to death. In the light of the observations we have made about the enclosed and self-referential nature of the English critical essay, this concern would have greater resonance. Not only is the object of study (the text) given, but the process of analysis is regarded as 'technical' and irrelevant. By contrast, Media Studies gives the students control over the choice of texts, and the method of analysis has a purchase on their own experiences. It was for this reason that Stephen described English as a 'specialist' subject:

> I think English A-level is a bit out of date, quite frankly. See, English is always treated as a general subject: everybody should do English, English is not specialist. But English A-level to me is very specialist, and yet it's not recognised as a specialist subject . . .

Stephen's argument here extended to a criticism of the lack of vocational relevance of English when compared with Media Studies:

> When I say that a book is a story, what I'm trying to say is, how does your ability to analyse a story, yeah, where does that put you in the

> work market, the job market? Now, if you have a story in Media Studies where you can recognise certain audiences, you know the whole advertising side of it, the whole commercial side of it, plus you understand some of the politics of business . . . you understand how it works, and you are better placed to go into work. Say you just did English A-level . . . that gives you a very big experience of what area of work you want to go into, doesn't it? I mean, what are you gonna be, a book reviewer?

It would perhaps be logical to expect students of Media Studies to end up deconstructing English. It seems inevitable that the students themselves will not submit to the process of becoming literate in English (at least not without considerable cynicism) if all that means is a socialisation into a very narrow, class-bound form of personal judgment and taste. In that respect, we are bound to admit that Stephen's own development also reflects our own personal histories, even if we did not ourselves encounter Media Studies until well after the end of our compulsory schooling. Of course, Stephen knows what we want to hear, although he also knows that he does not have to tell us any of it. And what he says may well be partly motivated by his desire to distance himself from his parents' values. In the end, though, what convinces us is the way he provides us with arguments that we had not thought of ourselves.

Conclusion

Rationales for teaching about popular culture often involve a great deal of rhetoric about the personal, social and political implications of being 'critical', and what it might actually do for our students. However, the process of 'becoming critical' has rarely been studied or defined. In particular, it remains unclear whether being critical should be seen as a state of mind or as a social practice. On the one hand, becoming critical could be seen simply as a matter of learning to reproduce the terminology and discourse structures of particular kinds of conventional critical writing — and thus, in Bourdieu's terms, of acquiring a kind of cultural capital. From this perspective, the consequences of becoming critical would need to be seen in terms of the broader politics of subject disciplines, and the distribution of power within society. On the other hand, the growth of critical understanding could be seen from a Vygotskyan perspective: as a matter of cognitive or conceptual development. This account would emphasise the way in which critical understanding offers the individual a degree of power and control over his or her own thought processes.

Our account in this chapter has retained a theoretical ambiguity about these different notions of what it might mean to be critical. This is partly because we do not perceive the issue in terms of an either/or choice. On the contrary, it may well be that this dichotomy between conceptual and discursive development is itself unnecessarily opposed. As we have argued, students need to imitate the processes they set out to learn as a vital part of that learning process. Instruction, as Vygotsky argued, must precede development. There is a dynamic interplay between the learning process and the entry into any discourse, let alone the politically privileged one of being 'critical'.

In the next chapter, we will continue to build on this debate about the relationship between language and learning by examining how students learn from practical media production. What we need to take forward from our study of Stephen's critical development is the sense that we cannot be absolutely unquestioning about any of the radical shibboleths of Media Studies, not even for a student whose work is such a great advertisement for the subject.

Notes

1. See Sefton-Green (1992) for a fuller description of the simulation and the task that led to Stephen's opening chapter.
2. A 'genre scheme' refers to the different types of writing (i.e. essays, letters, stories, etc.), while the 'discourse structure' refers to the component parts within each genre scheme. See Smith (1982).
3. See Richards (1929).
4. Ed. McGough (1986).
5. See Buckingham (1993c).
6. See Bordwell and Thompson (1979).
7. This piece of misinformation derives from our own teaching. To our chagrin, we have subsequently discovered that Todorov was not Russian but a French-naturalised Bulgarian! Thanks to Ken Jones and Phillip Drummond for background research. 'Nuff respect.
8. See Vygotsky (1962); although it is worth noting the apparent contradiction between this argument and Vygotsky's insistence on the limitations of the 'direct teaching' of concepts, noted in Chapter 8.
9. For insightful observations on the invisibility of theory in English, see Eagleton (1983) and Moss (1989).

Chapter 10

Solving the Theoretical Problem?: Positive Images and Practical Work

The 'theoretical problem' was in fact the way Stephen described his final A-level assignment; and it is the students' work on this assignment that forms the basis of this penultimate chapter. We would not claim that this work provides a theoretical solution to the problems we have raised — or indeed that there is any single solution. Nevertheless, we would argue that practical media production of the kind we will be considering here offers a distinctive mode of investigation, which should stand alongside the forms of critical analysis considered in the previous chapter. As we have suggested, it is in the *dialogue* between these different practices that significant learning may occur — although, as we shall indicate, the relationship between 'theory' and 'practice' is unlikely to be a straightforward one.

In his evaluation of this assignment, Stephen argued that it had differed in kind from the other practical projects (including those described earlier in the book) that he had undertaken during his four years of Media Studies. In this instance, he said, 'solving the theoretical problem [took] priority over creativity'. This question of the relationship between the theoretical and the creative has been one of the most debated issues in media education.[1] We need to outline the main arguments here in order to contextualise our study.

Broadly speaking, it is possible to distinguish between a 'progressive' and a 'radical' notion of the role of practical work, in the terms introduced in Chapter Seven. The progressive notion would emphasise the importance of 'creativity' and 'learning through doing'. Practical production would be seen as a process of open-ended exploration and self-expression, in which the students were encouraged to give voice to their own concerns and perspectives. By contrast, the radical notion would see practical work as another means of developing a critical analysis of dominant media forms, and hence of challenging the ideologies they are seen to convey. Practical work here would be strictly subordinated to the central task of theoretical investigation.

Thus, the notion of media education as a form of radical 'demystification', which was prevalent in the 1970s and early 1980s, offered a powerful challenge to what were seen as woolly-minded, liberal notions of 'creativity' imported from English or Art teaching.[2] Practical work was seen as a form of 'deconstruction' in which particular media conventions were systematically varied, and their meanings analysed. As critics have subsequently argued, this approach runs the risk of reducing practical work to a mere illustration of theory, in which the motivations and interests of the students are neglected in favour of the teacher's own theoretical agenda.[3] In fact, what underlies this approach is a fundamental suspicion of practical work, which derives from much broader concerns about the ideological effects of the media. The danger of practical work, it would seem, is that it encourages students to imitate dominant forms, and hence merely to reproduce the ideologies they are seen to contain. Here again, there are significant similarities between this approach and the 'cultural heritage' version of English teaching, to which it is outwardly quite opposed. Len Masterman, for example, offers a typical condemnation of students' creative work — 'an endless wilderness of dreary third-rate pop shows and derivative documentaries'[4] — in terms which clearly have much in common with a Leavisite perspective.

In recent years, however, practical work has come to be recognised as a central aspect of media teaching — not least because of the increasing accessibility of the technology.[5] In some instances, most notably in 'vocational' courses, this has provoked fears that media education will be reduced to a form of technical training in which theoretical or critical perspectives are marginalised.[6] Nevertheless, at school level, and particularly in the context of GCSE and A-level courses, there has been a central emphasis on the integration of 'theory' and 'practice': most Media Studies syllabuses at this level include a practical component which counts for anything between one-third and one-half of the final assessment. Yet despite these developments, the issues raised in those earlier debates about practical work have not really been resolved. The question of what students might learn from practical work, and how that learning might be evaluated, remains a central concern, not least in terms of assessment.

Inevitably, these issues have been framed rather differently by English teachers. While there remains a similar anxiety about the dangers of 'imitation', this is posed more in terms of an opposition between the personal and the generic. The 'personal growth' model of English teaching is based on an almost fetishistic notion of individual creativity, in which learning to master generic conventions or write in different styles is valued merely on the level of a artisanal skill. The collective nature of media production almost inevitably calls into question these assumptions about individual creativity; although there is also some important work on children's fictional writing that has begun to move beyond this approach.[7]

In this chapter, we want to explore some of the broader issues at stake in these debates through a detailed analysis of two production projects. Our account is organised in terms of three fundamental oppositions that appear to underlie the debate: the personal and the social; the expressive and the imitative; and the creative and the theoretical. In exploring these distinctions in relation to our students' work, we also want to challenge some of the grounds on which they come to be made.

Positive Images

The work we are going to discuss was produced in privileged circumstances, as part of the 'Advanced Production Module' for Media Studies A level. Despite its essentially practical nature, the criteria outlined in the syllabus for this module appear to derive from the 'radical' approach defined above: the project is seen as a kind of application of academic theory, and as such it necessarily involves a disavowal of the personal. The syllabus requires the project to be based on an explicit consideration of one aspect of Media Studies theory. Its implicit model would appear to be that of the political avant-garde — for example, the work of the British independent film and video movement of the 1970s and early 1980s — with its emphasis on self-reflexivity, formal experimentation and direct opposition to the pleasures of popular culture.

We chose to focus on the theme of representation and realism, and specifically on the debates around 'positive images', for several reasons beyond the constraints of the syllabus. The positive images debate is itself a major theme within popular discourse about the media;[8] and it has particular resonance within public-sector institutions, not least schools. It derives essentially from feminist and black activist traditions, although it has recently extended to include issues such as ageism, sexual orientation and disability. The central thrust of this work has been to draw attention to the negative effects of stereotyping and misrepresentation (or indeed invisibility) in the mass media; and it seeks to reverse these effects through providing positive representations of marginalised social groups. The notion of 'positive images' was enthusiastically embraced by the 'politically correct' Left in the late 1970s and 1980s as a means of effecting ideological change; and it became an object of ridicule in the right wing press of the Thatcher years.

As we described in Chapter 1, the school in which we were working has a remarkably diverse population, at least in terms of the ethnic backgrounds of the students. The community in Tottenham, as in other parts of inner-city Britain, is politically sensitive and self-aware — not least because of events in its recent history. This, we felt, made it possible for the students to engage with ideological issues while simultaneously utilising personal experience and emotions. In different ways, all the work described in previous chapters has dealt with popular culture within a broad framework of cultural politics and power — be they the gender relations invoked in photostories like *The Chippendales* or the ethnically based youth culture of 'Finesse FM'. What this assignment aimed to do was encourage a more direct and explicit political engagement with such issues, while continuing to base the content within the students' own cultural experiences.

This, at least, was the intention. We spent two weeks discussing notions of realism and the 'positive images' debate, for example in relation to films like *Handsworth Songs* (directed by the Black Audio Film Collective) and the very different anti-realism of Spike Lee's *Do the Right Thing*. We also looked at the use of images in 'equal opportunities' campaigns — for example, the Haringey Council posters that adorned the walls of the school — as well as at 'independent' photography, such as David Hevey's account of disability imagery and the work of black British photographers.[9] We then set the practical assignment, for which the students were required to produce a video, or series of images, that engaged with the representation of 'hidden' minorities or groups while simultaneously working against the dominant conventions of realism. This was a demanding task, and the results were significantly varied.

The first group produced a 15-minute video entitled *Muggers Morality* that aimed, in their words, 'to . . . challenge the dominant representation of black youth and . . . examine the role the police play in the criminalisation of black youth'. This was an ambitious short film, modelled on *Do the Right Thing,* following the descent into crime, and the eventual imprisonment of a female rapper. While the first part of the film used familiar documentary conventions, the second part undermined these with a more direct, Brechtian address to the viewer. The second group produced a collection of posters aimed at raising the profile of the Chinese community in Britain, using a much more didactic 'positive images' approach. And finally, the third group produced a magazine, called *Slutmòpolitan,* which aimed to be 'a direct parody of the monthly glossy publication "Cosmopolitan"'.

We will be looking in detail at these last two print-based productions in terms of the oppositions identified above. Some of the work is reproduced here, although again we will have to describe some of the material at relevant points in our account. Before doing so, however, it is important to note some of the differences between the work discussed here and the productions described in the first part of the book. Although most of that work was produced in Media Studies classrooms, it also used forms that young people might (and do) employ in their leisure time, as part of their everyday participation in popular culture. Ponyboy wrote *Plaz Investigations* by himself over a lonely holiday; the magazines and raps of 'Hardcore Rappin' were, it can be argued, already in production before being steered towards A-level assessment; and the photographs considered in Chapter 5 built on the everyday practice of photography. By contrast, it should already be clear, even from our brief description of the work in this unit, that the students were being placed in a different position as cultural producers. Nevertheless, we shall argue that the formal requirements of this situation built upon students' existing forms of expression and cultural investments in a powerful way.

This is evident from a brief comparison with the earlier work carried out — say, for example, the photography of the younger students discussed in Chapter 5. Although we argued that the work considered there engaged with the power relations of gender and race, it did so largely in an implicit way. The in-jokes of many of the photostories emerged from the mix of genres and forms, and from a kind of play with identity, through dressing up and 'posing' — all within the shared context of the peer group and the school. The positive-images work differs from this by virtue of its explicit grasp of larger social structures (even if the *issues are* effectively the same) and its self-conscious adoption of a 'position', expressed critically and directly as ideology. We would see this as a highly *political* form of Media Studies — although whether the proponents of the radical tradition would accept it as such is perhaps another matter.

The Creative Process and the Place of Theory

One of the most striking differences between the Chinese poster work and *Slutmo* was in terms of how the two groups approached their task. The Chinese poster group comprised four students with an equal gender split: two of the students were from Hong Kong Cantonese backgrounds, one was from a Greek Cypriot background and one was a white working-class student. (Of the four young women who worked on *Slutmo,* three came from Turkish homes, while the other was white British.) The Chinese poster group spent the first five weeks of the project agonising over a choice of topic and engaging with a highly theoretical set of arguments. They ended up with four finished posters, two aimed at art galleries, one modelled along local-authority equal opportunities styles (two of these three are reproduced on page 192–3), and one a collage of Chinese faces with the question 'Are they the same?' written in both English and Cantonese. The group produced many discarded draft versions and substantial written accounts of the project. These begin to explain the difficulties they had:

> The group started to examine the way in which black people were represented by people which were not black, however we soon decided against this idea because none of us were black and we would be just a group of people investigating another group we knew a little about.
>
> . . . we could not find any representations of Chinese people in Britain in the mainstream media. This meant that theories had to be

> borrowed from the discussion around the representation of black people because the same things are relevant.

In this extract, Stuart describes an apparently objective and de-personalised move from the study of black people (which was obviously a major theme in our class work) to, as it were, a gap in the market: the Chinese community. The application of academic theory (mainly derived from texts like *The Critical Decade*, on black photography)[10] in itself raised a whole host of abstract arguments. Antonia, for example, refers to:

> . . . [the] essay by Eddie Chambers [in *The Critical Decade*] in which he asks whether it is possible to subvert negative black imagery, such as the golliwog image, to progressive anti-racist work. This theory is one which we took into consideration for our product.
>
> I found it extremely difficult to invent images that would represent the Chinese community since it is an invisible minority.
>
> It is very hard to destroy stereotypes that have settled in our society; making people aware of how a minority group has been victimised through racial oppression takes many, many attempts.

These comments show a serious engagement with the political and academic arguments. However, it is notable how the students in this group were almost paralysed by the weight of this kind of abstraction, and initially found themselves unable to actually make anything.[11] The decision to focus on the Chinese community came about through a tortuous process of elimination, which saw the group moving from black to Greek minorities. However, as Stuart explained: '. . . one member of the group [Antonia] was Greek and I felt she was uncomfortable with the group studying the race of which she belonged . . . she thought Greek people were represented realistically.' The eventual choice of topic was made possible by virtue of Mei King's personal investment in the subject: 'As a member of the minority group we chose to study I found that I was insistent on providing the group with favourable views and arguments for the Chinese people.' Even so, once the theoretical terrain had been cleared, it was difficult to imagine what could be put in its place. It was easy criticising negative stereotyping: 'The stereotypical representations of Chinese people are having slanted eyes, using chopsticks to eat, straw hats, buck teeth, Kung Fu, working in take-away's/restaurants and being short in height.' But it was less clear how to reverse the process.

We would argue that this was due largely to the lack of an existing (or at least a widely shared) cultural form in which their ideas could be embodied. Because these students were, in effect, inventing a form of expression to encapsulate their ideas, they did not have the security and knowledge of familiar generic conventions, as was the case with the work considered in the first part of this book. Despite their attempts to define an audience for their work in art galleries or local authority workplaces, making posters to express abstract ideas resulted in abstract products. Furthermore, like the political avant-garde of the 1970s and 1980s — for example, in the case of *Handsworth Songs* — the concern to engage with factual (mis)representations led to a documentary style of presentation.

The *Slutmo* group, on the other hand, wanted to make a magazine as their starting point. Their 'way in' to the project was through a desire to work in a recognisable genre or cultural form — in contrast to the Chinese poster group, who effectively had to invent the form of the product to fit the theory. There was a theory behind *Slutmo,* but it only emerged *during* the process of production and (as we shall see) with considerable contradictions. The following piece of dialogue, which took place in the classroom one day, begins to articulate a resistance to academic theory on a number of levels:

> JSG: So you're criticising the representation of femininity in woman's magazines?
> Clare: We just want to have a laugh.

The over-serious media teacher is clearly being satirised here, in the best time-honoured tradition. But a number of further implications seem to be present in this exchange. We have the problematic situation of the male teacher explaining feminism to the female student — motivated, perhaps, by a fear that her work might not be as 'politically correct' as he (and indeed the examiner) would like it to be. And we have the student resisting the theoretical (and ideological) appropriation of her work through an emphasis on fun and 'having a laugh', thereby opposing the teacher's insistence on serious, academic discourse.

'Having a laugh', not taking things seriously, very effectively provides a kind of ambiguity, a space for play, in which meanings cannot be fixed once and for all. As we shall argue, the kind of parody produced by these girls can be read in a variety of ways, not just by us but also by the girls themselves; yet in a sense, this is precisely the point of it. The possibilities here are very different from the privileged 'critical' discourse discussed in the previous chapter; yet the extent to which 'having a laugh' may in fact enable students to engage with the serious issues raised by academic theory is one of the key questions of this chapter.

Either way, the *Slutmo!* group began with an existing cultural form, in much the same way as the work discussed in the first half of this book. What is striking, however, is the convergence of academic theory with questions of identity and reading in an indissoluble whole:

> The magazine would be a direct parody of the monthly glossy publication 'Cosmopolitan'. In the real world we like to think these things [cooking, looks, etc.] don't matter too much but these magazines are so powerful . . . that these faults are seen as things that desperately need to be changed . . . Even the most confident and

> feminist of us are entitled to worry that we are not as perfect as we would wish to be . . . It is the utter hypocrisy of such magazines that led us to produce an anti-realist magazine and play around with the conventions in order to expose their hidden values.

There is a striking contrast between this nexus of ideas and the starting points of the Chinese poster group. In a sense, the difference here is between abstract theory and what we might call personally grounded theory, much like the development we observed in Stephen's critical writing. It is also clear that where the creative starting point is culturally predetermined, where the shape of expression is partly given, the theoretical issues have very different points of entry and engagement.

From the Personal to the Social

As we have already implied, it was Mei King's personal investment in the Chinese poster project that galvanised the group to produce some work. While the group produced only four posters, there were many more unfinished ideas. By far the most powerful were the two posters produced by Mei King, in particular the East-West picture (see Figure 10.1). Unlike the poster masterminded by Antonia (see Figure 10.2), which was explicitly modelled on David Hevey's work[12] and almost amounted to an exploration in an 'equal opportunities' genre, Mei King foregrounds herself in the narrative. She describes the image as follows:

> The main question to be asked here was whether having a choice between two cultures was really a struggle or an opportunity to be a part of both worlds — to pick and choose aspects from two different worlds to suit their personal tastes as individuals. This poster is systematically divided into two; the right hand side — signifying the 'East' — shows various Chinese features (culture/tradition, zodiac, art and entertainment); the left hand side — symbolising the 'West' — shows the Western versions of these same features. In the middle of these juxtaposing images sits a Chinese person facing alternate ways (left and right), reflecting a choice between two styles. This Chinese person sits in a relaxed manner and wears a genuine smile on her face to show she is happy to have these choices open to her.

We are struck by two points in this account. The first is the atavistic reference to the notion of the first-generation immigrant being 'between two cultures'; and the second is the fact that the 'Chinese person' is Mei King herself.

Figure 10.1 East/West, Mei King

The notion of 'between two cultures' stems from a common-sense understanding of the position of the immigrant, which was prevalent in the 'race relations' discourses of 1970s sociology. It stands in contrast to the 'syncretic' model of cultural identity, which emphasises the greater diversity of options available, and the active agency of ethnic groups themselves.[13] However, the clarity of this explanation and indeed of the whole poster

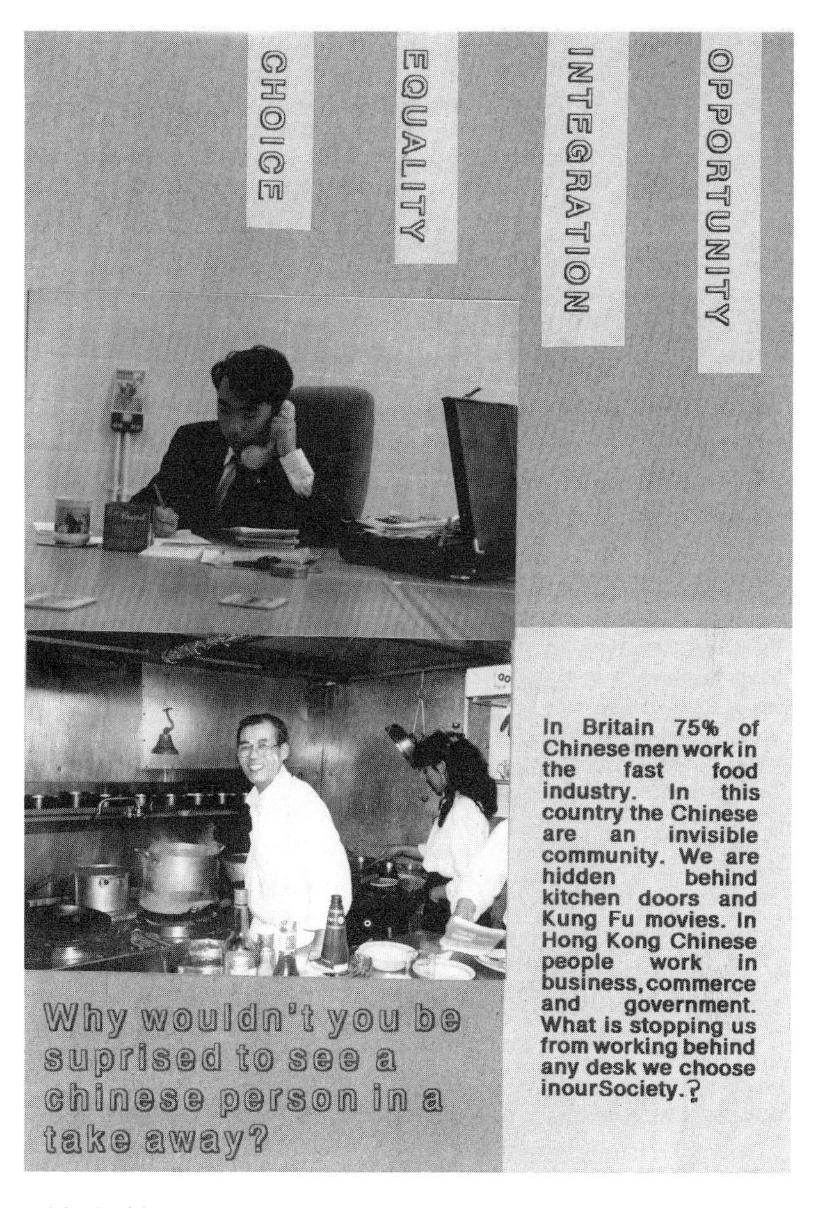

Figure 10.2 Positive Images, Antonia

indicates a kind of intellectual control over the project which almost renders the product itself redundant. The conscious, strategic manipulation of the signifiers of East and West makes the work an ideal exposition of media theory. Yet the schematic binary oppositions of the layout and the way in which the Chinese person faces both ways seem to eviscerate the product. In particular, the parity of explanation between the writing and the image points to the way in which the theory preceded the product, rather than emerging through reflection. It seems a purely didactic, intellectual statement, and as such it makes us question what actually *making* the product achieved in terms of these students' learning. If Mei King understood all these issues at the beginning of the project how did the process of making the poster develop that understanding — as distinct from even the ways that displaying the work validated her position within the class?

In this respect, the way in which Mei King uses the third person to describe herself is particularly significant. It is used, we would suggest, to confer the *gravitas* of authority — as though, if we knew it was her in the picture, the work would only have artistic merit. In that sense, Mei King seeks to authenticate the work through reference to external conventions rather than personal verity. (This is similar to the process described in the previous chapter where Stephen sought to create an authentic first person in his critical writing.) Yet her writing (and that of Ka Wai, the other Chinese member of the group) claims authority for the work through precisely this kind of appeal to personal experience. Ka Wai wrote:

> Being Chinese myself at first I really felt uncomfortable tackling this work . . . I could see certain advantages and connections I had. It was interesting to explore the different ways in representing my culture and at the end of the day I came up with the right minority group to represent. I also found that the fact I had a say in the representation of my own culture, the posters couldn't really be criticised as a misrepresentation of the Chinese.

Likewise, Mei King argued that 'If, however, we had decided to study the representations of another minority group I might not have been able to contribute as much.' The hesitancies and uncertain claims for credibility also reflect the unease both students felt about perceiving themselves as the 'Other' of dominant discourse.[14]

In order to explain this, we need to go back a little. We have already described the way in which the group searched for a topic of study. As we noted earlier, when the group moved from black to Greek minorities, Antonia argued strongly against using her culture as the focus of the project. Part of this stems from a very reasonable anxiety about being the 'object of study' — although this is not the case, in our experience, with black students. Part of the resistance may have been simply 'personal' — not wanting to be the 'centre of attention' — which, in the context of schooling again seems perfectly understandable. However, we also detected an unwillingness on Antonia's part both to construct herself as 'other' and indeed to conceptualise Greek ethnicity as 'ethnic' (which is perhaps similar to Harry's anxiety about his ethnic identity, discussed in Chapter 4). We have already seen how difficult it was for the Chinese poster group to make visible the invisible. The presentation of the self might bring benefits in terms of authentication and self-expression, but it also exposes individuals to potential criticism. Nevertheless, Mei King and Ka Wai moved from this kind of personal expression to a much more impersonal definition of their identities in broader cultural terms, which in many ways was a considerable act of bravery. We were never sure whether Antonia was being (reasonably) self-protective, or whether she genuinely could not conceptualise herself in terms of ethnicity.

This ability to conceptualise oneself as part of the larger social formation, which we discussed in some detail in Chapter 6, is taken up from the opposite point of view, as it were, in Stuart's final comments on the project. He wrote:

> I have learned a great deal of knowledge from this interesting project but some would view me as the British (white) colonialist who is racist, etc. At times it was hard for me to fit into the group because I am not from a minority group but I wasn't rejected from the others and I worked with the group who treated everyone equally.

It is very striking that Stuart was able to conceive of himself as the voice of the dominant discourse — which is also, in a sense, a way of seeing oneself as 'other' — and yet find a way of deriving pleasure from the experience. One could argue that Stuart is just being excessively polite, and that his use of terms like 'interesting' is merely an appropriate bourgeois form of deference to the inverted political order of media theory. Yet, almost by definition, this is an issue on which we will never find certainty.[15] In reality, students will take up a number of different positions, and express a range of opinions; and how they work through the implications of each position in their own lives is ultimately beyond our control. And yet, however 'sincere' he may be, the fact that Stuart could consciously reflect on his own position in this way seems to us to be a positive form of learning — and in this sense, it represents something that Antonia was unwilling or unable to take on.

The way in which Stuart rationally positions himself within the theoretical framework of this project (and it should be emphasised that he does so without the spotlight really being on him) provides an interesting comparison with the work discussed in Chapter 6. There, the students were invited to take up distanced positions as researchers. The 'academic' authority to treat other people as objects of scrutiny provided an alibi for what could have been an uncomfortable process — even if, as we argued, the exercise allowed students to develop an understanding of the relationships between the 'personal' and the 'social'.

In contrast to this distanced perspective, we have the extraordinary involvement of the *Slutmo* group. This group had worked before on magazines, and as we have already indicated, they got straight into the process of production without spending any time explicitly considering the theoretical ramifications of the project. It was precisely because of this kind of work that they had wanted to take Media Studies in the first place — even if their lack of interest in contemplating theory could be seen to reveal a lack of *nous* about how to succeed in the examination. This is not to suggest, however, that they had an untheorised approach to the topic. As Clare's comments (quoted above) clearly indicate, women's magazines are already a site of interrogation and conflict about gender roles. The fact that there was a shared understanding in the group about the ideological terrain meant that they did not need a laborious academic map to show the uninitiated around.

We can see quite how emotive and shared the understanding of the ideological conflicts was from Zerrin's account of the magazine. The account is worth quoting at length because it is an extraordinary piece of writing on any terms: the fact that it was produced within the potentially dry confines of an exercise on positive images shows that we cannot simply divorce theoretical analysis from the 'personal' aspects of the work.

> . . . the most original idea was to undermine the other women's magazines, we didn't want to aim for the 'working girl' image and definitely not for the 'housewife and Mummy' look so we decided on having the whole magazine based on the idea of being a slut, who's so outrageous you couldn't believe your eyes. This meant we'd be mocking the other magazines with a 'Tarty' theme with the magazine aimed at the women whose skirt is never short enough, who's worried about her nails breaking and whose dress sense could have been thrown off the back of a lorry instead of just dropped, her lipstick was the cheapest thing going apart from herself that is, and most of all if she looked hot enough for the men?
>
> For this to work as a group we had to think hard of examples of what is slutty/Tarty, it wasn't that hard since being girls, it was easy to think of things that we would never do or wear, we thought of things like ESSEX girls e.g. SHARON and TRACY[16] which was really stereotypical. Also images of white stilettos and black fishnet tights were head off the list, also bright coloured clothes with childish play-like jewellery e.g. plastic earrings, yellow beads, plastic rings, etc.
>
> Its always been easy thinking of slutty things since there's so many things that are considered so-called 'Slutty'. Its even worse to think of why these stereotypical views and ideas are slutty anyway . . . How does anyone know if the way I dress is slutty or not? I expect these views come from old values and expectations of women being 'virgin' who's clean, respectable (listens to parents) and generally does what is seen proper to do. Now young lady/woman in traditional views would be seen as a respectable lady who's willing to keep her legs firmly shut until she gets married to the man of her dreams!!!? Also she must love children, cleaning, sewing, cooking and be a brilliant lover to husband! She must not spend money like there's no tomorrow seeing as she has to make sure there's food to be

eaten, also no unnecessary leaving of the house. Then the final thing is she should dress appropriately e.g. long skirt, shirt, hair back, basically no make-up and no bright pink lipstick . . .

So its easy just think in the completely opposite of these views and you'll have everything to know about sluts/tarts and how to be a slut, that is. So a slut is a woman who can't control her urges, who pastes make-up on, who flirts, who goes out, who drinks, smokes, buys outrageous clothes, with no dress sense, long nails, short skirts, big earrings, fishnet tights, and white stilettos . . .

The contradictions here are obvious enough. If one wants to, it is easy to relate the expectations of Zerrin's repressive Muslim home to the pent-up feelings of this outburst. The compulsive repetitions (there are even more in her original account), the lavish itemising of 'white stilettos' and the detailed descriptions of clashing colours are unsettling for us as male researchers and teachers. Yet before we become consumed by voyeuristic angst, it is worth considering that this may be part of the object of the exercise from Zerrin's point of view. In other words, the piece is as self-consciously resistant as it is expressive;[17] and, as the male readers to whom it is immediately addressed, we are being deliberately implicated in its exploration of sexual identity.

The project clearly allows Zerrin to negotiate her sexuality, and to make connections between media consumption and personal freedom. What is less clear is what she thinks *Slutmo* is aiming to do. Although she appears to acknowledge the parodic intentions of the magazine, she cannot argue through the power relations of being a 'slut':

> We then moved onto the articles that we thought would suit the magazine e.g. the representation of women from this magazine had to be a sexy object, can't do a thing, useless, only good at one thing. Well things like 'How to cook peas in under 3 hours', 'How to replace a light bulb', 25 ways to keep your man', etc. The articles were exaggerated so much so as to look and sound really perfect.

The sheer pleasure Zerrin has derived from being allowed to explore 'sluttishness', and the power she seems to have acquired from simulating oral sex in an imitation 'Flake' advertisement (see Figure 10.3) is only implicitly measured here against the 'respectable' educational discourse. This leads to considerable intellectual confusion. It is not clear whether 'sluts' really do or do not exist, whether they are powerful or powerless, or whether the alternatives to being a slut are actually preferable. Neither is it clear whether the magazine is satirising 'sluts' themselves or those people who are critical of them and who have constructed the stereotype in the first place. Unlike Madonna (the unspoken presence here), Zerrin cannot explicitly acknowledge the 'slut' in herself, and is therefore unable to explain how the magazine uses the slut figure in its satirical message — although, as with

Figure 10.3 Slutmopolitan — Flake advert

Madonna, it is the fundamental ambiguity of the process that is essential if it is to serve the functions that it does.

Broadly speaking, we would argue that the experience of the *Slutmopolitan* project gave Zerrin an unrivalled opportunity to explore issues of gender and sexuality on both a personal and a wider social level. Yet what is puzzling is the extent to which the project 'empowers' Zerrin — whatever we might take that to mean. And what is even more difficult to ascertain is the kind of 'media learning' that might be going on here (and the relationship of that learning to any kind of empowerment). If Zerrin cannot disentangle the levels of parody and power explicitly in her writing, what can one claim for the educational value of the activity? Of course, this question raises a secondary one: the educational value *for whom*? Zerrin, as a 17-year-old girl from a Turkish family, and ourselves, as rapidly ageing, middle-class, male Media Studies teachers, inevitably have different agendas to explore. We can obviously value the way the project gave Zerrin opportunities to explore these issues — although its value for her, like that of *The Rude Boy Serial Killings* or *The Click* (from Chapters 4 and 5), depends largely on its status as a piece of creative work rather than on any attempt to generate a distanced, rational account in the accompanying writing.

This kind of conclusion might appear to reinforce a model of media education that emphasises the merits of academic discourse as the only 'proper' medium for understanding. Yet we would also want to support the very real possibilities that can be offered by this kind of work. What Zerrin was attempting to do here was something rather more complex than simply 'finding a voice'. If anything, what she was finding was a set of multiple, conflicting voices, in which the positions that were available to her were far from stable or fixed. The confusions inherent in her written account reflect the difficulty, but also the honesty, of her attempt to conceptualise herself in broader social terms. The moves in her writing between the personal and the analytical do, like Mei King's account above, indicate an ability to view herself, especially facets of her gender and sexuality, as 'other'. Unlike Antonia's caution about conceptualising herself in other people's ethnic categories, Zerrin leaps into the pleasures of positioning herself in other people's categories of gender. On one level, this difference might be seen to reflect broader social understandings of gender and race, and a sense in which the former may be less socially threatening than the latter. Yet working on the project has clearly allowed Zerrin a comparatively 'safe' space in which she can play with the range of gender positions that are available to her and reflect upon their contradictory possibilities and consequences.

The Meaning of Parody

Slutmopolitan is a complex and thorough piece of work. It comprises 16 pages in full colour. There is a front cover (see Figure 10.4) followed by an advert for 'Tina's Tights', and a back cover which takes the form of a full-page ad for Flake. Inside, there are a number of problem pages, including 'Dear Doreen', who deals with 'the dreaded broken nail'; 'Clare's Clever

Cookery Page', which describes how to cook frozen peas (Figure 10.5); and 'Deirdre's Do-it-Yourself', which explains the complexities of changing a light bulb. In addition, there is a comics page entitled '25 ways to keep your man', as well as letters, beauty and horoscope pages. All in all, *Slutmo* inspired an incredible amount of activity, and its level of detail and production quality bear testimony to the enthusiasm and commitment shown by its authors. The girls used weekends when parents were at work to black out bedrooms for covert photographic sessions, and appeared to work full time for seven weeks on the magazine. There was a very strong sense of shared friendship during this period, although this was, sometimes, tinged with tension. This tension often stemmed from the relationship between the young women as authors and their roles as actors in the various adverts or photo plays in the magazine.

We have already quoted Zerrin's account of the magazine's genesis, and commented on the intellectual contradictions in her writing. But the piece is also remarkable for its sense of excitement and personal involvement in, what was (if only superficially) an academic exercise. Her account makes it almost impossible to distinguish between her subjective investment in the project as a piece of self-expression and her objective interest in the project's avowed intent, which is to parody women's magazines.

However, another perspective from which we could consider the parodic intent of *Slutmo* (and it is one which unites both form and content) is Judith Butler's combination of postmodernist concepts of parody and feminist psychoanalytical theory.[18] In *Gender Trouble,* Butler argues that gender is in itself the 'foundational illusion of identity'. She builds on the concept of the masquerade in Lacan, Riviere and Irigary to develop 'a critical reflection on gender ontology as parodic (de)construction'. This means that gender should be seen not just as a form of behaviour, or as a personal attribute, but in itself as a form of parody that undermines essentialist views of identity or femininity. Using postmodernist theory, she argues that parody is not an imitation of an original but an imitation of a copy whose original can never be discovered. Thus, gender is a continual 'practice' that parodies 'the very notion of an individual'; that is, it functions as a way of exposing identity as fabricated and possessing no 'depth or inner substance'.

It is her comments on the way the body is used in constructing identity that reveals the relevance of her theory to our understanding of *Slutmo*. She writes:

> Gender is the repeated stylisation of the body, a set of repeated acts within a highly rigid regulatory frame that congeal over time to produce the appearance of substance, of a natural sort of being.
>
> (p. 33)

Page after page of *Slutmo* repeats precisely this kind of stylised regulation, as we are shown eye make-up, hair care, nails and laddered stockings, all

Figure 10.4 Slutmopolitan — Front Cover

formulaically laid out and ritualised. The women under attack in the magazine are thus undergoing the process of congealing that Butler describes; and the project of *Slutmo* parodies the surface structures of femininity to expose the constructed nature of gender itself. Thus, one of the ways in which we might read Zerrin's long outburst above is as an articulation of the

Clare's Clever Cookery Class

Hi! I've had plenty of letters from our Clare's Clever Cookery Class fans crying out for my help on cooking those troublesome frozen peas. So here's my very own recipe for all of you who have written to us. You need to put quite a bit of time aside to follow this recipe but we at Slutmopolitan' think that you'll find it worthwhile and quite peasing!!
(You're fired - Ed)

Preparation:

Actual cooking time : about six to eight minutes.
Serves: Measure peas according to number of people present for meal.
Calories per portion: Five.

1.) Gently remove frozen packet of peas from freezer,
2.) With scissors, snip corner of packet and slowly pour however many peas needed into prepared saucepan.
3.) Walk over to your sink and hold saucepan of peas under the COLD WATER tap.
4.) Turn on the cold water tap and fill the saucepan with enough water to cover the peas.
5.) Switch off tap and slowly carry saucepan over to cooker/hob.
6.) Turn on gas/electric to medium heat and place saucepan on hob, making sure it's the same part of the cooker which you have just switched on. A lot of our readers seemed to have this problem, finding dinner parties ruined,
7.) Leave to cook for six to eight minutes, making sure the water does not boil over, or until the peas are reasonably soft.
8.) Remove saucepan from gas and after draining the water, serve.

Clare's Handy Cooking Tips:

* It's worth your while to measure out the peas before cooking. Fill two tablespoons of peas per person and carefully pour into saucepan.
* For extra flavour, place a knob of butter on the peas after you have cooked them, stir with a wooden spoon and serve.

An all time classic, but even great recipes can benefit from a pinch of imagination.

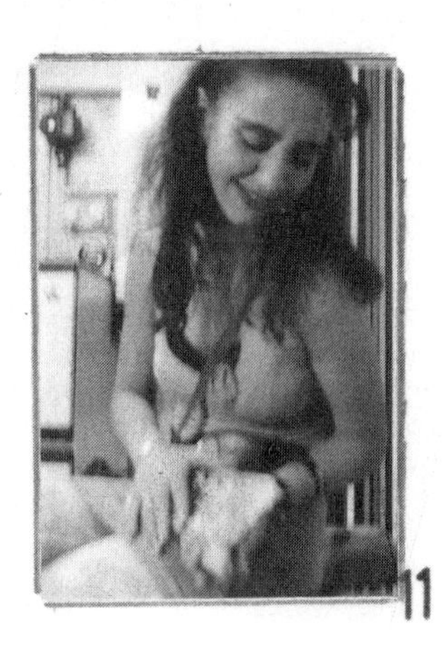

11

Figure 10.5 Clare's Clever Cookery Page

constructed nature of gendered identity. Her repeated attention to the artificial and stylised nature of 'the slut' bears out Butler's argument — even if Zerrin's investment in such a position would be different from Butler's.

As the above would imply, the project raises a number of questions about the role and meaning of parody within the educational process, as well as the forms of distanciation and ambiguity it relies upon, on the part of both readers and writers. The reception of *Slutmo,* and indeed of most of the projects described earlier in the book, foregrounded this double level of meaning. When the work was displayed in class, it attracted a high level of interest from other students in the school, and yet their comments often articulated a critical double standard. Personal comments about the looks or actions of the participants pointed to a secondary level of meaning which was often inaccessible to us as teachers. We have already commented in Chapter 5 on the ways in which peer-group relationships provided their own frame of intertextual reference: from the students' point of view, this level of audience reception was equally as important as our responses to their work, and indeed, their own expectations about its meaning. In this sense, Zerrin's confusions in her written account reflect a recognition that she will ultimately be unable to control the ways in which her peers might read her work.

Slutmo is, like *Viz* or even classic satire like *Gulliver's Travels,* a single extended joke. The fact that the authors and readers found so much pleasure in this extended, almost repetitive, structure is significant because it shows the purchase that the project's thesis has with its audience. As we have already indicated, though, the butt of the joke shifts between the magazine and the putative reader. Thus, on the horoscope page, we have 12 *identical* star signs, because as Clare wrote:

> For the horoscope section I studied several magazines including *Just 17* and *More!* I noticed that most of the horoscopes for each Zodiac sign basically boiled down to the same observation, so I exaggerated this observation so that all twelve Zodiac signs were exactly the same.

Here, the parody is explicitly aimed at the magazines and the genre is wittily and succinctly 'exposed'. The detail of each month's predictions, however, creates ambiguity about the identity of the inscribed reader:

> Love:
> I foresee the man of your dreams entering your life around the 29th. of this month. Be subtle in your approach, he is easily scared. Keep yourself well dressed for an unexpected visitor around the 20th.
>
> Wealth:
> A visit to King's Cross, London will revive your empty purse, but be careful all at once or you will find yourself falling back on financial hardship once again.
>
> Health:
> It's about time you went on a diet. Some of you are looking so flabby and its nearly Christmas! Remember to work on your tan in time for

> the festive season. A good work-out with the muscleman at the local gym would do you the world of good.

If the overall effect of this page, with its neatly laid-out identical predictions, is to satirise the practice of horoscope pages, and thus by implication the gullibility of female readers, the addressee of the actual content is a very different kind of person from the real reader of *Slutmo*: this putative reader is the 'slut' of Zerrin's outburst, the slut who makes money at King's Cross, a well-known haunt of prostitutes, and needs a fake tan for the festive season, presumably for display at the office party. The actual reader would, in effect, be laughing at the inscribed reader — the 'slut' — and it is from this that the irony derives.

Nevertheless, this level of complexity almost seemed to confuse the authors of *Slutmo*. For example, in their analysis of the front cover, which shows the top half of a female torso, revealing bra straps and tattoo, with a dangling CND pendant, two of the authors came up with radically different interpretations. Emma wrote that:

> The . . . photographic text usually marketed an idealised image of a woman for potential readers to desire, identify with and expect to attain through consuming the image.
>
> To contradict this we looked for an upper body shot, without showing the face, of a person purposely dressed in clothes that look sexually expressive. We did this by showing our model wearing a top slipped 'off the shoulder' with her bra straps showing. This being overtly sexual . . . because we are showing a part of a woman's clothing . . . which is usually hidden . . .
>
> The tattoo is again suggesting that the model is sexually overt and undermines the traditional view of a woman as the tattoo is often stereotypically shown as being something a man has. The point that a woman has got a tattoo is showing that she is not a stereotypical woman even though she is dressed and posing in a pejorative manner. Consequently the fact the tattoo is on the model's breast shows she is sexually drawing in the 'gawping' eyes of men to look at this open part of her body.
>
> In accordance, . . . the chain with the CND symbol can show that the woman on the cover is involved and highly intelligent enough to believe in a cause that is often classed as supported by men and strong-feminist women.

This description uses a broadly semiotic approach, and implicitly draws on various academic sources — a point to which we shall return below. The cover, Emma argued, was clearly planned, right down to its use of colour: 'Once more we disputed the traditional view of the way the magazine should look by intentionally using colours that did not match, for example red and luminous orange.' However, this kind of semiotic analysis was also used to support a radically different reading on the part of Clare. Her account of the front cover stated that:

> . . . the purpose of [the CND pendant] was to give the impression that the 'tart' was wearing it for fashion purposes rather than endearment towards the cause of nuclear disarmament.

We could argue, from these accounts, that Emma and Clare both demonstrate a detailed analytical capacity to deconstruct the front covers of women's magazines; but their differing interpretations of the meaning of the CND pendant stem from the ambiguous way in which *Slutmo* offers a range of ironic reading positions.

Ultimately, the fact that they can make such a complicated product does not mean that they can understand it with the same degree of complexity — or at least (and this is a crucial distinction) *demonstrate to us* that they can understand it. This apparent contradiction calls into question what it might mean to 'understand' their reading and writing in this context. There is clearly a level of 'understanding', operating here, which allows them to make the cover, with all its attention to semiotic detail in the first place; but that level is not necessarily replicated in the language of critical reflection. In a sense, however, this notion of understanding only becomes an issue if we take *our* reading of the magazine as in some way offering a higher level of truth, one which the students are slowly labouring to reach — or in other words, if we simply measure their understanding against ours, and take ours as the aim of the exercise. Given their subjective and ideological investment in this project, is it in any way reasonable for us, as male teachers, to make our reading of the project its preferred meaning? And how, then, do we locate the learning in this form of complex parody?

It is perhaps surprising, given the importance of parody in students' work and the ongoing anxieties about the dangers of 'imitation', that this question has not been explored in any great detail. Gemma Moss's work, for example, offers a broadly positive account of the ways in which students can use popular genres in their writing, but largely avoids this issue.[19] To an extent, as we have implied, the problem is a methodological one. On the one hand, we might say that parody — and hence the learning that might be seen to derive from parody — is in the eye of the beholder.[20] Yet on the other hand, the issue is also one of intent and explicitness. In what sense, and on what level, does the parody contain a critique of what it seeks to criticise? This then raises the question whether one can criticise through parody or whether it is an intermediate stage in the development of critical awareness. Can one mock something without understanding why? Or can one imitate without understanding? And from whose point of view can these questions be answered — that of the addressee of the imitation or that of the author? We will look at a few more pages of '*Slutmo*' to pursue the argument.

Some of the most effective pages in *Slutmo* are the advice columns. 'Clare's Clever Cookery Class' (Fig. 10.5) describes how to cook frozen peas. The illustrated page opens with a direct address from Clever Clare:

> Hi! I've had plenty of letters from our Clare's Clever Cookery Class fans crying out for my help in cooking those troublesome frozen peas. So here's my very own recipe for all of you who have written to us. You need to put quite a bit of time aside to follow this recipe but we at *Slutmopolitan* mag think you'll find it worthwhile and quite peasing!! (You're fired — Ed)

There then follow eight step-by-step instructions on how to open a packet of peas and boil them. The use of alliteration, innuendo, clichés ('those troublesome frozen peas') and a condescending tone ('you need to put quite a bit of time aside') all point immediately towards a certain level of parody. In addition, there are the stylistic echoes of other magazines — '(You're fired — Ed)' — as well as the absurd illustrations of a scantily dressed model attempting to open a packet of peas in a 'provocative' pose. Yet, the page could be seen to be mocking *both* the style of cookery pages and the putative readers, who could not do anything as basic as open a packet of peas.

There is a similar mode of parody in operation in the photostory/problem page 'Dear Doreen', which deals with the trauma of the broken nail, and in the 'Deirdre's Do-it-yourself' section, which tells you how to change a light bulb. Again, innuendo is a vital part of the humour, as Deirdre advises readers to 'practise screwing and inserting techniques'. Somewhat more pointed, however, is the feature on '25 ways to keep your man'. This is a series of comic drawings and *bon mots* which mix the absurd — 'Cut off his legs' — with the smutty — 'Screw him to the back of the door (then do it literally!!!)'. The cruel and the comic climax with the 25th piece of advice: 'MARRY HIM'.

As these examples suggest, there is no consistent mode of parody in the magazine. We have concentrated on the verbal humour because it is less contentious to argue its satirical intent. The visual dimension is equally important, but because the codes of visual parody remain unstated, they can often pass unnoticed. (Thus, for example, the layout for a jumper was elaborately contrived to look like the classic knitting feature.) The satirical poses of the models are fairly obvious, although there may be further level of parody in the colour combinations (as noted by Zerrin above) that we at least find much harder to spot.

The question of intent is clearly crucial to our reading of parody. Parody only becomes parodic, it is assumed, if it is conscious and deliberate: otherwise, it is imitation, and could be criticised for merely reproducing what it seeks to mock. But it is clearly diffic ılt for us to determine such parodic intent in the case of a cultural form, women's magazines, with which we are bound to have a very different relationship compared with the authors. Of course, on one level, this difficulty can be magically resolved through reference to the students' written accounts. There, the discourse of rational explanation can reassure us that the parody is deliberate and also that it stems from a coherent and intellectually respectable theory about the representation of women. And the parody could then be seen as a stratagem aimed at the heart of patriarchy.

The problem, of course, is that the accounts do not say this, or at least not as explicitly as we would like. Even if, like Mei King's account, they were to explain the theory and relate it, with equal precision, to the product itself, then the product would not be able to contain the depth and variety of meaning that we have argued it does. In other words, the parody enables us to explore contradictions and multiple readings precisely *because* we cannot anchor its meaning; whereas theoretical discourse has problems with more than one idea at a time. Theory might reassure *us* about the ideological positions that our students are taking up; but that may not be the aim of the students in this kind of practical work — even if we think it ought to be.

The other point to make is that theory is, with due deference to our readers, boring. It is, by definition, the very opposite of 'having a laugh'. As we argued in Chapter 8, one of the weaknesses of a Vygotskyan approach is that it privileges the cognitive over the affective. It offers us no way of making sense of humour, which we would argue is often central to learning, particularly when it concerns questions of cultural identity. The 'laugh' had by all the *Slutmo* group is about more than just having a good time. As Bakhtin argued in his analysis of Rabelais, the carnival allows structured subversion of the dominant order. If we search for evidence of learning only in the domain of rational discourse, this is bound to limit the kind of learning that we can find. In that sense, parody (despite or perhaps because of, its essential ambiguity) offers a qualitatively different kind of evidence of critical understanding. *Slutmo* might well be seen as a kind of carnival or 'heteroglossic' (multiple-voiced) text; and as such, it embodies its own form of critical discourse.[21]

Of course, it is true that Emma's writing does make explicit reference to semiotic theory, and uses a number of relevant academic texts in its analysis of *Slutmo*.[22] It seems to us that this does slightly more than just reassure uncertain examiners or readers of the magazine that it really is as 'right-on', in its own way, as *Feminist Review*. Emma has learnt to make explicit reference to larger bodies of ideas, and to use concepts such as ideology; and while we would not want to make enormous claims for this, it does seem to us that it has made a difference. In a sense, however, the crucial question is whether the reverse is true: does Zerrin, whose writing does not begin to approach Emma's objective and rationalistic critique, really 'understand' what she has been doing? And if her understanding is 'only' on the level of parody, rather than explicit critique, or 'merely' a matter of felt experience, does this necessarily make it any less significant than Emma's? The obvious answer is that it is different; but how *we* interpret that difference may only say more about the ways in which *we* value particular kinds of knowledge and discourse than it does about our students' own understandings and pleasures.

Politics, Popular Culture and Learning

Before we move towards our conclusion, we want to consider some of the more specific implications of our arguments in these last two chapters. First of all, we want to distinguish between the notions of carnival and play that we have employed in our analysis of *Slutmo* and the ways in which these ideas are sometimes used in debates about popular culture. John Fiske, for example, uses Bakhtin in support of an argument that comes close to being an uncritical celebration of popular culture.[23] In this account, 'the people' are invested with a mythical and hedonistic power to resist, appropriate and subvert dominant discourses and power relations. We have argued that, although *Slutmo* does possess many features that would support Fiske's viewpoint, it is still a fraught and contradictory text, one which appears simultaneously to reproduce and to subvert 'dominant values'. Our interest here is not in developing a totalising theory about the cultural significance of such texts. On the contrary, we have been at pains to delineate their local and contingent meanings, showing how they are situated within the specific social relationships of production and consumption. More to the point, we are interested in what the students might *learn* from producing such texts: and here too, we are regarding meaning not as something contained within the text but as part of a broader social and pedagogic process.

In the last chapter, we argued that 'becoming critical' was by no means a simple process that could be deduced from the outward form of critical writing. In this chapter, we have suggested that there may be other ways in which one can become critical — for example, through parody and humour. Yet this is also a process that we need to evaluate and to question. The 'critical' nature of practical work in Media Studies, like the critical nature of theoretical writing, is bound to be determined by those discourses and social contexts in which it is produced. 'Being critical' is not a higher state of grace into which the elect are received. On the contrary, it is a social practice which takes place within specific social contexts and relationships.

Ultimately, what lies at the heart of our investigation is a deep scepticism about the role of academic theory, and its claim to serve as the privileged means of social change. Academics in Cultural Studies have often been keen to carve out dramatic political roles for themselves — yet they have rarely shown more than a token interest in the processes by which their students might learn theory, or make sense of it in terms of their own lived experiences. There is an implicit vanguardist politics here, according to which academic theory is seen to have the power to dispel the illusions of ideology from which other people suffer. Elizabeth Ellsworth's critique of 'critical pedagogy' is relevant in this context.[24] She acutely exposes the power relations implicit in the so-called radical practice of 'teaching for liberation', and argues that such practice often presupposes

> a teacher who knows the object of study 'better' than do the students . . . The discourse on student voice sees the student as 'empowered' when the teacher 'helps' students express their subjugated knowledge.
>
> (pp. 308–9)

Ellsworth moves towards arguing for 'a pedagogy of the unknowable', in which the knowledge and the discourse of the teacher is no longer privileged over those of the 'oppressed' groups themselves. We would be deluding ourselves if we imagined that *Slutmo* 'empowered' its authors by transforming them into feminists — and indeed, that was a label that the authors themselves were keen to refuse. As Chris Richards[25] points out, the notion of 'empowerment' often rests on the peculiar assumption that students will perceive teachers and their knowledge as powerful and then seek to gain access to it for this reason. Yet, while the idea that knowledge is power may be reassuring for those who possess educational capital, it may not necessarily be shared by those who lack economic capital.

We have argued that learning about popular culture can provide important opportunities for exploring questions of identity and subjectivity, as well as their relationships with broader social forces. We would see this as an inherently political process — although whether it ultimately makes any difference to the students' personal or social lives must remain an open question. The work recorded in this book may have demonstrated local and partial gains in confidence, argumentation and expression, but what the future pay-offs may be it is impossible to say. Clearly, it would be mistaken to confuse critical awareness with political change. Yet in the end, such issues merely serve to beg even larger questions about how political change might occur in the first place. The work that we have done certainly seems to have energised and motivated working-class students whose life chances are severely crippled in the current political climate. Yet, in the end, this may simply be a depressing reflection on how ineffective schools have been in engaging with these students' perspectives and concerns.

Notes

1. For an overview, see Buckingham (1987b); and for an early account of the differences between 'progressive' and 'radical' (or 'alternative' and 'oppositional') approaches, see Collins (1976).

2. The most notable example here is Ferguson (1981)
3. See Buckingham (1987b) and Stafford (1990).
4. See Masterman (1980, Ch. 6).
5. See Stafford (*ibid*).
6. See Buckingham (1994 forthcoming).
7. Notably Moss (1989); and for a discussion of children's reading of popular genres, see Sarland (1991).
8. See Buckingham (1983) and Sefton-Green (1990).
9. See Bailey and Hall (1992) and Hevey (1992).
10. See Bailey and Hall (*ibid*).
11. For a parallel discussion of problems faced by Media Studies students in higher education, see Williamson (1981/2).
12. See Hevey (*ibid*).
13. See Gilroy (1987) and Gillespie (1994, forthcoming).
14. For a highly theoretical account of this notion, see Bhabha (1986).
15. This could be seen as one of the most prevalent neuroses of media teaching: see, for example, Williamson (1981/2) and Richards (1990).
16. 'Essex girls' were effectively invented by the popular press in 1992, as a local variant of the 'bimbo/slut' stereotype. 'Sharon and Tracy' may be a reference to the characters in the BBC series *Birds of a Feather*; however, while these characters do come from Essex, they do not really fit the image that Zerrin is describing here. Alternatively, these names are often used disparagingly as identikit white working-class names; and perhaps this is how Zerrin is using them here.
17. This could be related to the ways in which working-class girls are seen to use traditional forms of sexuality as a means of self-empowerment: see Payne (1980).
18. See Butler (1990).
19. See Moss (1989).
20. This issue is considered briefly in Buckingham (1990b, Ch. 2).
21. See Bakhtin (1968). This analysis could be extended by considering the powerful role of the body in *Slutmo*, given Bakhtin's observations about the role of the body in the carnival.
22. See, in particular, McCracken (1993).
23. See, for example, Fiske (1989).
24. See Ellsworth (1989).
25. See Richards (1992).

Chapter 11

Conclusion: Dialogues with the Future

The notion of learning about popular culture as a form of dialogue has been a central theme of this book. Indeed, the book itself could be seen as a further move in a continuing dialogue about the relationship between education and culture — a dialogue that has taken on an urgent political significance in recent years, but which continues to be dominated by abstract rhetoric. By contrast, we have sought to ground our arguments in a detailed account of our own teaching experience; and it is partly from our reflections upon this experience and from our close reading of the data we have collected that our theoretical positions have emerged. Nevertheless, our arguments have also arisen from a history of dialogues with other theoretical perspectives; it is this history that has equally determined how we make sense of our experience and our data.

Thus, in considering our students' readings and uses of popular culture, we have argued against the behaviourist assumptions of 'effects' theory, as these are manifested both in academic and in popular debates about young people and the media. In particular, we have challenged the assumption that young people can be seen simply as ideological dupes or victims of media influence. On the contrary, we have argued that young people *actively* use popular media as symbolic resources for creating their own meanings and social identities. Yet we have also sought to distance ourselves from a celebratory account of this process, which would see young people as wholly autonomous and popular culture as a form of 'resistance' to dominant ideologies. As we have shown, the ideological consequences of 'activity' on the part of audiences cannot be determined in the abstract: 'active' readings are of course not necessarily 'resistant' or 'empowering'. Young people's use of the media often involves both 'resistance' *and* 'reproduction'; and its ideological significance needs to be interpreted within the social contexts and interpersonal relationships in which it is situated.

Similarly, in making a case for teaching about popular culture, we have challenged the élitism and irrelevance of the 'cultural heritage' approach embodied in the revised National Curriculum for English. At the same time, we have also questioned the 'radical' notion of media education as a form of 'demystification', which will liberate students from the false ideologies that the media are seen to impose upon them. As we have argued, these seemingly opposite views have a great deal in common, particularly in terms of their view of young people as passive, uncritical consumers of the media, and of teachers as the bearers of objective political or cultural values. On the other hand, we have also pointed to the dangers of a 'progressive' approach to teaching about popular culture; while we would accept the need to recognise and to validate students' existing knowledge, we want to do more than simply leave them where they already are. In critically applying a Vygotskyan approach, we have sought to offer an alternative theory of 'media learning' that moves beyond the opposition between these perspectives and emphasises the importance of reflection and of the dynamic relationship between different language modes.

It is through this implicit (and occasionally explicit) dialogue with these alternative positions that we have attempted to define our own approach. Yet in the process, we have also sought to draw attention to questions which we feel are in need of further debate and investigation. We have questioned the way in which media education often appears to privilege rationalistic theory, and to neglect the potential of practical production; yet we have also pointed to the difficulty of identifying what students might actually be learning from either aspect. We have focused on the theoretical problems of 'reading' and evaluating students' work, and have questioned the ways in which, as teachers, we need to have our students' learning 'demonstrated' to us.

Above all, perhaps, we have sought to question what it means to be 'critical' about popular culture. Is teaching about popular culture simply a way of initiating students into another academic discipline, another form of cultural capital, that will serve to distinguish the 'haves' from the 'have-nots'? Some of our students have certainly perceived it in this way; we have taught them the discourse of academic Media Studies, and they have used it in their writing with a degree of knowingness, even cynicism. One of the things that we have all learnt is that you get extra marks for using words like 'deconstruction' and 'ideology' — even if (and this is definitely our cynicism speaking) you don't really understand what they mean. Is Media Studies (or Cultural Studies) anything more than 'low culture for highbrows', to use the slogan of the *Modern Review*? Is it just about learning to 'talk posh' — as our students would say — about things that everybody else just talks about normally?

This is an issue which is, if anything, even more urgent for those involved in teaching and studying popular culture in higher-education. Certainly in Britain, Media and Cultural Studies courses in universities are booming. Yet there are important questions to be asked about the functions of these courses for students — both in broader political terms, and in terms of eventual employment. The study of working-class popular culture clearly has a very different significance for middle-class university students, as compared with the students described in this book, and we might feel even more justified in questioning its political consequences. Is Media Studies at this level simply a form of 'initiation into that new elect of justified sinners, the culturally undoped', as James Donald[1] has put it? And how effectively have such courses managed to relate 'theory' and 'practice', or the 'academic' and the 'vocational' aspects of the subject? These are clearly issues that raise much broader theoretical and political questions, of the kind that we have sought to address here: questions about the relationships between the subjective and the social, the rational and the emotional, and the cognitive and the discursive, and indeed about the value of such distinctions in the first place. Yet these issues also imply a need for honest, detailed investigation of one's own teaching, of the kind that academics in Cultural Studies have rarely attempted.

The increasing popularity of media education is, of course, a response to changing circumstances. While the burgeoning growth of such courses has been partly 'market-led' — in the sense that they almost invariably attract students, and hence resources — it must also be seen as a response to much more fundamental cultural changes. Despite the reassertion of a 'cultural heritage' model of English teaching in the revised National Curriculum, the days of English as an academic discipline are clearly numbered. And in terms of compulsory schooling, the need for a fundamental reconsideration of notions of culture and literacy — and hence of the aims and methods of the central discipline of English — is rapidly becoming an urgent priority.

It is in the interests of promoting this broader reconsideration of literacy that we have constantly returned to metaphors of reading and writing. In common with a growing body of research, we have argued that literacy should not be narrowly defined in terms of instrumental skills, as much current public debate is inclined to do. Rather than regarding literacy as an act of individual cognition, we have consistently sought to locate it within a wider set of social practices and relationships. The empirical studies in the book have attempted to identify the dynamic structures of such a social conception of literacy.

In arguing for a wider, contemporary definition of literacy, and for a curriculum that is responsive to the changing cultural competencies of young people in the late 20th century, we cannot afford to remain tied to a unitary, inflexible notion of 'media literacy'. On the contrary, we need to ensure that we are able to engage with those radical and diverse notions of reading and writing that are emerging from current social and technological changes.

A particular example of these new notions of reading and writing can be found in Alan Durant's exploration of changing definitions of literacy in relationship to contemporary music-making.[2] Examining the influence of technological developments in music making, he argues that the digitalisation of sound and the computerisation of composition methods means that 'reading' music is no longer a matter of interpreting musical scores, but is now crucially dependent upon a knowledge of the relevant software programmes. Equally, the nature of 'writing' music is shifting away from the specialised knowledge of traditional musical notation and towards 'sampling', or creative production. In this context, even 'listening' to music takes on a different meaning from traditional concepts of musical literacy.

This more flexible notion of media literacy has implications for both 'production' and 'consumption' — and indeed for the changing relationship between them. The notion of the 'postmodern' provides one possible means of defining these developments — although, of course, there are some very diverse and competing definitions of that term. Studies of 'postmodern' texts from a wide range of media have identified a repertoire of distinctive features that will come to determine the ways in which young people learn to 'read' in future decades. For example, Jim Collins' *Uncommon Cultures* identifies several facets of the postmodernist text, many of which we have observed in our discussions of students' work.[3] Thus, for example, deconstructing the authority of the law is a feature of Ponyboy's story writing; and self-reflexivity is common to many of the photostories analysed in Chapter 5. Collins describes as follows the complex web of intertextual relationships he finds in modern culture:

> . . . the post-modernist text constructs *polylogic* rather than dialogic relationships with 'already saids', where the relationship between past and present coding is based on interaction and transformation instead of simple rejection.
>
> (p. 134)

This kind of argument might well be applied both to the parodic text of *Slutmo* and to the complex social processes by which the meanings found in *Slutmo* are constructed.

In common with many other accounts of postmodernity, Collins' book argues strongly for a rejection of élitist and sterile oppositions between high and popular culture; postmodern culture is seen here not as a reflection of alienation and meaninglessness but as vibrant, diverse and creative. Our students' 'failure' to engage in debates about high and low culture at the end of Chapter 7 may not only point to the fact that such debate is in itself the concern of the few but may also indicate a genuine democratisation in the sphere of culture. We may well be moving beyond such traditional binary oppositions and towards a much more pluralist — or indeed 'multicultural' — model of culture.

Yet, literacy in the postmodern age will be determined not only by the structure of texts but also by the situations in which we encounter them, as well as by the technologies by which they are produced and distributed. The changing nature of the domestic and social contexts in which texts are used and read, combined with the increasing dominance of digital technologies, is altering the very acts of reading and writing. Thus, developments in 'interactive' media forms, from home shopping through computer games to hypertext, all imply a very different relationship between reader and text than is the case in relation to print. Hypertext provides an extreme example of this. Defined as simultaneously 'a form of electronic text, a radically new information technology and a mode of publication', it is both a way of reading and a description of 'text'.[4] It has been described as the embodiment of Barthes' 'writerly' text, giving the reader the power almost to construct what she or he wants to read. And as the CD ROM format grows in popularity, so, it is argued, we will move from the expectation that narrative is linear to a new model of reader-centred circularity.

This in turn challenges established notions of what exactly constitutes texts and readers in the first place. For example, in what sense can we talk about a computer game or a hypertext package as a 'text'? Super Mario and his rivals would seem to be caught up in a much broader move in children's culture, towards what has been termed 'trans-media intertextuality' — in effect, a blurring of boundaries between texts and between media:[5] the computer games obviously borrow from other media sources — from films, comics and books — and the computer-game characters reappear in television programmes and in films. Yet the games are also part of a wider system of cross-media merchandising (namely of posters, stickers, clothes, lunch boxes, toys and even food); and this is reinforced by economic diversification and integration, and the increasingly complex patterns of cross-ownership among media corporations. We are rapidly reaching the point where it is impossible to talk about these media separately, or even to begin by focusing simply on texts.

In combination with other forms of digital technology, particularly hypertext, the popularity of computer games has brought about a fundamental change in notions of reading and authorship.[6] Computer games are not obviously 'authored', nor are they 'read' in the same way as books or even television programmes. The increasing availability of reproduction technology — computers, video recorders, photocopiers — has resulted in a massive increase in piracy and copyright theft, which may eventually undermine the notions of intellectual property and authorship that formed the basis of print culture. New production technologies, particularly the bringing together of sound, image, text and moving image into multimedia, may also be contributing to this fundamental blurring of the distinction between consumers and producers; and their availability in schools and perhaps increasingly in the home has profound implications for the content and pedagogy of media education.

Of course, these technological developments cannot be seen in isolation: they need to be situated within the broader social and cultural changes of which they are a part. Yet the signs here are, to say the least, contradictory.

On the one hand, it is possible to identify a broadly positive account, like Collins', which emphasises the democratic potential of such developments, as well as the potential diversity of expression and communication that they may permit. Thus, it is argued, these new production technologies may begin to abolish distinctions between readers and writers or between consumers and producers; they can permit new kinds of lateral communication, as opposed to vertical, top-down communication. Combined with the gradual restructuring of the major broadcasting institutions, and with much greater reliance on freelance labour throughout the media industries, they may be contributing to a blurring of the division between 'amateur' and professional production, and to a much more diverse and heterogeneous public sphere in which previously marginalised cultural identities can now be asserted and developed.

Other critics, however, have argued that there is a much more pessimistic account which emphasises the growing fragmentation of contemporary societies and the increasing control of commerce. From this perspective, such technological developments would be seen as part of a more disturbing reduction of the public sphere, in which collective leisure is increasingly privatised and forced back into the home. Critics of such developments point to the possibility that all forms of cultural expression will degenerate into empty pastiche, an endless self-referential manipulation of pre-existing images. In many ways, computer games, hypertext and multi-media do seem to represent a technological embodiment of this postmodern nightmare, in which images have become unhinged from meanings and the boundaries between reality and virtual reality are dissolved. Far from envisaging more active forms of citizenship, this account sees the individual as reduced to a mere consumer, 'zapping' aimlessly in front of the flickering screen.

At present, however, the major problem with most accounts of postmodern culture is that of sufficiency of evidence. The 'turn to postmodernism' in Cultural Studies often seems to have resulted in a retreat into mystical abstractions that precisely fail to engage with the cultural developments they are supposedly analysing. Theoretical notions of 'the end of the social' or 'the destruction of meaning' are, we would argue, simply rhetorical fancies that are of little value in attempting to explain the complex role of popular culture in those technological developments described above. Ultimately, they reflect the unreality not of the lives of ordinary people but of the self-regarding discourse of academics themselves.

What the best accounts of postmodern culture seem to represent is not an abandonment of explanation, or a dissolution of everything into infinite difference and meaninglessness.[7] On the contrary, they offer a detailed account of economic changes in patterns of work and leisure in the organisation of production, distribution and exchange, and the cultural implications of those changes. These accounts point to the increasing mobility of post-industrial societies, the blurring and breaking down of traditional boundaries, and the dissolution of familiar identities both at the level of the community and of the nation. But they also identify continuing inequalities of power, not least in terms of traditional categories such as gender, social class and ethnicity.

Any discussion of the complexities of these debates, or of their broader political implications, is well beyond the scope of our study here. Nevertheless, we should not underestimate the massive social dislocations that will result from these changes, and their fundamental educational implications. If the curriculum is to equip students for an increasingly technological, media-oriented society — not merely in the field of work, but also in that of leisure — it will need to be based on much broader notions of literacy and culture than those which currently prevail. In general terms, the vital need is surely to preserve what is good and valuable about print literacy while at the same time embracing the egalitarian and creative potential of the new media technologies. The notion of English teaching as a means of preserving an atrophied cultural heritage, a notion currently being reasserted in the revised National Curriculum, offers no position from which to accomplish this. It represents a view of English that fundamentally neglects the cultural experiences and competencies of the vast majority of young people; as such, it will merely result in irrelevance and incoherence.

Ultimately, media education itself will also need to be redefined. It will need to move beyond its traditional focus on texts and pay closer attention to the ways in which texts are socially circulated and used. In this context, the specialist study of particular *media* will need to be located within the broader study of cultural processes: Media Studies (like English) will need to become part of a broader discipline, one which might be termed *Cultural Studies.* Yet, as we have consistently argued in this book, this is not to call for yet another academic discipline, or for the transmission of a different body of academic theory. On the contrary, any such development will need to be based on a thorough understanding of, and respect for, the 'everyday' competencies and theories that students develop through their own cultural experiences. The social and cultural worlds in which these students will come of age is going to be radically different from ours. If our teaching is to enable them to participate in these new worlds, we need to begin a dialogue not just with the past but also with the future.

Notes

1. See Donald (1990).
2. See Durant (1990).
3. See Collins (1989).
4. See Landow (1992).
5. See Kinder (1991).
6. See Tuman (1992).
7. See, particularly, Harvey (1989).

References

ADORNO, T. and HORKHEIMER, M. (1979) *Dialectic of Enlightenment*, London: Verso.

ALVARADO, M. (1981) Television Studies and Pedagogy, *Screen Education* **38**, 56–67.

ALVARADO, M., GUTCH, R. and WOLLEN, T. (1987) *Learning the Media*, Basingstoke: Macmillan.

ALVARADO, M. and BOYD-BARRETT, O. (Ed.) (1992) *Media Education: An Introduction*, London: British Film Institute/Open University Press.

ANG, I. (1985) *Watching Dallas: Soap Opera and the Melodramatic Imagination*, London: Methuen.

ANG, I. (1989) Wanted: audiences — on the politics of empirical audience studies. in SEITER, E. *et al* (Ed.) *Remote Control: Television, Audiences and Cultural Power*, London: Routledge.

BAILEY, D. A. and HALL, S. (Ed.) (1992) *Critical Decade: Black British Photography in the 80s*, Birmingham: Ten 8.

BAKHTIN, M. (1968) *Rabelais and his World.* Iswolsky, H., Cambridge, Mass.: MIT Press.

BAKHTIN, M. (1981) *The Dialogic Imagination.* Emerson, C. and Holquist, M., Austin: University of Texas Press.

BALL, S., KENNY, A. and GARDINER, D. (1990) Literacy, politics and the teaching of English, in GOODSON, I. and MEDWAY, P. (Ed.) *Bringing English to Order*, London: Falmer Press.

BARKER, M. (1993) Seeing how far you can see: on being a 'fan' of *2000AD*, in BUCKINGHAM, D. (Ed.) *Reading Audiences: Young People and the Media*, Manchester: Manchester University Press.

BATSLEER, J. *et al* (1985) *Rewriting English: Cultural Politics of Gender and Class*, London: Methuen.

BAZALGETTE, C. (Ed.) (1989) *Primary Media Education: A Curriculum Statement*, London: British Film Institute.

BERNSTEIN, B. (1971) *Class, Codes and Control, Volume 1*, London: Routledge and Kegan Paul.

BETHELL, A. (1981) *EyeOpeners*, Cambridge: Cambridge University Press.

BETHELL, A. (1984) Media Studies, in MILLER, J. (Ed.) *Eccentric Propositions*, London: Routledge and Kegan Paul.

BETHELL, A. (1985) *The Media Tapes*, London: Methuen.

BEZENCENET, S. and CORRIGAN, P. (Ed.) (1986) *Photographic Practices*, London: Comedia.

BHABHA, H. (1986) The other question: difference, discrimination and the discourse of colonialism, in BARKER, F. *et al* (Ed.) *Literature, Politics & Theory: Papers from the Essex Conference 1976–84,* London: Methuen.

BILLIG, M. *et al* (1988) *Ideological Dilemmas,* London: Sage.

BLANCHARD, T., GREENLEAF, S. and SEFTON-GREEN, J. (1989) *The Music Business; a Teaching Pack,* London: Hodder and Stoughton.

BORDWELL, D. and THOMPSON, K. (1979) *Film Art: An Introduction,* Reading, Mass.: Addison-Wesley.

BOURDIEU, P. (1977) *Reproduction in Education, Society and Culture* (trans. Nice, R.), London: Sage.

BOURDIEU, P. (1984) *Distinction: A Social Critique of the Judgement of Taste* (trans. Nice, R.), London: Routledge and Kegan Paul.

BOWKER, J. (Ed.) (1991) *Secondary Media Education: A Curriculum Statement,* London: British Film Institute.

BRITZMAN, D. (1991) Decentering discourses in teacher education: or, the unleashing of popular things, *Journal of Education (Boston),* **173**, (3), 60–80.

BROOKER, P. and HUMM, P. (1989) *Dialogue and Difference: English into the Nineties,* London: Routledge.

BUCKINGHAM, D. (1983) Positive images? Some observations on racism in educational media, *Multicultural Teaching,* **2**, (1) 20–29.

BUCKINGHAM, D. (1986) Against Demystification, *Screen,* **27**, (5) 80–95.

BUCKINGHAM, D. (1987a) *Public Secrets: EastEnders and its Audience,* London: British Film Institute.

BUCKINGHAM, D. (1987b) Unit 27: Media Education, EH207 Communication and Education Course Unit, Milton Keynes: Open University Press.

BUCKINGHAM, D. (1989) Television literacy: a critique, *Radical Philosophy,* **51**, 12–25.

BUCKINGHAM, D. (1990a) English and Media: Making the Difference, *English and Media Magazine,* **23**, 8–12.

BUCKINGHAM, D. (Ed.) (1990b) *Watching Media Learning: Making Sense of Media Education,* London: Falmer Press.

BUCKINGHAM, D. (1991) Teaching about the media, in LUSTED, D. (Ed.) *The Media Studies Book: a Guide for Teachers,* London: Routledge.

BUCKINGHAM, D. (1992) Sex, lies and newsprint: Young people reading *The Sun, English and Media Magazine,* **26**, 38–42.

BUCKINGHAM, D. (1993a) *Changing Literacies: Media Education and Modern Culture,* The London File: papers from the Institute of Education, London: Tufnell Press.

BUCKINGHAM, D. (Ed.) (1993b) *Reading Audiences: Young People and the Media,* Manchester: Manchester University Press.

BUCKINGHAM, D. (1993c) *Children Talking Television: the Making of Television Literacy,* London: Falmer Press.

BUCKINGHAM, (1993d) Just Playing Games, *English and Media Magazine,* **28**, 20–25.

BUCKINGHAM, D. (1994 forthcoming) Media education and the media industries: bridging the gaps, *British Journal of Education and Work.*

BURGESS, T. (1993) Reading Vygotsky, in DANIELS, H. (Ed.) *Charting the Agenda: Educational Activity After Vygotsky,* London: Routledge.

BUTLER, J. (1990) *Gender Trouble, Feminism and the Subversion of Identity,* London: Routledge.

CARR, W. and KEMMIS, S. (1990) *Becoming Critical,* London: Falmer Press.

CARTER, R. (Ed.) (1990) *Knowledge about Language in the Curriculum: the LINC Reader,* London: Hodder and Stoughton.

COHEN, P. (1988) The perversions of inheritance: studies in the making of multi-racist Britain, in COHEN, P. and BAINS, H. (Ed.) *Multi-Racist Britain,* Basingstoke: Macmillan.

COHEN, P. (1990) *Really Useful Knowledge,* London: Trentham Books.
COLE, ?. (1990) Cognitive development and formal schooling: the evidence from cross-cultural research, in MOLL, L. (Ed.) *Vygotsky and Education,* Cambridge: Cambridge University Press.
COLLINS, J. (1989) *Uncommon Cultures: Popular Culture and Post-modernism,* New York: Routledge.
COLLINS, J. (1991) Batman: the movie, narrative: the 'Hyperconscious', in PEARSON, R. and URICCHIO, W. (Ed.) *The Many Lives of the Batman: Critical Approaches to a Superhero and his Media,* New York: Routledge and British Film Institute.
COLLINS, R. (1976) Media Studies: alternative or oppositional practice?, in WHITTY, G. and YOUNG, M. (Ed.) *Explorations in the Politics of School Knowledge,* Driffield: Nafferton Books.
CORCORAN, B. and EVANS, E. (Ed.) (1987) *Readers, Texts, Teachers,* Milton Keynes: Open University Press.
CULLINGFORD, C. (1984) *Children and Television,* Aldershot: Gower.
DAVIES, B. (1989) *Frogs and Snails and Feminist Tales,* Sydney: Allen and Unwin.
DEWDNEY, A. and LISTER, M. (1988) *Youth, Culture and Photography,* Basingstoke: Macmillan.
DONALD, J. (1990) Review of Allen's *Channels of Discourse* and Fiske's *Television Culture, Screen,* **31**, (1), 113–118.
DOYLE, B. (1989) *English and Englishness,* London: Routledge.
DURANT, A. (1990) A new day for music? Digital technologies in contemporary music making, in HAYWOOD, P. (Ed.) *Culture, Technology and Creativity in the Late Twentieth Century,* London: John Libbey/Arts Council.
EAGLETON, T. (1983) *Literary Theory,* Oxford: Basil Blackwell.
EDWARDS, D. and MERCER, N. (1987) *Common Knowledge: the Development of Understanding in the Classroom,* London: Methuen.
ELLSWORTH, E. (1989) Why Doesn't This Feel Empowering? Working through the Repressive Myths of Critical Pedagogy, *Harvard Educational Review,* **59**, (3), 297–324.
FERGUSON, B. (1981) Practical work and pedagogy, *Screen Education,* **38**, 42–55.
FERRARI, L. and JAMES, C. (Ed.) (1989) *Wham! Wrapping: Teaching the Music Industry,* London: British Film Institute.
FISKE, J. (1987a) *Television Culture,* London: Routledge.
FISKE, J. (1987b) British cultural studies, in ALLEN, R. (Ed.) *Channels of Discourse: Television and Contemporary Criticism,* London: Methuen.
FISKE, J. (1989) *Understanding Popular Culture,* London: Unwin Hyman.
FRASER, P. (1990) How do teachers and students talk about television?, in BUCKINGHAM, D. (Ed.) *Watching Media Learning, Making Sense of Media Education,* London: Falmer Press.
FRASER, P. (1993) Chaucer with chips: right-wing discourse about popular culture, *English and Media magazine,* **28**, 16–19.
FRITH, S. (1983) *Sound Effects: Youth, Leisure and the Politics of Rock 'n' Roll,* London: Constable.
FRITH, S. (1988) Playing with real feeling: jazz and surburbia', in *Music for Pleasure: Essays in the Sociology of Rock,* Cambridge: Cambridge University Press.
FRITH, S. (1992) The cultural study of popular music, in GROSSBERG, L., NELSON, C. and TREICHLER, P. (Ed.) *Cultural Studies,* London: Routledge.
FRYER, P. (1984) *Staying Power: The History of Black People in Britain,* London: Pluto.
GALLIMORE, R. and THARP, R. (1990) Teaching mind in society: teaching, schooling and literate discourse, in MOLL, L. (Ed.) *Vygotsky and Education,* Cambridge: Cambridge University Press.
GERAGHTY, C. (1991) *Women and Soap Opera,* Cambridge: Polity.

GILBERT, P. (1987) Post reader-response, in CORCORAN, B. and EVANS, E. (Eds) *Readers, Texts, Teachers,* Milton Keynes: Open University Press

GILLESPIE, M. (1994 forthcoming) *TV, Ethnicity and Cultural Change: an Ethnographic Study of Punjabi Londoners,* London: Routledge.

GILROY, P. (1987) *There Ain't No Black in the Union Jack.* London: Hutchinson.

GOODSON, I. and MEDWAY, P. (Ed.) (1990) *Bringing English to Order,* London: Falmer Press.

GRAFF, H. (1979) *The Literacy Myth: Literacy and Social Structure in the 19th Century City,* New York: Academic Press.

GRAHAME, J. (1990) Playtime: learning about media institutions through practical work, in BUCKINGHAM, D. (Ed.) *Watching Media Learning: Making Sense of Media Education,* London: Falmer Press.

GRAHAME, J. (Ed.) (1991) *The English Curriculum: Media 1,* London: The English and Media Centre.

HALL, S. and WHANNEL, P. (1964) *The Popular Arts,* London: Hutchinson.

HARAWAY, D. (1991) *Simians, Cyborgs and Women: the Reinvention of Nature,* New York: Routledge.

HARGREAVES, D. (1982) *The Challenge for the Comprehensive School,* London: Routledge and Kegan Paul.

HARRIS, D. (1992) *From Class Struggle to the Politics of Pleasure: the Effects of Gramscianism on Cultural Studies,* London: Routledge.

HARVEY, D. (1989) *The Condition of Postmodernity: an Enquiry into the Origins of Cultural Change,* Oxford: Blackwell.

HEATH, S. B. (1983) *Ways with Words,* Cambridge: Cambridge University Press.

HENRIQUES, J. *et al* (1984) *Changing the Subject: Psychology, Social Regulation and Subjectivity,* London: Methuen.

HEVEY, D. (1992) *The Creatures Time Forgot: Photography and Disability Imagery,* London: Routledge.

HEWITT, R. (1986) *White Talk Black Talk: Inter-Racial Friendship and Communication amongst Adolescents,* Cambridge: Cambridge University Press.

HODGE, B. and TRIPP, D. (1986) *Children and Television,* Cambridge: Polity.

HOGGART, R. (1957) *The Uses of Literacy: Aspects of Working Class Life with Special Reference to Publications and Entertainments,* Harmondsworth: Penguin.

JONES, K. (1990) *Right Turn: the Conservative Revolution in Education,* London: Hutchinson.

JONES, K. (Ed.) (1992) *English in the National Curriculum: Cox's Revolution?,* London: Kogan Page.

JONES, S. (1988) *Black Youth, White Youth: the Reggae Tradition from JA to UK,* Basingstoke: Macmillan.

JORDIN, M. and BRUNT, R. (1988) Constituting the television audience: a problem of method, in DRUMMOND, P. and PATTERSON, R. (Ed.) *Television and its Audience: International Research Perspectives,* London: British Film Institute.

KENYON, D. (1992) *Inside Amateur Photography,* London: Batsford.

KINDER, M. (1991) *Playing with Power in Movies: Television and Video Games from Muppet Babies to Teenage Mutant Ninja Turtles,* Berkeley: University of California Press.

KOZULIN, A. (1990) *Vygotsky's Psychology: a Biography of Ideas,* London: Harvester Wheatsheaf.

KRESS, G. (1993) Genre as Social Process, in COPE, B. and KALANTZIS, M. (Ed.) *The Powers of Literacy: a Genre Approach to Teaching Writing,* London: Falmer Press.

LANDOW, G. (1992) *Hypertext the Convergence of Contemporary Critical Theory and Technology,* Baltimore: John Hopkins.

LEAVIS, Q. D. (1932) *Fiction and the Reading Public,* London: Chatto and Windus.

LEWIS, G. (1987) Patterns of meaning and choice: taste cultures in popular music, in LULL, J. (Ed.) *Popular Music and Communication,* Beverly Hills: Sage.

LIEBES, T. and KATZ, E. (1990) *The Export of Meaning,* Oxford: Oxford University Press.

LORAC, C. and WEISS, M. (1981) *Communication and Social Skills,* Exeter: Wheaton.

LULL, J. (Ed.) (1987) *Popular Music and Communication,* Beverly Hills: Sage.

LULL, J. (1990) *Inside Family Viewing,* London: Routledge.

LUSTED, D. (1986) Introduction — Why Pedagogy?, *Screen,* **27**, (5), 2–14.

MANDER, M. (1987) Bourdieu, the sociology of culture and cultural studies, *European Journal of Communication,* **2**, 427–53.

MASTERMAN, L. (1980) *Teaching About Television,* Basingstoke: Macmillan.

MASTERMAN, L. (1985) *Teaching the Media,* London: Comedia.

MATHIESON, M. (1975) *The Preachers of Culture: a Study of English and its Teachers,* London: Allen and Unwin.

MCCRACKEN, E. (1993) *Decoding Women's Magazines: From Mademoiselle to Ms,* Basingstoke: Macmillan.

MCGOUCH, R. (Ed.) (1986) *Strictly Private,* London: Penguin.

MCROBBIE, A. (1990) *Feminism and Youth Culture,* London: Macmillan.

MEEK, M. (1988) *How Texts Teach What Readers Learn,* London: Thimble Press.

MIDDLETON, R. (1990) *Studying Popular Music,* Milton Keynes: Open University Press.

MIEDZIAN, M. (1992) *Boys will be Boys: Breaking the Link between Masculinity and Violence,* London: Virago.

MOLL, L. (Ed.) (1990) *Vygotsky and Education: Instructional Implications and Applications of Sociohistorical Psychology,* Cambridge: Cambridge University Press.

MORGAN, D. (1992) *Discovering Men,* London: Routledge.

MORLEY, D. (1986) *Family Television: Cultural Power and Domestic Leisure,* London: Comedia.

MORLEY, D. (1992) *Television, Audiences and Cultural Studies,* London: Routledge.

MOSS, G. (1989) *Un-Popular Fictions,* London: Virago.

MOSS, G. (1993) Girls tell the teen romance: four reading histories, in BUCKINGHAM, D. (Ed.) *Reading Audiences: Young People and the Media,* Manchester: Manchester University Press.

MULHERN, F. (1979) *The Moment of 'Scrutiny',* London: New Left Books.

NAVA, M. (1992) *Changing Cultures: Feminism, Youth and Consumerism,* London: Sage.

NEALE, S. (1980) *Genre,* London: British Film Institute.

NEWMAN, F. and HOLZMAN, L. (1993) *Lev Vygotsky, Revolutionary Scientist,* London: Routledge.

PALMER, P. (1986) *The Lively Audience: a Study of Children Around the TV Set,* Sydney: Allen and Unwin.

PAYNE, I. (1980) A working-class girl in a grammar school, in SPENDER, D. and SARAH, E. (Ed.) *Learning to Lose,* London: Women's Press.

PEARSON, R. and URICCHIO, W. (Ed.) (1991) *The Many Lives of the Batman: Critical Approaches to a Superhero and his Media,* New York: Routledge & British Film Institute.

POTTER, J. and WETHERELL, M. (1987) *Discourse and Social Psychology: Beyond Attitudes and Behaviour,* London: Sage.

REDHEAD, S. (1990) *The End-of-the-Century Party: Youth and Pop Towards 2000,* Manchester: Manchester University Press.

REID, I. (Ed.) (1987) *The Place of Genre in Learning: Current Debates,* Geelong, Centre for Studies in Literary Education: Deakin University Press.

RICHARDS, C. (1990) Intervening in popular pleasures: media studies and the politics of subjectivity, in BUCKINGHAM, D. (Ed.) *Watching Media Learning: Making Sense of Media Education,* London: Falmer Press.

RICHARDS, C. (1992) Teaching popular culture, in JONES, K. (Ed.) *English and the National Curriculum: Cox's Revolution?,* London: Kogan Page.

RICHARDS, I. (1929) *Practical Criticism,* London: Routledge and Kegan Paul.

ROE, K. (1987) The school and music in adolescent socialisation, in LULL, J. (Ed.) *Popular Music and Communication,* Beverly Hills: Sage.

ROSE, D. (1992) *A Climate of Fear: The Murder of P.C. Blakelock and the Case of the Tottenham Three,* London: Bloomsbury.

SARLAND, C. (1991) *Young People Reading: Culture and Response,* Milton Keynes: Open University Press.

SEARLE, C. (1989) *Your Daily Dose: Racism in The 'Sun',* London: Campaign for Press and Broadcasting Freedom.

SEFTON-GREEN, J. (1990) Teaching and learning about representation: culture and *The Cosby Show* in a north London comprehensive, in BUCKINGHAM, D. (Ed.) *Watching Media Learning: Making Sense of Media Education,* London: Falmer Press.

SEFTON-GREEN, J. (1992) Publishing: the book and the reader, in ALVARADO, M. and BOYD-BARRETT, O. (Ed.) *Media Education: An Introduction,* London: British Film Institute/Open University Press.

SEFTON-GREEN, J. (1993) Untidy, depressing and violent: a boy's own story, in BUCKINGHAM, D. (Ed.) *Reading Audiences: Young People and the Media,* Manchester: Manchester University Press.

SEGAL, L. (1990) *Slow Motion: Changing Masculinities, Changing Men,* London: Virago.

SHARP, R. and GREEN, A. (1975), *Education and Social Control: a Study in Progressive Primary Education,* London: Routledge and Kegan Paul.

SKEGGS, B. (1991a) A spanking good time, *Magazine of Cultural Studies,* **3**, 28-33.

SKEGGS, B. (1991b) Five of the best: feminist rap?. *Magazine of Cultural Studies,* **4**, 10-11.

SMITH, F. (1982) *Writing and the Writer,* Oxford: Heinemann.

SONTAG, S. (1979) *On Photography,* Harmondsworth: Penguin.

SPENCE, J. (1986) *Putting Myself in the Picture,* London: Camden Press.

SPENCE, J. and HOLLAND, P. (Ed.) (1992) *Family Snaps: the Meanings of Domestic Photography,* London: Virago.

SPICER, A. (1987) Necessary opposites? Media Studies and literature in secondary schools, *Literature, Teaching, Politics,* **6**, 43-51.

STAFFORD, R. (1990) Redefining creativity: extended project work in GCSE Media Studies, in BUCKINGHAM, D. (Ed.) *Watching Media Learning: Making Sense of Media Education,* London: Falmer Press.

STANLEY, L. (Ed.) (1990) *Feminist Praxis: Research, Theory and Epistemology in Feminist Sociology,* London: Routledge.

STEEDMAN, C. (1982) *The Tidy House: Little Girls Writing,* London: Virago.

STREET, B. (1984) *Literacy in Theory and Practice,* Cambridge: Cambridge University Press.

SWINGEWOOD, A. (1977) *The Myth of Mass Culture,* London: Macmillan.

Talk, Workshop Group (1982) *Becoming Our Own Experts,* London: Talk, Workshop Group.

THOMPSON, D. (Ed.) (1964) *Discrimination and Popular Culture,* Harmondsworth: Penguin.

THOMPSON, J. B. (1990) *Ideology and Modern Culture,* Cambridge: Polity.

TUDGE, J. (1990) Vygotsky, the zone of proximal development and peer collaboration: implications for classroom practice, in MOLL, L. (Ed.) *Vygotsky and Education,* Cambridge: Cambridge University Press.

TUMAN, M. (1992) *Word Perfect: Literacy in the Computer Age,* London: Falmer Press.

TURNER, G. (1990) *British Cultural Studies: An Introduction,* London: Unwin Hyman.

VAN DIJK, T. (1987) *Communicating Racism,* Beverly Hills: Sage.

VYGOTSKY, L. (1962) *Thought and Language* (trans. Hanfmann, E. and Vakar, G.), Cambridge, Mass.: MIT.

VYGOTSKY, L. (1978) *Mind in Society* (trans. Cole, M. *et al*), Cambridge, Mass.: Harvard University Press.

WALKERDINE, V. (1984) Some day my prince will come, in MCROBBIE, A. and NAVA, M. (Ed.) *Gender and Generation,* Basingstoke: Macmillan.

WALKERDINE, V. (1986) Video replay, in BURGIN, V., DONALD, J. and KAPLAN, C. (Ed.) *Formations of Fantasy,* London: Routledge.

WERTCH, J. (Ed.) (1985a) *Culture, Communication and Cognition: Vygotskian Perspectives,* Cambridge: Cambridge University Press.

WERTCH, J. (1985b) *Vygotsky and the Social Formation of Mind,* Cambridge, Mass.: Harvard University Press.

WERTCH, J. (1990) The voice of rationality in a sociocultural approach to mind, in MOLL, L. (Ed.) *Vygotsky and Education,* Cambridge: Cambridge University Press.

WEST, A. (1992) How we live now, *English and Media Magazine,* **26**, 4–12.

WETHERELL, M. and POTTER, J. (1992) *Mapping the Language of Racism,* London: Harvester Wheatsheaf.

WILLIAMS, R. (1958) *Culture and Society 1780–1950,* London: Chatto and Windus.

WILLIAMS, R. (1961) *The Long Revolution,* London: Chatto and Windus.

WILLIAMSON, J. (1981/2) How does girl number 20 understand ideology?, *Screen Education,* **40**, 80–87.

WILLIS, P. (1990) *Common Culture,* Milton Keynes: Open University Press.

WOBER, M. and FAZAL, S. (1986) *Children and their Media,* London: Independent Broadcasting Authority.

WOOD, J. (1993) Repeatable pleasures: notes on young people's use of video, in BUCKINGHAM, D. (Ed.) *Reading Audiences: Young People and the Media,* Manchester: Manchester University Press.

Index